Also by
The Beardstown Ladies' Investment Club

The Beardstown Ladies'
Common-Sense Investment Guide

The Beardstown Ladies'
Stitch-in-Time Guide to Growing Your Nest Egg

The Beardstown Ladies' Guide to Smart Spending for Big Savings

The Beardstown Ladies'

GUIDE TO
SMART SPENDING
FOR BIG SAVINGS

How to Save for a Rainy Day without Sacrificing Your Lifestyle

The Beardstown Ladies' Investment Club
with Robin Dellabough

A SETH GODIN PRODUCTION

NEW YORK

LIBRARY OF CONGRESS CATALOGING-IN-PUBLICATION DATA

Beardstown Ladies Investment Club.
    The Beardstown Ladies' guide to smart spending for big savings :
how to save for a rainy day without sacrificing your lifestyle /
the Beardstown Ladies' Investment Club with Robin Dellabough.
       p.   cm.
   "A Seth Godin production."
   Includes bibliographical references and index.
   ISBN 0-7868-6265-3
   1. Finance. Personal—United States—Handbooks, manuals, etc.
I. Dellabough, Robin.   II. Title.
HG179.B348   1997
332.024'01—dc20   96–35857
                                                  CIP

FIRST EDITION

10 9 8 7 6 5 4 3 2 1

We dedicate this book to Helen B. Kramer, loving friend and charter member of the Beardstown Business and Professional Women's Investment Club. Helen's death on April 2, 1996, saddened our hearts. She was an active participant in the club and always enjoyed sharing her knowledge with others in our programs. Helen's Christian manners enriched each one of our lives.

—The Beardstown Ladies

ACKNOWLEDGMENTS

From the Beardstown Ladies:
Our families—each and every one.
Thank you for continuing support and love. We bask in your pride of our accomplishments.

Homer G. Rieken, Broker, A.G. Edwards & Sons, Springfield, Illinois
Homer helped us organize our club; recommended that we join the National Association of Investors Corporation and continues to be a loyal friend and supporter.

Havana National Bank, Havana, Illinois
For continued involvement in the club's book promotions and investment programs and wonderful book-signing receptions.

Beardstown Chamber of Commerce, Beardstown, Illinois
Donna Strieker, Secretary
For continued trust in our success and for Donna's untiring efforts in the distribution of our books and responding to myriad inquiries.

City of Beardstown, Beardstown, Illinois
For recognition of our success.

Central Illinois Public Service Company, Beardstown, Illinois
For providing a spacious meeting room for our "guest nights."

Fourth Street Evangelical Lutheran Church
For providing a meeting room.

DeSollar Insurance Agency
For professional contributions to the insurance-related content of our book.

Beardstown Community Unit School, District #15
For continuing support.

From the Writer:

At Hyperion
Thanks to Laurie Abkemeier and Brian DeFiore for their continuing publishing support and editorial teamwork.

At Seth Godin Productions
Thanks to Julie Maner, Sarah Silbert, Lisa Lindsay, Nana Sledzieski, Nicola Coddington, Andrew Pearlstein, Anne Shepherd, Susan Kushnick, Leslie Sharpe, Karen Watts, Malcolm Faulds, Wendy Price, and especially Seth Godin and Lisa DiMona for their hard work, esprit de corps, and faith.

Thanks to Jon, Joel, Flynn, and Fergus for riches money can't buy.

Special Thanks:

We wish to thank Keith Colter and Carolyn Patterson of Central Picture Entertainment, Inc., who created the award winning video production, "Cookin' Up Profits on Wall Street."

CONTENTS

THE BEARDSTOWN LADIES' INVESTMENT CLUB   xiii

INTRODUCTION   1

CHAPTER ONE
The Spending Pyramid   7

CHAPTER TWO
House-Proud and Home Free   21

CHAPTER THREE
Saving on Auto Spending   45

CHAPTER FOUR
How to Make Appliances Work for You   65

CHAPTER FIVE
The Insured Life   85

CHAPTER SIX
Utilize Your Utilities   105

CHAPTER SEVEN
Bank on This   117

CHAPTER EIGHT
Tax Breaks for Ordinary People   133

CHAPTER NINE
First-Class Travel at Half the Price   147

CHAPTER TEN
How to Love Your Children for Less   171

CHAPTER ELEVEN
Your Health: Physical and Fiscal   195

CHAPTER TWELVE
The Times of Your Life   209

CHAPTER THIRTEEN
And While We're at It—Shopping for Everything Else   225

CHAPTER FOURTEEN
Time Well Spent: The Volunteer Habit   237

APPENDIX I
Your Letters   245

APPENDIX II
Worksheets   253

RESOURCES WE RECOMMEND   259

INDEX   279

THE BEARDSTOWN LADIES' INVESTMENT CLUB

Ann Brewer, 62, secretary, charter member.

Ann Corley, 68, retired homemaker, member since 1985.

Doris Edwards, 76, elementary school principal, charter member.

Sylvia Gaushell, 85, retired art teacher, member since 1991.

Shirley Gross, 79, retired medical technologist, charter member.

Margaret Houchins, 55, former gift and flower shop owner, member since 1991.

Ruth Huston, 77, retired owner of a dry-cleaning business, charter member.

Carnell Korsmeyer, 69, hog farm owner, President of the National Pork Board, charter member.

Hazel Lindahl, 89, retired medical technician and school nurse, charter member.

Carol McCombs, 47, insurance agency employee, Elsie Scheer's daughter, member since 1993.

Elsie Scheer, 79, retired farmer and teacher's aide, charter member.

Betty Sinnock, 64, bank trust officer, charter member.

Maxine Thomas, 75, retired bank teller, charter member.

Buffy Tillitt-Pratt, 43, real estate broker, member since 1987.

The
Beardstown Ladies'
Guide to
Smart Spending
for Big Savings

INTRODUCTION

IF YOU'RE LIKE MANY PEOPLE, YOU SPEND virtually everything you earn. You admire people who have managed to grow a nest egg, but no matter how hard you try, you don't seem to end up with any money left to save.

You're not alone. According to the U.S. government, the average American has less than $2,000 in savings. Think about that for a second. Every ten years, the average American earns about $200,000. Yet after expenses and taxes, there's only $2,000 left! How did this happen? How did the people of a nation of industrious and productive hard workers end up spending everything they earn?

One reason is that you've been conditioned to believe that spending money will make you happy. Last year, more than one million commercial messages told you to buy things. The advertisers tried as hard as they could to make a connection between buying their product and your well-being. Buy this insurance and your family will love you more. Buy this car and your neighbors will like you more. Buy this soft drink and your life will be more exciting.

The advertisers are half right. Acquiring things can help make you happy, if you spend money on the right things. A comfortable house can contribute to a better life. Driving to work can be more fun than taking the bus and walking in the rain. Having nice clothes can make you feel better about yourself. But we take this idea to extremes.

If you try to follow the advertiser's advice and buy your way to happiness, you'll ultimately fail. There isn't enough time or enough money in the world to buy everything you might ever want. Instead, you're going to have to pick and choose. You're going to have to determine what really makes you happy, and why. And you'll have to balance the pleasure you get from purchasing "things" with the stress and discomfort that come from debt and from a lack of retirement savings.

There are families who feel they are just scraping by on $150,000 a year. Can you imagine? Most of us would feel rich beyond belief on $150,000 a year. But these families have trapped themselves in an endless cycle of expenditures to maintain their lifestyles. Faced with mounting debt and the stress that goes with it, they no longer enjoy anything they buy.

This is a book about two things: *what* you buy and *how* you buy it. In your lifetime, you'll have a limited amount of money. You'll need to spend that money on shelter, food, recreation, health care, education, and more. Throughout the book, we're going to ask you to think hard about how you spend your money.

Spending smart is a combination of several factors. First, you've got to be educated. Knowing the ins and outs of the industry you're shopping in will save you time and money.

Second, you've got to know *why* you're buying. If going to the movies is a carefree treat for the family, you don't want to ruin it by smuggling in your own popcorn or calculating the cost per ounce of different sizes of soda. You're there to enjoy yourself!

Third, you have to consider whether you get more satisfaction from the buying process or the actual owning. Some people love to shop—but once they get the item home, the satisfaction is gone.

Fourth, you've got to make intelligent decisions without letting your emotions influence you too much. You need to be aware of when you're letting a feeling override your common sense.

Have you ever bought something to get rid of a pesky salesman? Or because you're tired of shopping? Have you ever purchased an expensive item to cheer yourself up at the end of a hard day, or reward yourself at the end of a good one? When you and your spouse purchase something expensive, do you discuss your objectives ahead of time, or do you argue about them as part of the shopping expedition?

Our goal is to teach you to use money as a *tool* to get the things you want. By learning how to focus on the issues that matter a lot, you can let the little ones slide. You'll end up spending *less* time shopping, less time feeling stressed about your purchase, and more time enjoying yourself. And that's the whole point of spending money, isn't it?

We know a 40-year-old husband and wife who live in a small, comfortable home in a nice neighborhood. Their son attends one of the best private high schools in the country. Their daughter takes art classes and has a purebred dog. They feel safe enough to walk the dog at night and in the nearby woods. Both parents have jobs they love, but which give them enough flexibility to spend a lot of time with their kids. They drive a minivan large enough to hold the soccer team the dad coaches. They eat well, enjoy good wine, go to the theater, and never feel deprived. But it's not because they're wealthy. In fact, their joint income is far less than that of most of their neighbors and less than that of many of their friends. Yet their neighbors and friends are constantly complaining that they don't have enough money, whereas our young couple feel they have plenty—for the truly important things.

This couple practiced smart spending for big savings every step of the way. It no doubt helped that the husband inherited a few genes from his parents, the 68-year-old retired milkman and secretary we described in the beginning of *The Beardstown Ladies' Stitch-in-Time Guide to Growing Your Nest Egg*. Their son and daughter-in-law carefully weighed what was important to them and what they could let go of. They started out by keeping their wedding costs to a minimum. They asked friends to provide everything from champagne to food to music in lieu of wedding gifts. That enabled the parents of the bride and groom to help pay off their graduate student loans instead of spending money on a lavish wedding. So the couple started off their marriage free of debt. That in turn enabled them to buy a house sooner than a lot of their friends. The house they live in is close enough to a train station that they only need one car, and they've driven that car for six years. They also bought the car for $3,000 less than the sticker price because it had been driven 150 miles and was considered "used." When the bathroom in their house needed remodeling, the estimates came in at $10,000. Our friends decided to reglaze the bathtub instead. The $9,700 they saved bought them their beloved dog, a trip to Europe, and summer camp for their children. They have functional but pleasant furniture, a lot of which came from relatives. No one in the family wears designer clothes, but they feel suitably dressed for their lifestyles.

A couple of years ago, they noticed mortgage rates had gotten really low, so they refinanced their loan. They were able to lower their mortgage payments by $300 a month. Now that amount is automatically deducted from their paychecks and invested in a mutual fund, so their retirement nest egg is growing slowly but surely. They feel their lives are full and rich today and because of their investments, they don't worry about tomorrow.

This family made a major compromise on their most expensive purchase—their house—and it paid off in a hundred ways, each of which made their lives more enjoyable. That's the message in this book: No matter what your income is, if you apply the lessons and information we're about to provide, you can come closer to the kind of lifestyle you want. We think you can shop carefully, invest what you save, and enjoy your retirement. In our first book, we showed how a little common sense turns a minimal investment into maximum returns. In the second book, we presented the basic tools everyone needs to manage their finances and to save for retirement.

Since the publication of those two books, the question people ask us most often is: How do we find the money to invest? It doesn't magically appear. As Ann Corley's husband always said, "It's not how much money you make, it's what you do with it after you make it." We like to save as much as we can wherever we can in order to have more to invest. You do have to want those investment dollars and then plan and work to save more of your spending dollars. We try to save when we spend large amounts of money on major consumer purchases.

Chances are, every time you buy a car, a house, an appliance, or insurance, you spend money unnecessarily. Money that, if saved in an interest-bearing account, could help produce a comfortable retirement. We know. Between us, we've bought nearly 50 homes;

almost two hundred cars; countless refrigerators, washing machines, air conditioners, etc. Lately, we've even bought a few computers! We've traveled many, many miles on airplanes, buses, trains, and automobiles. We've raised 29 children and helped put another generation through college. We didn't do all this by being tightwads or by looking at thriftiness as a sport. We simply tried to spend our money on what mattered.

Spending and saving the Beardstown way is not a hobby that relies on reusing broccoli bands. Rather, it's an overall attitude toward money. It's a way of looking at your life, figuring out where things fit into it, and what really matters to you. You don't have to clip coupons for tuna fish each week if you save enough on a once-a-year purchase. It's not necessary to count pennies or save soap slivers. That's not the good life—that's a life with too much time on its hands! We like to think in terms of "clipping coupons" for large items where we really save a lot. Saving $1,000 when you buy a car is twice as good and lots faster than saving by clipping coupons.

Entire books just on mortgage tips or buying cars are readily available and jammed with tips. We list them in the Resources section at the back of this book. Our book is more of a primer to help you realize how important it is to practice what we preach. It's designed to help you avoid "situational" or emotion-based spending by learning a simple formula. We call it *STOP, LOOK,* and *LISTEN.* This is how it works:

STOP and consider before you buy anything. Do you really want it? Can you afford it? Is it the best value for your money? Are there other things you'd rather spend money on? How will you feel about the purchase tomorrow, when it's not new anymore? In one, five, or ten years, will it have changed or improved your life?

LOOK before you leap. You wouldn't think of investing in the stock market without finding out as much as possible about the stock. You wouldn't send your child to a college you hadn't visited. Think of everything you buy as an investment. Look around, comparison shop, do your research.

LISTEN to yourself. You usually know exactly what you should be spending, or what you should be doing to save money. Why don't you? Because you're cold, hot, hungry, tired, bored, or cranky. You're in a store, and although you know you don't really need that $300 gas barbecue grill, your emotions get the better of you. If you listen to yourself, it's easier not to let spending money be a substitute for recreation, personal satisfaction, or other kinds of needs. You hear the difference between, "I really *need* that" and "I just *want* that." Then you can ask yourself whether you want to spend money on one thing more than another.

Carnell Korsmeyer likes to tell a story about buying a new car once when her daughter was young. They were driving the new car home and her daughter asked if they could stop and get a root beer. Carnell told her, "I don't have any money, do you have any money?" Her daughter said, "No, I don't have any money." Carnell said again, "Well, I don't have any money." Her daughter thought about this for a few minutes, and then replied, "Are you telling me that you have enough money for a new car, but not a nickel for a root beer?" Lest we get too caught up in saving big money at the risk of sacrificing life's small pleasures, Carnell says, "Remember that it's important to have those nickels for a root beer, too."

Read carefully, and you'll discover that by focusing on the big things, the little ones can take care of themselves.

CHAPTER ONE

THE SPENDING PYRAMID

*You can have the good life now and later
by spending to save and saving to spend.*

THE KEY TO OUR APPROACH IS BEST ILLUSTRATED by what we call
The Beardstown Ladies' Spending Pyramid. (See page 8 to see what
we mean.) It's a way of thinking about money and spending in a
general way, so that each time you make a financial decision, you
have a frame of reference. Putting most of your time and energy into
saving in those areas where you *spend* the greatest percentage of your
income should result in financial rewards for you. We suggest you
consider your financial goals, start at the top level, and work your
way down. A few smart decisions a month can make a significant
difference in stretching your income.

The Power of the Pyramid

Most people treat their shopping in exactly the wrong order.
We spend hours clipping coupons to save $30 or $40. We switch
dry cleaners to save a nickel on every shirt. It's easy to focus on
these little purchases. They're simple and provide immediate
gratification.

If you're good at managing the bottom tier of the pyramid,
you'll save a few hundred dollars a year. Nothing to sneeze at,
certainly, but it's not enough.

Look at the top of the pyramid. An extra few hours spent
negotiating on a house can save $5,000. Doing some research on

THE BEARDSTOWN LADIES' SPENDING PYRAMID

If you can put away an extra $5,000 a year, you'll retire with more than half a million dollars.

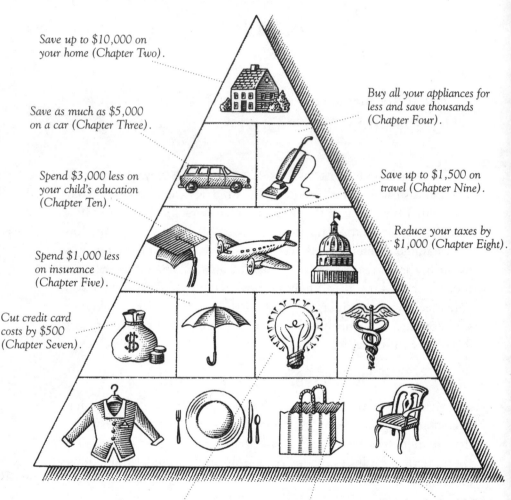

Save up to $10,000 on your home (Chapter Two).

Save as much as $5,000 on a car (Chapter Three).

Spend $3,000 less on your child's education (Chapter Ten).

Spend $1,000 less on insurance (Chapter Five).

Cut credit card costs by $500 (Chapter Seven).

Buy all your appliances for less and save thousands (Chapter Four).

Save up to $1,500 on travel (Chapter Nine).

Reduce your taxes by $1,000 (Chapter Eight).

Save $500 on utilities (Chapter Six).

Reduce health care expenses by $500 (Chapter Eleven).

Save hundreds of dollars on food, clothes, and furniture (Chapter Thirteen).

college grants can save $20,000. Calling insurance agents for a day or two can save you $3,000 a year. These are big numbers. It's like getting a huge raise—without having to work harder.

The pyramid is here to help you focus on the spending that matters, to demonstrate that it's worth investing your time and energy in discovering how to most effectively save money.

If you can change the top of the pyramid and save $4,000 a year (and put that money in a stock fund), you'll end up with *hundreds of thousands of dollars* for your retirement, or for the lakeside cabin you've always wanted, or to send your grandchildren to college.

A small change in the top of your pyramid can double or triple your disposable income. By adjusting the way you buy the big things—housing, transportation, insurance, education, etc.— you can free up enough money to *dramatically* increase your standard of living. Consider it a second job. If you learn how to think about money and do your homework on your purchases, you can find yourself with a lot more freedom and a lot more cash.

Carnell explains, "You need to be aware of exactly what it is you are buying. If you focus on buying a *car*, then perhaps all the extras look very attractive. But if you remember that you're buying *transportation* to meet your particular needs, then it's easier to sort out which of the niceties you really want to buy. The same thing can be said of housing. Instead of buying a *house*, you're buying *shelter* for your family. Picking out *colleges* for your children? Try thinking in terms of buying *education*. It gives you a different perspective."

Once you fill in your own pyramid, you'll be able to look at your overall financial picture, rather than see only the details. You'll know which categories matter the most to you. First, list all of your expenses. Look through bank and credit card statements for the last six months to get an average monthly amount for each area.

Monthly Expenses

House _____

Car _____

Education _____

Health _____

Utilities _____

Insurance _____

Taxes _____

Clothing _____

Groceries _____

Entertainment _____

Travel _____

Furniture _____

TOTAL _____

Now calculate what percentage of your total income each expense represents. Take the largest item and put it in the top of the pyramid. The smallest-percentage items should wind up at the bottom. It's been said before, but a picture really is worth a thousand words. When you can *see* where you spend your money, it makes it more compelling to be able to *save*.

Naturally, your pyramid will change over the years as your circumstances change, which is why we've included blank pyramids in Appendix II. Individual pyramids vary tremendously, too. None of ours are the same. The largest percentage of Ann Corley's income goes toward real estate and income taxes. Buffy Tillitt-Pratt says income tax is her biggest expense because she's managed to get everything else paid off.

Shirley Gross explains that she has five grandchildren, whom she is helping educate. The largest portion of her income is spent on their college tuition. Two graduated last May and another one is a senior in college, working towards a master's degree. One finished three years ago. A granddaughter just graduated from high school and wants to be an architect. "I have already provided for their education," says Shirley.

Many Americans would no doubt put their mortgage at the top of their pyramid. As for many of us, we paid for our homes years ago. Sylvia Gaushell, for example, has lived in her home for 55 years, so utilities and long-distance calls to her children are her biggest expenses. Betty Sinnock's home in Beardstown is mortgage-free. Her daughter and family live there. Paying the mortgage on her second home in Havana, Illinois, is near the top of her pyramid now. Betty adds that putting back as much as possible into their investments is a close second.

Maxine Thomas points out that when she had a mortgage, the biggest percentage of her income was definitely her house. "We bought our home in 1940, right after we were married. We remodeled the whole house, thinking that would be more economical than building a new home." Remodeling her home is Ruth Huston's top pri-ority. Hazel Lindahl's car is at the top of her pyramid. At age 89, she doesn't have too many other big expenses.

BEARDSTOWN TALES

My dad was a Ford dealer. My mom used to say, "I raised you kids to be poor. I didn't raise you to think 'Oh, our dad can buy us anything.'" If you earn a nice income, but are raised to live on a small amount, it leaves you money to buy things that will make you more money instead of frittering it away on consumer goods. Most millionaires invest all they can and they live on what's left over. I would rather spend on my rental properties, because that's going to make me money. Sometimes I'm a little too frugal for my own good. How little can I get by with? I want to shortcut myself on some things, and spend what I save on an invest-ment that will make me money.

BUFFY TILLITT-PRATT

Coupon Clipping for the Big-Ticket Items

"I would not drive to the next town to buy something that was a few cents cheaper," Betty says. "If I was going there for another purpose, that's fine, but I think too many people spend several dollars to save a few cents." Ann Corley's attitude is that if you have to save every cent, you won't be very happy. She thinks it's important to have those things that you want. Ann says, "I *could* get along without a VCR but I don't want to. I'm planning to get a second one. You want to be able to enjoy life."

Margaret believes in reading the fine print before buying anything. She uses a grocery store example to describe the process she goes through to find out if she's getting a true bargain or not. "Is the generic brand as good as or comparable in quality to the name brand? How important is that quality to you? If you're willing to compromise, you may have more money to go into your investments or your vacation or into a large purchase."

Sometimes it's not a matter of compromising on quality so much as considering the law of diminishing returns. What do we mean by that? Say you're in the market for a diamond ring. You see one that costs $500, one that costs $2,000, and one that costs $10,000. The difference between the $500 ring and the $2,000 ring is apparent at a glance. But if the only way you can tell the difference between the $2,000 ring and the $10,000 ring is with a microscope, is it worth it? They're both high quality. Is one that much better—$8,000 better? You need to decide if it's more important to enjoy *owning* the ring than it is to enjoy *buying* the ring.

A Shopping Profile

We've all made our fair share of mistakes and had to learn some lessons the hard way. That's the whole reason for this book. In order to get the most out of your money, you need to identify who you are as a shopper and as a saver.

Whether you are an impulse-buyer flitting from store to store, a frugal bargain hunter who buys only after careful consideration, or somewhere in between, will determine how you will apply the concepts we offer. What kind of shopper do you think you are? Fill out our shopper's profile on page 14 to find out.

Betty is the first to admit she really enjoys shopping. "I always said I'd like to be financially affluent enough that I could just walk into a store and buy what I wanted without asking the price," she says. Sylvia has no problem spending money on things she loves. "I buy just what I have the money for," Sylvia says. "That's why I don't have credit cards or go into debt. I don't go overboard on anything." In fact, she did once buy a brand new Cadillac. Despite its high cost, she felt the status and comfort were worth every penny—especially since she had the cash to pay for it.

It's important that you're honest with yourself about what gives you satisfaction. If buying groceries without looking at the price makes you feel content, then why force yourself to do price comparisons? If you've always dreamed of buying a bracelet from Tiffany's and bringing it home in that robin's-egg-blue box, then finding the exact same bracelet at a discount store will not fulfill your dream—even at half the price.

BEARDSTOWN TALES

I never had much jewelry as a child. My parents couldn't afford it. I just admired jewelry on other people so much that it does something for me to have it. I think Indian jewelry was one of my bigger expenditures. I bought it when Indian jewelry was very popular and the movie stars were all wearing it. I think it's one of the things that I pride most. These pieces were all less than $40. It's not an investment. It's just that I enjoy wearing it. It satisfies my ego, I guess.

HAZEL LINDAHL

Hazel was brought up strictly in the school of "stay within your income." Her advice today is to be practical when you start spending money. Don't overspend. But she also believes in listening to yourself in terms of what's going to make you happy. For Hazel, it's been costume jewelry. She buys what she likes and doesn't really budget for it. She does have her own version of checks and balances. She tries to equalize the amount she spends on personal pleasures with church giving. "I feel if I can gratify myself, why then I can certainly give more to church."

Making Choices

We have only a certain amount of money. We have to spend some on food and shelter, but beyond that we have choices. You can decide where you want to put your priorities. The main mes-

WHAT KIND OF SHOPPER ARE YOU?

1. *How often do you shop?*
____ A few times a year   ____ Once a month   ____ Once a week
____ Twice a week   ____ More than twice a week

2. *How much time do you spend on one shopping excursion?*
____ All day   ____ One or two hours
____ Six hours   ____ Less than one hour

3. *How much money do you spend each time you shop?*
____ It varies   ____ Less than $100   ____ More than $100

4. *Do you shop only when you intend to buy or when you feel like it?*
____ I only shop when I know what I want. When I find what I want, the shopping event goes no further.
____ I only shop when I know what I want, but I often end up shopping for other things as long as I'm out shopping.
____ I shop when I feel like shopping.

5. *Do you like to browse lots of stores or limit your destinations to a select few?*

6. *Do you consider shopping a social activity? Do you shop with groups of friends?*

7. *Do you enjoy shopping?*
____ Very much   ____ So-so   ____ Shopping is a necessary evil

8. *What type of merchandise do you shop for most often?*
____ Clothing   ____ Food   ____ Books   ____ Entertainment   ____ Other

9. *Do you save lots of coupons? Do you look out for sales?*
____ I buy only items that are on sale.
____ I try to look out for good prices, but I don't waste time looking around.
____ Quality is all that matters. Money is no object.

10. *How do you like to pay for what you buy?*
____ Credit card   ____ Cash   ____ Check

sage of this book is to think about what you're spending money on *before* you spend it and to realize that if you save in the places that are not important to you, you'll have extra to spend on something you really love.

Most of us have to make a choice between one area and another. We know a couple in New Jersey who live happily in a small apartment rather than a larger home. It's not that they can't afford a house. It's that they have made a conscious decision to spend their extra income on their extensive compact disc collection.

We're not suggesting that you can have everything you ever wanted no matter how little money you earn. You *can't* have it all. But once you prioritize what you *really* want, you will find you can make your way pretty far down the list.

Your Personal Priority Pyramid

By now you know where your money is going, and you probably wish you could divert some of it and rebuild your pyramid. To accomplish that, you need to think about where your savings and goals intersect, and about where you really want to spend money. That is why we provide a different kind of pyramid to fill in: the Personal Priority Pyramid on page 18. You'll notice that it's blank. After some careful consideration, fill it in by putting the things *you* most want to spend money on in order of importance, starting at the top and working down.

Ponder the things you feel most strongly about in your life. Maybe, like Maxine, you love to travel. Travel would go at the top of your Personal Priority Pyramid. Perhaps you're more like Doris Edwards, who likes to spend part of her income on gifts for her nieces and nephews. Shirley's top priority and biggest percentage of her spending is for her grandchildren's education.

The more your Personal Priority Pyramid and Spending Pyramid match, the more content you should be. Working toward that goal is yet another way to keep your spending in perspective. If travel is at the top of your Personal Priority Pyramid but it's on the bottom of your Spending Pyramid, what can you do to change that? How can you reduce the amount you're spending at the top of your Spending Pyramid? That's what *STOP* and consider means.

THE LADIES' RULES OF SMART SPENDING FOR BIG SAVINGS

Throughout this book, we'll be giving you insights into how to think about buying particular items. Each industry has its own language and customs. These insider tips make it easier and more profitable when you shop.

But there are some basic rules of thumb that apply to everything. Understanding these ground rules saves you money, whatever you buy.

1. Money spent today is worth more than money spent tomorrow.
In a nutshell, you will always pay more if you buy something over time or on credit. The opposite is also true. Many sellers will give you a break if you'll pay cash up-front.

2. When the demand goes up or the supply goes down, the price rises.
We've all heard the old saw about the law of supply and demand. But it really is a law. The more people want something, the more the price goes up. The more people are offering something, the more the price goes down.

Think about ice cream for a minute. If there's just one person at the beach selling ice cream on a hot day, he can raise the price and still sell out. If the day is cloudy and cold, or if there are a dozen people selling ice cream, the price better go down or there will be a lot of melted inventory!

When you shop for something, think about the season and every other element that contributes to supply and demand. Christmas wrapping paper is a lot cheaper in January, and houses are less expensive when too many are on the market.

3. The more unique it is, the less choice you have.
If you really want a Rolls-Royce, you don't have much choice. There's only one Rolls-Royce. When you buy a house or a car or life insurance, think hard about whether you need a particular brand or neighborhood, or if you can be flexible.

4. Insurance is expensive.
Most of us don't like risk. We don't want a car that might break down, or an appliance that will fall apart. We want some assurance that we won't find ourselves broke and homeless.

The price and quality of insurance differs. Buying a tool at Sears, for example, means you get a lifetime guarantee. A tool from the store down the street, on the other hand, might have only a one-year warranty.

While some insurance, like a Sears' warranty, is a great bargain, other types, like a dealer warranty on a stove, isn't. Figure out how much insurance you *really* need. Buy too much and you've wasted some money. Buy too little and you may have taken too much risk.

5. Sellers have to make money.
Understand that you can't get something for nothing. If you expect a store to be well lit, conveniently located, and have helpful salespeople and reasonable hours, you're going to pay more for it. You can't begrudge a salesperson his commission or a store its profit. That doesn't mean you can't use this to your advantage. If there are two people selling a similar item, and you're flexible about who you buy from, give them a chance to tell you how eager they are to sell to you.

6. Fashion always costs more.
Last year, teenagers were clamoring to buy a certain brand of shoe. Today, a store can't give away the same shoes. What changed? Fashion. A big portion of the price of many items we buy is based on how up-to-date the product is.

If you get pleasure from a fashion trend, buy it. If you don't see any difference, buy the newly *unfashionable*. The decrease in demand will save you money.

7. We all drive used cars.
Within five minutes of getting behind the wheel of your new car, it's used. Same for your house, your clothes—everything you own.

Before you rush to get something brand-spanking-new, take a few minutes to think about taking advantage of depreciation and buying a used one instead.

8. Don't borrow money to buy things that make your life only slightly better.
Cars and clothes wear out. If you borrow money to buy them, you'll be in a debt cycle that may last forever. Better to save first, then buy what you need with your own cash.

PERSONAL PRIORITY PYRAMID

How would you like to be spending your money? Fill in this pyramid in order of preference, from top to bottom.

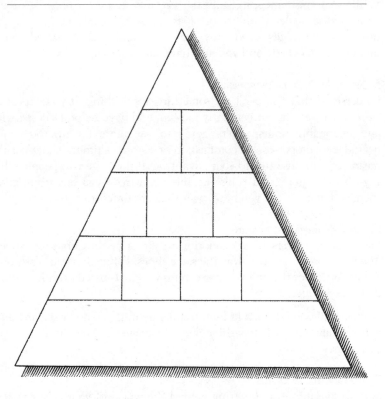

Spending and Investing

If you've read our first book, you already know how enthusiastic we are about the stock market. We believe that investing in common stocks is one of the smartest moves you can make. But investing isn't only about stocks, mutual funds, and municipal bonds. Everything we buy–everything we spend money on—is an investment. We invest our time and energy in shopping. If something breaks down prematurely and we need to repair or replace it, that's a bad investment. If we save thousands of dollars over the life of a mortgage because we shopped around for a lower interest rate, that's a good investment. The more we save whenever we can, the more we have to invest in stocks and bonds that will increase our future security.

In the same way we do our homework before we make any investments, we make it easier to spend wisely without undue sacrifice by *doing our homework*—another way of saying *LOOK* before you leap.

You don't have to read every consumer magazine before you spend a dime on any purchase. But spending a little bit of time can go a long way toward saving money. We research companies we invest in, and we like to check out products and services we buy.

Calculating Costs

You need some concrete strategies and information to begin saving for the items in your Personal Priority Pyramid. You need to know as much as you can before you spend a few hundred dollars here or there. But trying to do that yourself can be time-consuming and confusing, which is where this book comes in handy.

We've taken out our calculators for you and discovered how to think about what things *really cost*. We'll explain that buying a new car every few years ends up costing more than a college education—and what the alternatives are. We'll brave the thickets of buying life insurance, paying for college, and deciding which appliance warranties are worth it. And we'll give you hundreds of ways you can save big money.

Most of all, we'll keep reminding you to *STOP* and consider, *LOOK* before you leap, and *LISTEN* to yourself. Make a deal with yourself to pick a dollar amount—$25, $50, or $100—and anytime you're about to spend that much, *STOP, LOOK,* and *LISTEN*. We're willing to bet that if you start practicing this technique, by the time you've finished reading this book you will have saved money.

Getting Down to Brass Tacks

1. Determine where the greatest percentage of your income goes by filling in your Spending Pyramid.

2. Think about where you want to spend your money by filling in your Personal Priority Pyramid.

3. Start trying to make your pyramids match by practicing STOP, LOOK, and LISTEN whenever you shop.

CHAPTER TWO

HOUSE-PROUD
AND HOME FREE

*Paying attention to a small detail here can
save you thousands of dollars.*

OWNING A HOME IS USUALLY AT THE TOP of most Americans'
Spending Pyramid. It's the single most important area in which
to search for savings because it is probably your largest single
investment.

Unfortunately, a home is often your biggest emotional
investment. It's hard to think as clearly about saving money on a
house as on a washing machine. With an appliance, you care
most about how well it works. When it comes to a house…well,
a house is not just a house, it's your home. There are all kinds of
feelings that go into a home-buying decision, from security and
convenience to aesthetics and location.

It's possible for a single person to live in decent shelter for
just a few hundred dollars a month in rent. It's also possible for a
wealthy married couple to spend more than $30 million on a
house. You need to figure out what you want *before* you go shopping for a house.

Are you looking for a good school district for your children?
If so, do your homework before you go shopping. Visit schools
first, not houses. Compare test scores. Take a look at the difference in tax rates between a community with great schools and
one with not-so-great schools. How much more will you pay to

live there? Is it cheaper to live in a neighborhood with lower taxes and send your kids to private school?

A family with one child was looking for a home in the suburbs of Los Angeles. They liked a house in the neighborhood with the best schools, but were amazed to discover that property taxes for a house that fit their needs were $12,000 a year, and the house cost more than $600,000. A similar house just three miles away was one-third less, and the taxes were just $6,000 a year. By moving to the lesser school district, the couple saved more than $20,000 a year. They took half the money they saved and sent their son to a Catholic school. They invested the rest to finance four years at the best engineering college in the country. Basically, they bought a fine private school education with college thrown in for "free."

STOP!

Consider that the reasons you buy a home may include:

1. *Shelter.*
2. *Tax savings.*
3. *School district.*
4. *Convenience.*
5. *Investment.*
6. *Impress friends and family.*
7. *Neighbors.*
8. *Features and lifestyle.*
9. *Pride of ownership.*

There's nothing wrong with buying a house because it makes you feel good, because it will impress your friends, or because the neighborhood is beautiful. But understand that you're giving up something else. You may be trading a European vacation every year, or a new car, or an early retirement. Everything in the Spending Pyramid displaces something else.

Let's look at a concrete example. A simple house in the suburbs of Buffalo, New York might cost $50,000. With three bedrooms, a garage, a kitchen, and a family room, it's really all you need for hospitable shelter. The neighborhood is safe, and the schools are average. A few miles away, a grand showplace of a house might cost five times this. For $250,000, you get a prestigious neighborhood, a few extra bedrooms, a formal dining room, a study, an in-ground pool, and a three-car garage.

Buy the second house, and you'll have tremendous satisfaction from knowing you can afford such a great house. You'll have the peace of mind of knowing your kids are going to the very best public school. You'll impress your friends and relatives (and your mailman). So why not buy it if you can afford it?

Because by buying the expensive house, you've increased your mortgage from zero (assuming you had the $50,000 saved as a down payment) to about $2,000 a month. What else could you buy with $2,000 a month? You could buy a brand-new car every year—and give it away when you were tired of it. You could go to a different foreign country every summer. You could endow two college scholarships for needy students, or you or your spouse could quit your jobs and pursue creative endeavors.

We all make these choices, whether or not we're aware of them. If you aren't aware, you'll often make the wrong decision. So, ask yourself some hard questions. What's an extra bedroom worth? A swimming pool? That wonderful kitchen with the custom cabinets—is it really worth $50 a month for the rest of your life?

Once you and your family have figured out the trade-offs you're willing to make, write them down. Bring the list to your real estate agent and explain your requirements. Then stick with them. Don't start looking at houses that differ from your list.

Find the house that meets your needs. Compare it to similar houses. Then make a rational decision. If your final choice makes you sad that you don't have a bigger yard or a better

BEARDSTOWN TALES

When I shopped for a home, I went to a reputable real estate dealer who showed me a few houses. He then told me about a house that had not yet been placed on the market. When I heard the location I immediately wanted to see the inside of the house. I had observed it from the outside. Buying a house is one of the biggest investments a person makes in a lifetime, so I wanted another person with good judgment to give me an opinion. I asked my mother to come see the property. We could tell by the layout that a woman had had some input into its design. There was a large living room, a large kitchen, and a large utility room. There were three good-sized bedrooms and a big family room. We both were very impressed with what we saw. When the real estate agent said he had an appointment to show the house again in 20 minutes, I asked him the price and said, "Don't show it to anyone else. I'll take it!" I think I got a bargain. After 27 years that house is still my home.

DORIS EDWARDS

view, pull out your list and reevaluate the choices you made. If a bigger lawn is worth more than four years at a private college for your oldest son, then make the switch. Everyone has different priorities, and once you recognize yours, you can make them work.

There's nothing wrong with spending money. That's what it's for. But don't overspend for the wrong reasons or worse, without even realizing it. The biggest trap that home-buyers face is the phrase, "Well, if we're spending this much, we might as well get…" We disagree. Spending an extra $2,000 to get a stone floor in your kitchen is exactly the same as spending $2,000 for anything else in your life. Situational spending is costly every time.

As you look for a home, *STOP, LOOK*, and *LISTEN* before you spend anything on housing. *STOP* and consider: Is owning a home at the top of your Personal Priority Pyramid? If it is, then it makes sense for you to spend the biggest percentage of your income on a house. Once you stop and really think about it, maybe you'll discover that there are other things you'd rather do with your money. Then you'll want to make housing costs drop down a level or two on your Spending Pyramid. How?

One family we know reduced their housing costs slowly but surely by making several key decisions. First, they bought the "worst" home in the best neighborhood they could afford and fixed it up themselves. They took out a 15-year mortgage with the lowest interest rate they could find. As their three children grew, so did the husband's income from his law practice. The wife was an artist who chose to stay home. Five years ago, by the time their oldest child was 16, their house was completely paid off. That is when they made a critical choice. Instead of moving to a larger, fancier house, as almost all their neighbors had done, they decided that their old home was perfectly fine. They stayed put.

Mortgage-free, they now can afford luxuries their friends marvel at: paying their children's private college tuition, buying a boat, extensive travel, and the healthiest retirement fund you ever saw. They feel that they have so much wealth to share, they're about to adopt a child. Motivated by what was truly important to them, they saved on their home in order to spend on other parts of their life.

When and What to Buy

It's important not to *assume* that you want to buy a house. Instead of buying a home, you might be better off renting if:

- Rents are low.

- Interest rates are high.

- You have no down payment saved.

- You don't want the responsibility of owning property.

Consider meeting the following criteria before you buy a house:

- You can get 15 percent or more below fair market value.

- You are definitely staying in the area.

- You need to reduce how much income tax you pay.

- You want to accumulate equity and gain security.

- You are ready and eager to maintain your own home.

A couple in Ohio rented the top floor of a big Victorian house. Even after they had had two boys, they decided they were not interested in the hassle of owning a home. Besides, their rent was extremely low, only the husband worked so they didn't need the tax relief, and for a long time, interest rates seemed prohibitive to them. They looked carefully at their Personal Priority Pyramid, and a home was not at the top.

Another couple was the opposite. They were paying very high rent and living in an area where they could get a good rate on a mortgage. They desperately wanted a garden and backyard of their own to fix up. Finally, they were able to buy a house that had been foreclosed and was being sold at a greatly reduced price.

When you're first starting out, it might seem more difficult to narrow down your needs. When you're investing hundreds of thousands of dollars, it's worth spending time weighing needs and wants. Try to set aside plenty of calm, relaxed moments to discuss what kind of house you and your spouse, if you are married, want. You might come up with an unexpected list of requirements or things you *don't* care about. For example, how big a house do you want? How big a house do you *need*?

One of the simplest, fastest, most obvious ways to save money on housing is to buy less of it. We urge you to think through just how much space *you* need to be comfortable, rather than trying to keep up with the Joneses. Once you decide you and your family require a certain amount of space, you'll be in a better position to make sensible choices about what kind of house to live in and what you can live without. Say, for example, you don't cook much, so you don't care about a big kitchen. But you have three teenagers, so you need more than one bathroom. Or you would be happy living in a cozy little house as long as it had a nice garden.

Shirley had a very clear need in mind when she was shopping for a house. She bought her house because of her arthritis. It's all one level, with no basement or attic or steps. "It's easier for me. Before I had a carport, now I've got a garage," Shirley says. "Convenience was what I was looking for in a house."

The Down Payment

Many people don't think about *when* to buy a house. Timing can save you lots of money—but you have to be patient. We say, do not buy a house until the right time. This might mean waiting until you have a enough money for a large down payment to buy the home of your dreams. By avoiding the "starter" home syndrome and being patient, you will save money over the long haul. Waiting will mean you can buy a house to live in the rest of your life, instead of incurring the added expense of moving every five years. Of course, in a market where real estate prices are rising faster than investment earnings, you're better off buying now.

Another young couple we know in Colorado was married for seven years before they bought a house. They wanted to travel first. After awhile, their Priority Pyramid changed, when they had children and wanted a home. But they still waited until they could afford a charming four-bedroom house in the kind of neighborhood they liked. Because real estate prices were flat for the years they waited, they got a better house and a lower payment. They are satisfied with their house and will be mortgage-free when they retire.

It goes back to what we've been saying in our last two books: Pay yourself first. Shirley explains, "Build a nest egg. My advice is to make the largest down payment possible so that you can reduce your payments and maybe even shorten the payment period. Then you're not paying as much interest and at the end of so many years, you've got more equity in the house."

Ruth saved enough to put down half for the house she still lives in. She says, "It is a well-built home and still strong. My husband served in World War II, and I saved the allotment I received from him. I worked and lived on what I made, so, after the war, we could make a down payment."

If you can follow Ruth's example, and save up for a down payment in the short run, you'll be dollars ahead in the long run.

Looking for the Best Sellers

Remember the law of supply and demand? It works especially well for houses. A house in a desirable neighborhood sells for more, merely because so many people want to live there. A house being sold by someone who isn't moving for a year sells for more because the seller can afford to wait.

Searching out the most motivated sellers is a good way to get the most for your housing dollar. Look for houses being sold by people who need to move immediately because they've been transferred or have already bought a second home. Other good bets are homes that have been on the market for more than three months; foreclosures; and estate sales.

Can you find the "perfect" house this way? It depends on what you mean by perfect. If you are looking for the kind of house everyone else wants, it's unlikely you'll find a special deal. The market is too efficient—someone else is likely to find the house before you do.

If you're willing to buy an ugly duckling, live in a neighborhood in transition, in a very big or a very small house, or in a house near the highway, you may be able to find an overlooked house and a very desperate seller. When you do, you can save enough to allow you to live more extravagantly in other areas of your pyramid.

Margaret feels her house was the best deal she ever made, through a combination of savvy and luck. The house had been appraised for $36,000, they were asking $29,000, and Margaret and her husband paid $26,000 for it. The previous owners had been transferred, and their bank had taken over the house, which had been on the market for six months.

The time of year you buy a house can also affect the amount you spend a lot. If you have any choice, try to make an offer in the winter, when there are fewer buyers shopping for homes. Prices seem to drop in dreary weather, when a subtle psychological effect occurs. Houses look less "salable" without flowers blooming and the sun sparkling. Another good time to make an offer is over a holiday week or weekend. Again, you'll have less competition, so it will be more of a buyer's market.

Flexibility is a key factor when you buy a house. If you have a pre-approved mortgage and the ability to close now *or* later, you've just made yourself much more attractive to the seller. If you have your priorities straight and you're ready to move quickly, you'll find sellers much more motivated.

For Sale by Owner

Buying a house directly from its owner is a way to reduce your final price significantly. Real estate agents can charge 6 percent or more, and those selling houses without a broker are sometimes willing to share these savings with the purchaser. Beware, though, many sellers are trying to sell their homes themselves so that *they* can save money, not you.

Drive around neighborhoods you like, searching for "For Sale by Owner" signs. Check the newspaper listings. Let everyone know when you are ready to shop for a house. Word of mouth is often the fastest way to find a house without a broker. Carol has had the good fortune to buy from an owner twice. Her first house was advertised in the paper "For Sale by Owner." Carol says, "We were the first ones to call. This lady's husband had just died. She didn't want to stay there anymore and so we got a good deal on it." She bought the house she is in now from her sister. They both saved money by not using real estate agents.

You can go one step further. Once you find a neighborhood you like, try advertising that you'd like to buy a house there. Or place a flyer in mailboxes. Many home owners are excited and flattered to discover how easily they can sell their houses, and you may be able to find people delighted to sell without the hassle or uncertainty of listing their houses.

Ordinary Extras

Another often overlooked way to save money when you buy a home is to ask for more than just the house and property. If you can get a seller to include an item you would otherwise have to buy, it's as if you've just knocked money off the asking price. Usually a seller is more than happy to include an appliance or carpet or drapes or playhouse if it means the difference between selling and not selling a home.

Don't start out asking for anything extra, however. It's better to wait until you and the seller have gotten fairly close to agreeing on a price. Then, you're in a better position to say, "Okay, we have a deal but only on the condition that you'll give us this light fixture, too."

A woman we know in Oregon was buying her first house and didn't have any appliances. She asked the sellers, who were relocating and would have had to pay a hefty price to move them, to throw in the washing machine, dryer, refrigerator, and stove—all less than two years old. It was the equivalent of getting them to lower their selling price by at least $2,000. All she had to do was ask!

The Buyer's Broker

A money-saving techique that's rapidly growing in popularity is to hire a *buyer's broker*. Ordinarily, a real estate broker represents the person selling a house. This is true even if you go to a real estate agent and ask for help in buying a house: The seller is the primary client. In some states, the broker is a "dual agent" of both buyer and seller. An agent is required by law to reveal to the seller any financial information the agent discovers about the buyer. Naturally, such an agent is going to negotiate on the seller's behalf.

A buyer's broker, on the other hand, represents the buyer. This type of agent is required by law to get the best possible price and terms for you, the buyer. A buyer's broker does not have to reveal

BEARDSTOWN TALES

I wanted to know why my real estate assessment was so much higher this year. I filed a written complaint with the Cass County Real Estate Review Board. I had not made any improvements, and my location wasn't that ideal as now the main railroad line is across the street from my property. I want to pay my fair share, but this was quite a large increase. The Cass County Review Board answered my complaint stating that the fair market value was erroneously over-assessed. So one does have to be watchful.

MAXINE THOMAS

your financial information to the seller. According to one survey, people who use regular real estate agents pay an average of 96 percent of the list price of the homes they buy. Those who use buyer's brokers pay 91 percent on average. On a $100,000 home, you'd save $5,000! The buyer's broker's fee can be either an hourly rate or a flat rate. Even if it ends up costing as much as your share of the seller's agent's commission, it may be worth paying. A buyer's broker can be more objective when presenting you with potential properties and help you negotiate more aggressively.

How do you find such a broker in your area? Try asking your local board of Realtors®, large real estate agencies, or real estate teachers at colleges or universities, or call the Buyer's Broker Registry listed in the Resources section on page 259. Get a contract in writing before you work with any buyer's broker.

Financing a House

Before shopping for a house, it's worth investigating a pre-approved mortgage. This will give you a lot more clout in your negotiations, and possibly help you secure a lower price. Regardless of whether you're pre-approved, you'll need to make some important decisions about your mortgage. These decisions will have a huge impact on your income for years to come, so it's probably worth talking to a trusted lawyer, banker, accountant, or mortgage banker before you decide.

Mortgage payments include principal, interest, taxes, and insurance. It seems as if this is out of your control, and you can't lower your payment. In fact, you can control your costs in several ways:

- Pre-payments.

- Length of the loan.

- Adjustable rate versus fixed rate.

- Points.

Pre-payments

If you borrow $100,000 to buy a house and take a 30-year mortgage, *nearly half of your mortgage payments will go to the bank, not the house.* The amount of interest you will pay over the life of the mortgage is staggering, and you can make that number go down.

Consider the full impact of pre-paying even small amounts of the principal. For example, take a $50,000 mortgage at 8 percent for 30 years. Your monthly payment would be $366.88. Let's say you increased the monthly payment to $370, just $3.12 per month more. Do you realize this would reduce your loan repayment period by a full *year*? It's amazing what a small monthly increase in the principal amount does to the total life of a loan. Now imagine if you could pay an extra $20 each month (possibly from savings on insurance or real estate tax). You would cut five years off your loan and save $22,013 in interest, by paying $5 per week to accelerate your principal payment.

Buffy is a true believer in accelerating loan payments. Her theory is, "If you have something accumulating interest, pay it off as quickly as possible. Let's say the interest rate is 8 percent. If you continue to make payments to yourself, it's the same thing as putting money in an investment and trying to get 8 percent return. Accelerate payments as much as you can without hurting yourself."

There's an added bonus to paying ahead: It's great for your credit rating. When the credit companies check your credit history and see that you've paid ahead a certain number of times, it's a double-win situation.

By having lower payments you save thousands of dollars over the life of a loan. For example, say two couples decide to buy

MORTGAGE PAYMENT CHART

This chart shows you how much your monthly principal and interest payments for a 30-year, fixed rate mortgage and a 15-year, fixed-rate mortgage would be at different interest rates and different loan amounts.

Monthly Payments: 30-Year Mortgage

RATE OF INTEREST	AMOUNT OF MORTGAGE ($)						
	70,000	75,000	80,000	85,000	90,000	95,000	100,000
6%	419.69	449.66	479.64	509.62	539.60	569.57	599.55
6.5%	442.45	474.05	505.65	537.26	568.86	600.46	632.07
7%	465.71	498.98	532.24	565.51	598.77	632.04	665.30
7.5%	489.45	524.41	559.37	594.33	629.29	664.25	699.21
8%	513.64	550.32	587.01	623.70	660.39	697.08	733.76
8.5%	538.24	576.69	615.13	653.38	692.02	730.47	768.91
9%	563.24	603.47	643.70	683.93	724.16	764.39	804.66
9.5%	588.60	630.64	672.68	714.73	756.77	798.81	840.85
10%	614.30	658.18	702.06	745.94	789.81	833.69	877.57
10.5%	640.32	686.05	731.79	777.53	823.27	869.00	914.74
11%	666.63	714.24	761.86	809.47	857.09	904.71	952.32
11.5%	693.20	742.72	792.23	841.75	891.26	940.78	990.29
12%	720.03	771.46	822.89	874.32	925.75	977.18	1,028.61

Monthly Payments: 15-Year Mortgage

RATE OF INTEREST	AMOUNT OF MORTGAGE ($)						
	70,000	75,000	80,000	85,000	90,000	95,000	100,000
6%	590.70	632.89	675.09	717.28	759.47	801.66	843.86
6.5%	609.78	653.30	696.89	740.44	784.08	827.55	871.11
7%	629.18	674.12	719.06	764.00	808.95	853.89	898.83
7.5%	648.91	695.26	741.61	787.98	834.31	880.66	927.01
8%	668.96	716.64	764.52	812.30	860.09	907.87	955.65
8.5%	689.32	738.55	787.79	837.03	886.27	935.50	984.74
9%	709.99	760.70	811.42	862.13	912.84	963.55	1,014.27
9.5%	730.96	783.17	835.38	887.59	939.80	992.01	1,044.22
10%	752.22	805.95	859.68	913.41	967.14	1,020.87	1,074.61
10.5%	773.78	829.05	884.32	939.59	994.86	1,050.13	1,105.40
11%	795.62	852.45	909.28	966.11	1,022.94	1,079.77	1,136.60
11.5%	817.73	876.14	934.55	992.96	1,051.37	1,109.78	1,168.19
12%	840.12	900.13	960.13	1,020.14	1,080.15	1,140.16	1,200.17

houses. The Browns buy a $100,000 home. They've saved only $5,000 for a down payment, so they have to take out a $95,000 mortgage. It's a fixed-rate, 30-year loan at 8 percent interest. Their total bill will be $155,947. Their friends, the Clarks, also purchase a $100,000 house. But they've been paying themselves first for the last several years. They are able to put down $25,000 as a down payment. They take out a $75,000 mortgage at the same rate as the Browns. But at the end of the 30 years, the Clarks have spent $32,831 less for their home than the Browns.

Length of the Loan

The length of the loan, called the term, is another place you can dramatically reduce your overall financing costs. The difference between a 15-year and a 30-year mortgage is about 39 percent. How much money is that? If you take a $100,000 mortgage at 10 percent interest, you'll pay $193,430 for 15 years. In 30 years you'll spend $315,925, or $122,495 more. But, you say, how can I possibly afford a huge monthly payment on the 15-year mortgage? That depends. In reality, the shorter-term mortgage is only $197 more per month: $1,075 as opposed to $878. So if you can possibly squeak out the extra $197, it will be well worth your while.

Again, it comes back to your Personal Priority Pyramid and weighing how and when you spend your hard-earned cash. Would you rather skip restaurant meals for a few years now if it means eventually saving $122,495? Think of the kind of retirement you could afford if you invest that savings! On the other hand, if you are a real gourmet, maybe eating out today is more important to you than all the golf in the world tomorrow.

Fixed versus Adjustable Rate

Interest is generally the biggest expense home owners face in their monthly payments. The difference of a fraction of a percentage point in an interest rate can mean thousands of dollars over 15 or 30 years, not to mention substantially higher or lower monthly payments. You'd pay $109 less a month if you had a 30-year $100,000 mortgage at 8.5 percent as opposed to 10 percent.

Many people think that a fixed rate is the best bargain. They don't like the uncertainty as to whether or not their payments will go up if interest rates rise. An adjustable-rate mortgage generally has a lower interest rate than a fixed-rate mortgage. How much lower it is can determine whether you want to choose this route, but it can be a good choice. You need to look at the overall picture.

The adjustable-rate mortgages usually have a cap on them; they cannot increase more than 2 percent a year, or 7 percent over the life of the loan. If interest rates skyrocketed 3 percent in one year, for instance, the bank would only raise your payment 2 percent for the next 12 months. If you had a crystal ball and could forecast the upward and downward trend of interests rates, you could make a fortune. Don't rely on your intuition about interest rates and don't rely too much on analysts' predictions. The average home owner moves every seven years. If you think you will be moving within seven years, the 1 or 2 percent lower interest rate for an adjustable mortgage may be worthwhile to you—especially if it is 2 percent or more below the fixed rate. Interest rates have remained relatively stable during the past decade, and in no one year have they increased over 2 percent, so this is actually a safer method than it once was in the early 1980s when interest rates soared to 18 percent.

The bottom line here—if you're going to move soon, an adjustable-rate mortgage is probably right for you.

Pointers on Points

You can't calculate the total cost of your mortgage until you include any points your lender may charge. Points are a finance charge you pay at closing to increase the lender's profit above and beyond the stated interest rate of your mortgage. A point equals 1 percent of the total loan: one point of a $95,000 loan would be $950. When you are shopping for a mortgage, don't let a "no-points, no-fees" offer fool you. If the loan is at a much higher interest rate than one with points, you might be better off paying the points. For example, a mortgage with no points and an 8 percent interest rate is not as good a deal as a mortgage with one point and a 7.25 percent interest rate. *LOOK* before you leap.

The Biweekly Mortgage

A practically painless way to lower your interest costs over the life of the loan is the biweekly mortgage payment. Rather than making a full payment once a month, you make half a payment every other week. It is so simple that we don't know why everyone doesn't request it, but we do know why most banks don't suggest it. It is a terrible "interest income" loser for them! Since many people get a weekly paycheck, this may even fit into your budget in an easier fashion than the monthly payment. It also may seem easier to make half a payment every other week because it seems like less money. Here's an example of how staggering the savings actually are:

The monthly payment on a $50,000 mortgage at 8 percent for 30 years is $366.89. With the biweekly payment you could make a half payment of $183.45 every other week. With a once-a-month payment over the life of the loan, your total payments would be $132,078. Paying biweekly, you'd spend only $109,996. That's a savings of $22,082 in interest over the life of the loan. By paying every two weeks, you pay more on the principal faster because you are paying interest each period. The amount of interest goes down as the amount of principal goes up with each payment rather than only once a month. Also, by paying every other week you actually make 13 payments a year rather than 12. This accelerates principal payments and cuts almost seven years off the life of a 30-year loan, and it's relatively painless.

There is one catch: Most lenders want you to have the biweekly payments automatically deducted from a checking or savings account, rather than mail a check. They may charge a fee for this service too. There is more paperwork for twice as many payments, so they prefer it to be automated to cut down on their processing expense. This is only fair to the bank—you really are preventing them from making $22,000 in interest on your loan!

Taxes

Real estate taxes are computed differently from every other form of tax you pay. They're not based on your income, on how much you paid for your house, or even on how big your land is.

They're based on a very subjective judgment of what your house is worth relative to other houses. This is called an assessment, and it forms the basis for your real estate taxes. Surprisingly, most people don't know what their assessment is, and don't realize they can change it.

BEARDSTOWN TALES

I live in a home my late husband and I built in 1984. We spent more money on building our home than on anything else. Don did his own contracting, hiring electricians, plumbers, and carpenters. We got low prices or discounts on almost everything that went into our house. Our three sliding glass doors and the windows were half-price. And we got a good price on discontinued paneling. We knew how much money we wanted to spend building our home and knew as we went along what it was costing. I don't really need a three-bedroom home now, but I do enjoy it. It's nice when my children come for the holidays or when friends visit for a few days.

ANN CORLEY

How do you know if you are over-assessed? In Illinois, the assessment of homes is supposed to be one-third of their cash value. If you have purchased your home recently, say within the last five to seven years, you are probably currently assessed at close to one-third of the market value. If you have lived for many years in your home, and purchased it when prices were substantially lower, you may or may not be assessed at current market value. It depends on how good the county assessor is at keeping up with reassessment of market values. In small counties where there is one assessor, and no computerized system, the assessments may not be current. If you think you may be over-assessed there is a way to check, but it requires some work on your part.

The county keeps assessments on public record at the local courthouse. Go in and see how all properties in the county are assessed. While you are there, check your property record card. Do they have the correct size of your home? If they have more square feet on the card than your house actually has, you need to apply for a *certificate of error.* This may result in a lower tax for you immediately!

The trick is to find three or more homes that are very similar to your house. Check their assessments, and check the size from the property record cards. Divide the assessment amount by the square feet and see at what price they are assessed per square foot. Is your home over-assessed per square foot compared to neighbors' homes that are similar in quality and design? If so, you may do well to file a complaint to get the taxes lowered. This will necessitate appearing in person, or submitting a typed complaint before the local board of review.

It really is a simple method. Use the Property Tax Assessment Reduction Request Worksheet on page 38. First, enter the size of your home and total assessment. Divide the assessment by the square feet of your home. Now find three or more comparable homes, similar to yours. Check their size and assessment per square foot. It also is a good idea to calculate the percentage of discrepancy on assessments in relation to yours. Finally, ask for a specific assessment that you think is fair. Don't leave it to chance or to the discretion of the board of review. Ask for what you want. You may just get it. Even if you don't, you probably will get a reduction of some type, and that reduction will remain the next year and thereafter.

This will save you more than a few hundred dollars in taxes. Compound that savings by the number of years you live in the home, and you will see how many thousands of dollars you have saved. If the expense is offset by future tax savings, you may prefer to hire a local professional (attorney, real estate agent, appraiser) to do this work.

Insurance

When you borrow money to buy a house, the lender will require you to carry home owner's insurance. We recommend you get several estimates and make sure that you are not carrying excessive coverage. Remember, if you try to insure yourself for everything that *might* happen, you could end up having an insurance escrow as high as the taxes. Use common sense, since this is one area you can control. Don't leave yourself uncovered, and meet all requirements that your lender has on insurance, including liability insurance. (For more detailed insurance information, see the home owner's section of Chapter Five.)

WORKSHEET

PROPERTY TAX ASSESSMENT
REDUCTION REQUEST

Assessment Subject _____

Address _____

Assessment # of Subject _____

Name of Owner _____

	ASSESSMENT	÷	SQUARE FEET IN HOUSE	=	ASSESSED VALUE
Subject	$15,000	÷	1,000	=	15.00
COMPARABLE ASSESSMENTS					
Comp #1	$12,000		1,100		$10.90
Comp #2	$12,500		1,150		$10.86
Comp #3	$10,500		950		$10.52

Average of three assessments = $10.76 per square foot

Request assessment for [subject address] at 10,760 assessed valuation based on square feet in subject and average assessment per square foot.

Another type of insurance you may be required to purchase is private mortgage insurance (PMI), sometimes called mortgage insurance premium (MIP). When you make a down payment of less than 20 percent of the home's purchase price, your lender will make this part of your mortgage payment. In addition to private mortgage insurance, the government insures some mortgages through the Federal Housing Administration, the U.S. Department of Veterans Affairs, or the Farmers Home Administration. Anyone can apply for FHA insurance, while the others have more specific requirements. These government agencies enable people to buy homes with as little as 2 to 5 percent down payment.

Make no mistake: This is insurance for your lender, not for you. It's to protect the lender against losing money if you stop making mortgage payments. The amount ranges from 1/2 to 1 percent of the mortgage loan. Once you have paid off enough principal so you own 20 percent or more equity in your home, you usually don't have to continue carrying mortgage insurance. Keep track of how much equity you have so you can "remind" your lender to remove the extra fee at the appropriate time.

Control Your Closing Costs

Closing costs, also called settlement costs in some areas, can come as a shock if you aren't prepared for them. They are all the "extras" you are charged at the time you meet with the seller to do legal paperwork necessary for the transfer of the house. Closing costs run 2 percent to 10 percent of the price you pay for your house, so it's easy to see why keeping them to a minimum can save hundreds of dollars.

What are these mysterious closing costs? Sometimes, just that: mysteries! There's usually such a long laundry list of items and the buyer is so overwhelmed at the number of checks he or she is writing, that a few hundred dollars here or there hardly seems worth questioning.

You'll probably bring a lawyer with you to the closing. At times, it seems as though the lawyer is more interested in working with the other lawyers and the title company official than in representing your interests. Make it very clear to your lawyer before the closing that you want each and every questionable charge brought to your attention, and that you'd like her to work hard to negotiate these costs down. Oftentimes, the seller will pay for some of these costs as part of the sale. But you must *ask*.

Common closing costs include a loan origination fee—if it hasn't been paid already (ask!)—points (another term for a fee the lender charges the borrower on top of the actual principal and interest), prepaid home owner's insurance, appraisal fee, lawyers' fees, recording fee, title search and insurance, notary fee, transfer tax, tax adjustments, agents' commissions, mortgage insurance (if your lender requires it), and other miscellaneous expenses. These costs vary a lot from locale to locale, but there are two general principles you can apply no matter where your closing takes place:

1. *Watch out for plain old-fashioned errors.* Bring a calculator to your closing and re-check all the math on your closing sheet. Accountants and computers still make mistakes! We know a family who moved across the country a few years ago. They drove right to their closing their first day on the East Coast, arriving with two small, tired children. Much to the wife's chagrin, the husband took out his calculator and checked every single dollar and cent. Much to her delight, he found several errors and saved them several hundred dollars.

2. *Be aware of hidden, inflated, or unnecessary costs.* These may appear in the form of jargon such as "document transportation fee," or "escrow waiver fee." Or they may seem perfectly reasonable—say, flood insurance—until you realize you are buying a home in an area on top of a hill with absolutely no chance of ever flooding. Or there may be a charge of $100 for filing a title in a state that only asks $50 for that service.

Keep in mind that you are the consumer. You have the right to question everything, no matter how tedious or time-consuming it may seem. Don't let a room full of attorneys and bankers intimidate you. You may be surprised at how fast a lender will back down on a certain charge in order to salvage a closing.

Refinancing

If you already own your home, your mortgage is probably at the top of your Spending Pyramid. You should definitely think about how to save in that area. There is a way to reduce your monthly payments through refinancing. When interest rates decrease below what they were when you first took out a mortgage, it is a great time to cash in on this opportunity. Usually the rates have to be two percentage points lower than your current mortgage to make refinancing economical.

Not taking advantage of lower interest rates is like turning down thousands of dollars in savings. Yet many people don't get around to looking into it. It can seem confusing and like a lot of work at first. The trick is to figure out whether or not it's worth it to you, to *STOP*, *LOOK*, and *LISTEN*. Once you know for a fact that you'll save a specific amount of money, you may be much more motivated to make those phone calls to your lender. Should you want to refi-

WORKSHEET

MORTGAGE REFINANCING

Here is a sample worksheet to help you calculate how long before you realize savings from refinancing.

1. Present principal and interest payments on $45,000 at 9.5% interest:	$378.39
2. Proposed principal and interest payments on $45,000 at 8% interest:	$330.20
3. Subtract Line 2 from Line 1 for your monthly savings:	$48.19
4. Total closing costs from Bank Disclosure Statement:	$1,823.38
5. Amount of interest included in Bank Disclosure Statement:	$284.38
6. Subtract Line 5 from Line 4 for actual closing cost:	$1,539.00
Actual closing cost (Line 6):	$1,539.00
Divided by monthly savings (Line 3):	$48.19
Equals number of months before you start saving after refinancing:	32 months*

*31.93 round off to 32

nance, the easiest way to see if it is worthwhile is to fill in the Mortgage Refinancing Worksheet on page 257.

First you get the total cost of refinancing (closing cost disclosure) from the bank where you plan to obtain the loan. Then you calculate your savings on monthly payments by subtracting your estimated principal and interest payment (calculated by the bank) on the proposed refinance from your present principal and interest payment (ignore taxes and insurance for this exercise). Divide the refinance cost or closing costs disclosure by the monthly savings to determine how many months it will take you to make up the closing costs and *really start saving money*. If you will start saving within two to three years, refinancing is worthwhile.

GETTING THE MOST FOR YOUR HOUSE

Whether you are selling your home through a real estate agent or by yourself, using the following checklist can increase your sale price by hundreds—sometimes thousands—of dollars. So before you open your door to the first potential buyer, make as many of these improvements as possible. Remember, your house won't sell itself—you have to help it!

- *Paint, paint, paint.* Studies show that curbside appeal rises dramatically depending on the color of your home. If it's an odd or dreary color, it will seriously reduce your asking price. In that case, it's worth the investment to paint it a nice, light, neutral color such as white or beige.

- *If you don't want to paint the whole house, touch up the trim.* Concentrate especially on the front door. Be sure it looks great. Replace the doorknobs and locks if necessary.

- *Inside, check each room for peeling wallpaper or dirty painted surfaces.* Repaint or touch up.

- *Wash all the windows.* Open all the curtains and blinds. Let the light shine in to make your house look bright and appealing.

- *Put higher-watt light bulbs in all your fixtures.* This will also enliven your decor.

- *Put fresh flowers in halls and living and dining rooms.* Place potted flowers on the front porch or along the walkway.

- *Pack up a third of all your possessions in every room.* You'll be amazed at how much more modern and spacious your home will seem just by clearing away the clutter.

- *Check for anything broken*—leaky faucets, chipped cabinet knobs, a rusty fence post—and fix or replace if possible.

- *Take down and replace any special fixtures,* such as Aunt Margaret's chandelier, that you plan to bring with you. What the buyer doesn't see won't hurt your asking price.

- *Finally, one of the most neglected yet important things you can do: a smell check.* This is something that's difficult to do yourself because you've become accustomed to the smell of your own home. Find a relative or friend to come in and give you the straight scoop. If there is a pesky odor, either try to remove the source or disguise it by boiling cinnamon, cloves, and apples on the stove whenever prospective buyers come calling.

Refinance charges can cost anywhere from $500 to $2,000 and up. If you don't have this amount of cash available, most banks allow you to include the refinance charges in the new mortgage amount, provided you have enough present equity in your home.

Another important factor in deciding to refinance is whether or not you think you will be living in your present house for a certain number of years. Many of Buffy's clients have refinanced their homes to cash in on lower interest rates. Then they were transferred within six months and didn't get to enjoy the benefit of the lower interest. Some of them did not even get past the break-even point of the refinance charges. So don't rush to refinance because the rates are low. Look at the total picture, and take time to calculate your potential savings. Margaret, for example, has considered refinancing her home, but has held off because she and her husband are considering selling it and getting more acreage for their horses. She's wise to wait awhile.

Other reasons it might make sense to refinance include:

- If you have an adjustable-rate mortgage and want to convert it to a fixed-rate loan.

- If you want to change to an adjustable-rate mortgage with a lower cap or interest rate.

- If you want to convert to a shorter-term loan (a 15-year mortgage instead of a 30-year mortgage).

- If you want to draw on the equity in your house to finance other major purchases such as a college education.

Selling Your Home Yourself

Many people think that selling a home is quite simple, and that they would do just as well selling it themselves rather than listing with a broker. You may be tempted by the possibility of saving thousands of dollars in a broker's commission, but Buffy's professional opinion is to let a professional handle it.

Before you decide to sell your house yourself, you need to ask three important questions:

1. *Will a broker's connections and skills allow this house to sell for at least 6 percent more than I can sell it for myself?* If the answer to this question is yes, then using a broker is the smart choice. In many communities, the broker has built up a good network and learned enough about pricing to generate far more than 6 percent in additional value.

2. *Am I willing to spend the time and energy to do this right?* If you can sell your $100,000 home without a broker, you've just saved $6,000. Even if you spend $1,000 on advertisements, you still come out $5,000 ahead. That's a lot of income in exchange for 50 or 100 hours of work. But if you can't commit to doing the work, then don't try to do it yourself.

3. *Will the process make me miserable?* If the stress of selling your most expensive asset will cost you sleep, think twice about it. If you're the kind of person who will second-guess yourself for years about the outcome (or even worse, second-guess your spouse), then it's a false economy.

Selling a house yourself is a lot of work, and if you decide to do it, you should read several books on the topic, find other people who have recently gone through the process, and take a thoughtful, step-by-step approach.

Getting
Down To
Brass Tacks

1. *Shop for the shortest-term, lowest-interest mortgage you can afford to save tens of thousands of dollars.*

2. *Shop carefully for a real estate broker, or buyer's broker, or try selling your own home.*

3. *Consider refinancing if your new rate is at least two percentage points lower than your existing mortgage rate and if you plan to stay in your house for at least three more years.*

CHAPTER THREE

SAVING ON AUTO SPENDING

Did you know it's possible to save a quarter of a million dollars just by driving your cars a little bit longer?

THERE ARE ALMOST AS MANY REASONS TO BUY a car as there are kinds of cars, and understanding why you want a car is important. We don't drive cars only for transportation, or else we'd never see sports cars, convertibles, and limos.

Ask yourself: Would you drive a car with a big gouge in the door if the dealer took $1,000 off the price? $5,000? Does the color matter? Why? How important is safety to you—would you be willing to drive an older car if you knew it were safer?

Before you go car shopping, make a list of the things your car must do or have, and give each one a dollar value. For example, if air-conditioning were $5,000 extra, would you buy it? Most of us would say no, and that's a first step toward figuring out what each feature is really worth to you.

As you look at your Personal Priority and Spending Pyramids, think about what portion of your income you're willing to invest in each aspect of owning a car.

Once you've got an idea of what's really important and what's a frill, it will be much easier for you to identify an acceptable car for you. Then you can decide if you want to pay the extra money for the car of your dreams.

Before You Buy a Car

Think about the price of a new car, any make of car. So many Americans get caught in the habit of buying a new car every two years. But why? The instant you drive that shiny, brand-new car off the lot, it depreciates by 20 percent. Then add the fact that more than half the cost of owning a new car goes toward depreciation and interest on loan payments. Is it worth it? Are you any safer, more comfortable, or better off in a late-model car? You could have driven your cars a few more years and invested the difference.

STOP!

Consider that the reasons you buy a car may include:

1. *Transportation.*
2. *Flexibility.*
3. *Sex appeal.*
4. *Reliability.*
5. *Safety.*
6. *Impress friends and family.*
7. *The pleasure of driving.*
8. *Convenient features.*
9. *Inexpensive operating costs.*

"We own one car and one truck," Ann Brewer says. "We do not have to drive 'new' cars every year. We tend to drive our vehicles five or six years." Doris likes to buy her cars new—every five to seven years. Right off the bat she's saving those extra thousands of dollars she'd otherwise spend on replacing them more often. Ruth's car has about 97,000 miles on it. She says, "It's 10 years old and I do need a new one. But I don't travel out of town like I used to. I try to keep it up."

We Ladies tend to drive our cars a long time and repair them instead of trading them in at the first sign of wear. Maxine says, "I hate to invest in a new car, so I'm trying to keep mine up. With my eyesight I don't know how long I'll be able to drive."

Carol has five vehicles, including one she bought new. It's a 1988 model and has 123,000 miles on it. "We've had minor repairs. We change the oil regularly and keep it running."

By driving your car for even two more years than you used to, you can save a sizable amount—enough to become your retirement nest egg if you invest it. Instead of the high premium you pay for a brand-new car, you can buy a slightly-used car and take advantage of the incredible rate of depreciation yet still have that luxurious new-car feeling. You need to consider what you want out of a car, what you need, and then decide whether to buy

WORKSHEET
BUYING A NEW CAR

You may want to use this form to help you figure out how much leeway you have to bargain with a car dealer.

MODEL _____

	INVOICE PRICE	RETAIL PRICE
BASE PRICE	_____	_____

OPTIONS

AUTOMATIC TRANSMISSION	_____	_____
STANDARD TRANSMISSION	_____	_____
AIR-CONDITIONING	_____	_____
ENGINE SIZE	_____	_____
DIESEL ENGINE	_____	_____
CASSETTE PLAYER	_____	_____
POWER BRAKES	_____	_____
POWER STEERING	_____	_____
POWER LOCKS	_____	_____
POWER SEATS	_____	_____
REAR WIPER/WASHER	_____	_____
FULL SIZE SPARE TIRE	_____	_____
STEEL BELTED RADIALS	_____	_____
DUAL MIRRORS	_____	_____
REMOTE CONTROLLED MIRRORS	_____	_____
LUGGAGE RACK	_____	_____
SUNROOF	_____	_____
LEATHER INTERIOR	_____	_____
OTHER	_____	_____

a new car, how often to buy, what kind, or whether a used car might be a good alternative.

What Do You Need?

STOP and consider: Do you need a roomy car? A prestigious car? A comfortable car? Does your car need to be the least expensive one possible, the most fuel-efficient, or absolutely the safest model on the road? Do you haul groceries, lumber, dogs, or children in your car? The whole soccer team or office supplies for a small business? Does your car have to be a workhorse to get you back and forth to a distant job? Or do you use it to run errands around town? Do you take long, leisurely driving vacations or use your car for deliveries? In other words try not to think about your car as merely an object but about what you need it to do.

Carnell says it's important when buying a new car to assess your needs. Because she is on the road a lot, often by herself, it's most important she have reliable transportation. Each time you buy a car, it's a good idea to reassess your needs, which change over time. Sylvia had a Cadillac for awhile. But now that she doesn't do much driving, she says she "figured I didn't need such a powerful car. So, I bought a Buick instead."

Several of the Ladies need their cars for business purposes, and that determines much of their decision when it comes to what kind of car to buy. Buffy is a real estate broker and feels obligated to drive a large car. It has to be large and spacious and comfortable for her clients. "My car is a marketing tool. If I were not in this business, I'd only have a pickup truck."

When Ruth and her husband were in the dry cleaning business, they bought a new car every three years. "We used to deliver clothes in it," Ruth says. "We really put miles on it. My husband insisted on black, which you had to order. He used to have it washed every day for a dollar at the filling station across the street. He was so proud of his car."

Ruth's husband knew he wanted a spotless black car. It's as important to know what you *want* as it is to know what you *need* before buying a car.

What Do You Want?

In our recipe for investing, we look at 10 ingredients. One is personal preference. It's the same for buying a car—even more so! We spend so much time in our cars, we want to be sure we like what we're driving. The point is that even if you decide you want to drive a big, luxury car, there are still plenty of ways to reduce the cost. You need to know what you want first.

When Betty and her husband travel, they like to stop, buy what they want, and take as much luggage as they want. Betty likes a roomy car, so she drives a Mercury Grand Marquis. Maxine is the opposite. After her husband died, she knew she wanted a new car to avoid "any worries." She preferred a Pontiac because she was familiar with them. She wanted a much smaller car than the one she had owned with her husband. "I felt it would be easier to park and take care of."

Buffy, who owns the Lincoln for business, really is happiest in her old, $1,500 junker pickup truck. "I love it," she says. "I use it to carry my For Sale signs so that I don't get the Lincoln's trunk all muddy. I use it when I do work on my rental properties. I can haul junk and other stuff. When I work on my yard, I can fill the back end full of tools and fertilizer. I use it to save putting a lot of miles on my Lincoln. I try to put all my personal miles—hunting and fishing, country activities, working in the yard—on the truck. Those miles are non-deductible. They don't make me any money. Not that I drive my truck to church on Sunday!"

Do you *want* a new car or a used car? The answer to that often changes quite a bit. Sylvia buys new cars because she says she doesn't want "anybody else's troubles." Carnell and her husband bought used cars for many years. "We were raising children and we needed transportation. We didn't need the latest and best in cars. We wanted to economize. We started buying new cars when the children were in high school. Cars meant more to them than to us. Sometimes you spend more to improve family relations."

We know a young couple who set out to buy a $6,000 used Toyota and came back with a $24,000 new Saab. The thrill of the purchase made them shift their priorities about what was important to them in a car. Some people get a great deal of pleasure from buying a new car. They enjoy having a clean and shiny vehicle in their driveway, and it's worth the extra money to get a new one every two or three years. Remember, money is a tool to buy us what we like. Once you recognize that this is a luxury and one that you're willing to indulge, by all means do it!

The Beardstown Advantage

These days the typical American spends an average of $19,000 on a new car. For some people, a car is their biggest expenditure, amounting to 40 percent of their income. "Our largest purchase was our last new car in 1993," Ann Brewer says. "Since we purchased our house back in 1955, it takes a backseat to the purchase of an automobile."

Saving money on such a sizable investment is essential to our pyramid approach. Fortunately, when it comes to buying a car, a little *LOOK* before you leap makes a dollar go a long way.

Not long ago, Margaret Houchins told us that she was going to replace the minivan she uses to drive us to our speaking engagements and book signings. We could get seven Ladies in her van. We laugh, we giggle, we tell stories. It's helped us form such a good close relationship. If we have to take two cars, then we feel like we miss out. Although her husband really wanted her to go for a Lincoln or a Cadillac, Margaret decided to shop for a minivan—a red one, because that's her favorite color.

Margaret looked and looked for a red minivan. After haggling with the third dealer, she and her husband were getting pretty tired. Usually, shopping when you're tired leads to a bad purchase decision. But if you're prepared, it can help you end up with the right deal. Margaret describes what happened next:

"I was thinking, I'd rather be home. We asked to speak with the manager and told him that we knew what our bank was willing to loan us for this model and what our old van was worth. We told him what we were prepared to offer and asked if we had a deal. Usually we're not that aggressive. We had done our homework and were confident enough to negotiate.

"The manager recognized me as a Beardstown Lady. He said if I threw in an autographed copy of our book I had a deal. He got his book, I drove home in my red minivan, and we were both satisfied."

Even if you're not a Beardstown Lady, approaching a car dealer with specific needs and a lot of knowledge can get you the car you want.

Do Your Homework

In our first two books, we talk a lot about doing your homework. Perhaps nowhere is this more true than in buying a car. The more you know before you set foot onto a car lot, the more money you're likely to save. *LOOK* before you leap: Before you test drive a car, go straight to your library, magazine stand, or online service and start reading. We suggest *Consumer Reports* as a good starting place for narrowing down car models and options that fit your needs and budget. Try to arm yourself with figures to know what price you should be looking for. You also want to know how the car is rated on accidents and reliability. Check the Resources section on page 261 for a list of helpful publications.

Being flexible can help you find a better deal. That's what happened to Doris. "For years, I had driven Pontiacs. My 1987 Pontiac had been a good one, but it was getting quite a few miles on it. I started looking around. I was interested in front-wheel drive, power brakes,

BEARDSTOWN TALES

I live in the country and a car is of the utmost importance. I was driving a 1986 car and had promised to sell it to my granddaughter Cindy when she turned 16. Shopping for my new car was delayed for several months due to a hip injury. Time came when I needed to do my shopping pronto. I didn't need to go shopping around with a grandson selling cars at the Buick dealership. It was the fall of the year and new models were coming out, so I got a $1,500 bonus off the 1995 car along with an AARP discount of $1,000. Laughing we all called it the little grandma's car as it was a popular choice for people over 50. It doesn't have a lot of fancy doodads to fluster me. It fits my needs and I really like it. I feel I did get a good deal on my purchase.

ELSIE SCHEER

power steering, and four doors. I looked at Pontiacs and Buicks, but they didn't satisfy my expectations. At an Oldsmobile dealer I was greeted by a former student. Having known him, his parents, and his grandparents, I placed much trust and respect in his explanation of his cars. I found an Oldsmobile with all the features that I wanted."

The Invoice Price

Find out the invoice price of the model and each option you want. You can do this several ways. For a good approximation of what the dealer paid for the car, multiply the cost factor included in the *Consumer Reports* annual car profiles by the sticker price. For an exact factory invoice price, you can use one of the services, such as Edmunds' New Car Prices, listed in the Resources section. A nominal fee, usually $12 to $15, will buy you a printout on any model you wish.

It's also good to know the value of your old car before you shop for a new car. Even if you have decided to sell it yourself instead of trading it in, check classifieds in your area or the *Edmund's Used Car Guide* to get an idea of what it's worth. You may want to check with a loan officer at your bank to see how much you should expect in trade and what the car you are interested in should cost.

How to Buy a New Car

Here's our step-by-step process for buying a new car.

1. *Shop around. Compare models and final sale prices at different dealers.* When Betty and Bob were shopping for her Grand Marquis, for example, the first owner "talked like he would give us a real good deal. When we compared his deal with another one, it was not nearly as good. We do comparison shopping. We're not afraid to go to more than one place."

2. *Be ready to bargain.* Your goal should be to get the best possible price while still leaving the dealer some profit. Think up from the invoice price rather than down from the sticker price. We like to aim for 3 to 7 percent over the invoice price. "One of the things that amazes me in working with young people is how many are willing to pay the first price quoted," says Betty.

BUYING A NEW CAR

How Much Does It Cost?

When you ask the price of a car, the answer may be confusing unless you are familiar with the following terms and what they mean.

- *Invoice Price*: The equivalent to wholesale, this is the price the manufacturer or factory charged the car dealer. Often it is higher than the dealer's actual final cost because of rebates, allowances, discounts, and incentive awards for the dealer. The invoice price includes destination and delivery charges, also called freight.

- *Base Price*: This is the cost of the car without options. It includes standard equipment, factory warranty, and delivery charges. The base price should be printed on the Monroney sticker.

- *Monroney Sticker Price*: This is the price when the manufacturer's already-installed options are added to the base price. Required by federal law, this label is attached to the car window. It also shows the manufacturer's transportation charge, fuel economy or mileage, and the manufacturer's suggested retail price.

- *Dealer Sticker Price*: This is the Monroney sticker price with the dealer's suggested prices for other options such as preparation and undercoating. It is like the retail price and may include terms such as "additional dealer markup" or "additional dealer profit."

"It's a shame we have to bargain, but for the most part, we do when it comes to buying a vehicle."

3. *Keep coming back to the total price.* Don't let a salesman confuse you with numbers. The only number that matters is the final price.

4. *Walk in with a list of things you must have and politely refuse to pay for any feature not on your list.* Along the same lines, if you do not see a car with only the features you want on the dealer's lot, have it ordered. Although it will take longer, you won't end up paying for features you didn't want in the first place. Oftentimes, car dealerships will carry vehicles with higher-priced features on their lots in an effort to convince

you to pay the extra money and avoid the wait. Don't fall for this. Stick with your original list.

5. *Avoid discussing financing your new car or trading in your old car until the very end of your negotiation.* Adding those figures into the mix will only complicate an already complex bargaining position.

6. *Keep some information to yourself.* We don't mean you can't be friendly. We do mean you should stay on your toes. You certainly don't want to let on that you may be in a rush to find a specific model car in time for your daughter's high school graduation gift. Such information could be used against you, to strong-arm you into paying more than if you suggested you were willing to shop around. By the same token, don't mention other dealers' price quotes.

7. *Deal with the sales manager.* It's worth calling ahead to see whether you can make an appointment with him directly. If one dealership says no, try another. By avoiding the highly trained, high-pressure salesperson you will undoubtedly save money. For one thing, the manager can't use himself as an excuse to bully you, as in "Oh, I'd love to come down on the price for you, but my manager won't let me."

8. *Get everything in writing.* Once you have agreed on a deal, ask for it in writing. Verbal agreements, sad but true, are not going to hold up should you have a dispute. This applies to refundable deposits, price quotes, or any other promises made to you. Also, write everything down yourself as you gather information. Otherwise it's all too easy for a salesperson to "forget" that he had given you a quote of several hundred dollars less a few minutes ago.

All About Options

Manufacturers make a far greater profit on the options than on the car. Of course, some are important because they add safety and comfort to your car. Many experts recommend spending extra for such features as air bags—which have become standard and required in most cars anyway—antilock brakes, rear window wipers, and traction control. Carnell and her husband have "quite a few options because we're older. We like the automatic seats. As we travel, we can adjust these and we can drive longer periods comfortably. We're buying more comfort than we formerly did."

Other options just take money out of your pocket. Generally these are dealer-installed extras such as fabric protection, paint sealant, rustproofing, and pinstripes. They can add another $1,000 or more to the price of your car. When Ann Corley bought a car, the dealer suggested several options which she didn't need. "It runs the price of the car up too much. You might pay for a little stripe but it doesn't make the car worth any more."

For most people these days, buying extra rustproofing is not necessary. That's because most cars are made with fewer parts that can rust. Plus, they often come with rustproofing already, as well as rustproofing warranties.

We recommend that you avoid any pre-assembled option packages. They rarely are exactly the right combination for each individual. Although they may seem like bargains, they're not if you wind up with extras you never wanted. You need to decide which options make sense for you and say no to the rest. Doris is somewhat of an exception. When she bought her last car, it already had everything on it. That was important, she explains, "because every Sunday I visit relatives and family. They live about 70 miles from Beardstown—that's a long drive. So I want a nice, dependable, comfortable car with air-conditioning and everything automatic." Doris wants the options and is willing to pay for them. Good for her!

DOLLARS AND SENSE

Be on the alert if you hear the following from a car salesperson:

- *Shop around. I'll beat any offer.*

- *Your information is wrong.*

Try not to answer these trick questions— they'll cost you money:

- *If I can get you X amount on your trade-in, will you buy today?*

- *If we get your monthly payment down to X, will you buy today?*

- *How much would you pay for this car?*

- *How much do you think I should make?*

Warnings on Warranties

Every expert we've consulted has one thing to say about an extended warranty on a new car: Forget it. An extended warranty is one of the most expensive options a dealer can add. Not surprisingly, it's one the dealer will try to sell most aggressively because it provides a big profit. These warranties cost you from $300 to $1,000, yet their coverage is often useless. Either the repairs they include are so major that the warranty covers only a fraction of the total, or the deductible is too high to cover all the little nuisance repairs a new car is more likely to have.

Our advice is to skip such extended warranties and stash away some cash in an interest-bearing account instead. Then, in the unlikely event you do need a big repair, you'll still be okay.

What About Used Cars?

One of the easiest ways to save $100,000 to $200,000 over your working life is never to buy a new car. That doesn't mean you have to drive a beat-up jalopy—it just means that you let someone else bear the expense of a fancy new showroom car. Here's an example: According to a classified ad in a city newspaper, you can buy a one-year-old Taurus from a dealer for about $13,000. The same car, brand-new, would cost you $19,500 by the time you drive it away. Three years from now, when you sell the used car, you'll get about $2,500 less than the new car would fetch (because your car is a year older). The end result is you save up to $2,500 every time you buy a car. The savings are even greater if you buy a three-year-old car, and greater still if you buy it from an individual instead of a dealer.

As we said, buying used does not mean you have to settle for a lesser car. Take Buffy and her luxury Lincoln. She says she would never buy a new Lincoln at the full sticker price. Instead she always buys a "pre-owned" or "program" car. These are cars that the Ford Motor Company leases to or provides for their executives to drive for six months and then sells to dealers. They may be $10,000 below sticker price with up to 15,000 miles. Buffy's car is a '95. She says, "I bought it in 1995 with 13,000 miles on it. I paid $27,900 and the sticker price was $38,000. Now that's quite a substantial savings."

This strategy works equally well for more utilitarian vehicles. Margaret's "new" red minivan is a '95 previously leased car. It had 20,000 miles. "We wanted a car that was a year old," Margaret says. "Once you drive a brand-new car off the lot, there's going to be depreciation. You're continuously taking it back to the dealer to get all of those little bugs worked out. You've got your time spent, plus your depreciation, so I can't see that that is a very good buy. Unless you prefer to have a brand-new one."

Very slightly used cars or "demonstrators" are a subcategory. They may have only been driven off the lot a few miles. But because they are technically "used," you get to take advantage of that magical depreciation rate. Doris got this kind of good deal on her most recent "new" car purchase. "I bought a car that had been driven only 541 miles," Doris explains. "I was able to save $6,000."

Then there are old-fashioned regular used cars, which quite a few of us have owned. Some of us, like Shirley and Maxine, bought them when we were younger and couldn't afford anything else. Others, like Hazel and Ruth, buy them now since they seldom drive anymore.

BEARDSTOWN TALES

To me, a car has five wheels: four to ride and one to steer. I know nothing more about a car. It's transportation. I had a '72 car, and as it got older, the son of the man who had a filling station here in town nursed it along. When my car needed to be replaced, I told this dealer how much I could spend. He showed me what he had and I chose the white Chevy. I asked him if another man who I trusted could look it over before I made up my mind. He drove it and thought it was okay, so I bought it. Paid cash.

Now we have to take a driver's test every year once we're past a certain age. The day before I took my test, I checked to see where everything was on my new car. I couldn't find the horn. I went back to the salesman and said, "Where's the horn on this car?" He couldn't find it either. So he said, "Go ahead and take your test. They never ask about a horn." I went to take my test. The first thing she said was, "Sound your horn." I said, "There isn't any horn." She said, "Well, you can't take the test." I was disgusted. Finally, one of the salesmen took the horn off of his car and put that horn on my car. I would say when you buy a used car, make sure you have a horn.

HAZEL LINDAHL

Our advice: The single quickest way to improve your cash flow is to buy only used cars.

How to Buy a Used Car

You can buy a used car from a car dealer and pay up to 15 percent more than if you bought the same car privately from an individual. But that 15 percent will also buy you a warranty and protection against getting a lemon. You have to decide whether it's worth the risk of buying directly from a car's previous owner to save 15 percent or more. If you follow these guidelines it will help you reduce the possibility of being stuck with a lemon, no matter where you buy your used car.

1. *Ask to see the car's paperwork, including the warranty booklet or owner's manual, service records, and repair bills.* Checking the car's maintenance history is even more important than checking how many miles it's been driven. A car that's been well cared for and has 50,000 miles is a better bargain than one that's been neglected but has only 25,000 miles. Of course you do not want to buy any car that has been in a major accident. If you can, check with the previous owner.

2. *If you're buying from a dealer, be sure the mandatory Buyer's Guide sticker is on the window.* Required by the Federal Trade Commission, it provides information such as whether the car comes with a warranty; what protection the dealer offers; whether the car is being sold "as is" with no warranty; what some of the major problems are that may occur in any car; and other advice.

3. *Test drive the car.* This might sound obvious, but bears a reminder. Try to drive the car in good weather and in a variety of conditions, including on the highway, in stop-and-go traffic, up and down hills. As you drive, answer the following questions:

   • Steering: Does the car wander or pull to one side? Is there any vibration?

   • Engine: Is there enough power? Is the acceleration smooth? Is there any knocking, pinging, or other noise? Is there any black or blue smoke?

- Transmission: Does the car shift smoothly? Does the clutch slip?

- Brakes: If you put on the brakes while going 30 miles an hour, does the car stop quickly? In a straight line?

- Exhaust system: Does the car sputter or rumble? Again, do you see any smoke?

- Comfort: When you drive over bumps, does the car bounce too much? Are there squeaky sounds you wouldn't be able to stand?

4. *Have your own mechanic check it out.* If a seller won't let you do this, walk away. If you don't have a mechanic you trust, use the American Automobile Association's diagnostic test center program.

5. *Once you know you want the car, offer 15 percent less than the asking price.* Chances are you'll go up about 5 percent in your negotiations with the seller but you'll wind up with a hefty 10 percent savings. On a $5,000 car, that's $500.

6. *Get it in writing.* When you buy a used car, have the seller give you a written document saying that the car is in good, safe condition. Then continue to keep your own written records of all the paperwork as a backup measure should you have any problems.

How to Pay for Your Car

Shopping around for financing can save you as much money as shopping around for the car itself. Before you buy a car, compare financing costs from various sources. Start with yourself. That's what many of us have done over the years. We prefer to pay cash up front for our vehicles. As Doris says, "Why should I pay interest at the bank? I might as well save myself that money." Doris, along with Elsie, Hazel, Ann Brewer, Ann Corley, Buffy, and Shirley, start saving for their next car as soon as they have purchased a new car. Instead of making costly car payments with lots of interest, they make interest-free payments to themselves. And, being savvy Beardstown Ladies, they invest the money in the meanwhile. Not only are they avoiding paying interest, their money is earning interest!

In addition, we've found over the years that often when we offer cash we can get a discount. We know, however, that it's not always possible to save enough cash for such a big purchase. Especially these days, when cars often cost more than $20,000. If you do need to take out a loan, try to avoid those from the car dealer. Car dealers are like restaurant owners: Restaurants make more from selling alcohol than they do from serving food. Car dealers make their biggest profit from the extras such as financing and warranties rather than from the cars themselves. Don't assume the dealer will give you the best deal. In general, banks or credit unions will do one or two percentage points better than the dealers. If you read our previous book, you will remember how much even one percentage point can add up because of compounding. Every now and then, a dealer may offer a special promotional loan rate. If it happens to be on the make of car you want anyway, count yourself lucky—and wealthier. As always, the idea is to shop around, compare rates, and only then decide your best bet for financing.

DOLLARS AND SENSE

The best time to buy a car is the last hour of the day, the last day of the week. Reason: Salesmen are tired at the end of their work week and easier to bargain with.

The best day to buy a car is the last day of the month. Reason: Dealerships have to meet monthly sales quotas.

The best month to buy a car is the last month of the year. Reason: Managers want to dump end-of-year inventory.

Try to get a bank loan approved a week or two before you buy your car. The larger your down payment and the better your credit rating, the lower your interest rate will be. Remember too that the shorter the period of your loan, the less you will wind up paying in interest. Since car interest is not tax-deductible—unless you use your car for business—it doesn't make sense to extend the duration of the loan. For example, say a two-year loan rate is 6.25 percent. A five-year loan rate is 7.5 percent. Now say you're financing a $15,000 car. Your monthly payments would be $666.50 for two years or $300.59 for five years. Guess how much that $15,000 car would wind up costing if you took out the five-year loan? An astounding $18,035 compared to $15,996 for the two-year loan. You'd be much better off putting the money you'd save into an investment if you were able to make the larger payments.

You might want to consider a home-equity credit line to finance your car. This can be a great way to pay for it. There are two advantages: First, the interest rate may well be lower than a car loan rate. Second, the interest *is* tax-deductible on your income tax. You'll save a lot in taxes by having this amount to deduct.

Another simple cost saver is easy to overlook: Whether you finance through the dealer or a bank, turn down credit, life, and disability insurance. This insurance, which pays off your loan if you die or become disabled, is available through other policies you already own. Watch out for it. Often it's automatically included so unless you specifically ask to have it dropped, you'll wind up paying unnecessary premiums. No matter what the car dealer tells you, this kind of insurance is not required and is better bought as regular life and disability rather than through consumer loans. Make sure you check your loan contract for such a policy. You can save a few hundred dollars over the life of your loan by omitting the insurance you don't need.

Leasing versus Buying

Did you know that the number of new cars being leased has increased by 15 percent in the last five years? And why not? With no down payment and lower monthly payments, it's obvious how consumers are tempted into leasing cars. Especially when they fall in love with luxury cars they otherwise could never afford to drive.

What does a lease really cost? According to consumer analysts, leasing costs 20 percent more than a regular purchase if—and this is a big if—the lease is for three or more years. If you are in the habit of buying a new car every one or two years, however, leasing may save you from $200 to $1,000 or more. One reason for the increased savings in recent years is that car makers have begun subsidizing leases. It's in their own best interest to encourage you to keep switching cars every year or so.

Is it better to lease than to buy a car? It all depends. The problem is that it's very difficult to size up lease agreements. They can vary tremendously in length, terms, subsidies, and how they are calculated. You need to understand the following before you can make a decision:

- The lease rate is like the annual percentage rate on a car loan. It can be called the money factor, the monthly lease charge, or the service fee.

- The residual value of the car is what the leasing company estimates the car will be worth at the end of the lease term. Usually, the higher the residual value—the less a car depreciates—the lower your monthly lease payments will be.

- There are extra charges a dealer can try to get you to agree with that are equally negotiable as those options on a car you buy. Security deposits, document charges, end-of-lease charges, paint protection, and rustproofing fall into this category. Resist!

- Leases contain annual mileage limits which you need to carefully evaluate according to your driving habits and needs. If your daily commute is 100 miles, for example, you're likely to drive at least 25,000 miles a year. If the limit is 12,000 miles a year and you will be charged up to 25 cents a mile over the limit, you can see how that could cost you $3,000 in a year. On the other hand, if you only drive to the grocery store and back, you may be "paying" for the privilege of miles you don't need.

- The lease contract will have a wear-and-tear clause. How is excess wear and tear defined? It's important to consider how hard you drive a car and what your risk may be to avoid being charged a high excess wear-and-tear bill at the end of the lease term.

- If you want to end the lease agreement early, you may pay a penalty or even be forced to keep making all the monthly payments. Check your contract.

- Insurance to cover the difference between what you owe on a lease and what the car is worth in the event the car is stolen or damaged is essential. Some leases include such "gap" insurance while others charge you extra. It's worth shopping around to get this coverage for free if possible.

WORKSHEET

SHOULD YOU LEASE OR BUY A CAR?

This worksheet is designed to help you fill in all the numbers you need to do a thorough cost comparison of leasing and financing for a two-year period.

24 MONTHS	LEASING	FINANCING
STICKER OR INVOICE PRICE	_____	_____
FINAL DEALER OR SELLING PRICE	_____	_____
REBATE	_____	_____
DOWN PAYMENT	_____	_____
FEES, LICENSE	_____	_____
STATE SALES TAX	_____	_____
LOAN OR LEASE MONTHLY PAYMENT	_____	_____
TOTAL PAYMENTS FOR 24 MONTHS	_____	_____
LEASE TERMINATION FEE	_____	_____
RESALE VALUE OF OWNED CAR	_____	_____
YOUR TOTAL COST	_____	_____

- You want to be sure the manufacturer's original warranty will cover your lease term as well as however many miles you estimate you will drive the car.

As you can see, leasing is fraught with hidden pitfalls. Luckily, as leasing has become more common, state governments have begun to legislate consumer protection laws. In 1995, New York was the first state to require comprehensive lease disclosures and give consumers legal rights. Check with your state attorney general's office to see whether similar legislation can help you.

Getting Down to Brass Tacks

1. Select the model and make of car that is best for you and then drive it for five to seven years.

2. Comparison shop to save hundreds of dollars.

3. Consider a pre-owned or slightly used car to save thousands of dollars.

CHAPTER FOUR

HOW TO MAKE APPLIANCES WORK FOR YOU

Did you know that the cost of running your appliances may total five times or more the amount you paid for them?

APPLIANCES ARE PART OF ALMOST EVERYBODY'S Spending Pyramid. Most of us don't think we could live without our washing machines or refrigerators. Nor do we need to unless we want to go back to prehistoric times. You wouldn't think of going to a car dealer and simply picking out a nice-looking car on the spot. Yet people often do that when it comes to buying an appliance. Before you buy, you need to know what your personal preferences are so you can evaluate an appliance against your standards.

STOP and consider: Are aesthetics important? Do you have to have a refrigerator to match your cabinets? Or would you rather sacrifice your decor to get a lower price? If you are a true gourmet cook, maybe you want to invest in a chef's-quality stove. But if all you ever do is boil water for spaghetti, you don't need a fancy stove. Do you really need an automatic ice maker, or would you rather spend that $300 on something else and make your own ice? Do you have family members at home all day using dishes? Then a good dishwasher is a must. If you're a single, working person, maybe you don't even need a dishwasher. How about noise? A sensitive person might want to spend the extra money on the most quiet model dishwasher possible.

This chapter will explain how to shop smart for appliances. Otherwise you might suffer the fate of one young woman we know.

With a husband, two children, and a mud-loving dog, she was doing more than a load of wash a day. The same day her old washing machine broke down, she marched into the nearest appliance store, ready to buy a new washing machine. Only she really wasn't ready. She hadn't taken the time to read about the latest models, research brands, figure out which features her family could truly use, or even price machines in several locations. She had no idea about energy efficiency or how big a capacity she needed.

STOP!

Consider that the reasons you buy an appliance may include:

1. *Save time.*
2. *Save effort.*
3. *Aesthetic appeal.*
4. *Reliability.*
5. *Save money.*
6. *Convenient features.*
7. *Unobtrusive, quiet, small.*

The salesman sized her up and tried to sell her an expensive machine with a lot of extra cycles and speeds. At least she knew she didn't need them. She asked him to show her a cheaper model, and she said she'd take it. Feeling smug at having saved a few hundred dollars, she drove home and got the new machine the next day.

Unfortunately, her impulsive purchase has cost more than a few hundred dollars in the first year alone. Turns out it has a transmission-driven agitator that is so powerful it shreds anything she puts in. The wear and tear has prematurely aged the family's wardrobe, producing holes in almost-new clothes. The towels now look like rags. Bed sheets are threadbare.

She needed to *STOP, LOOK,* and *LISTEN.* Once you buy an appliance, you're not necessarily finished paying for it. You could say an appliance has a second price tag: the cost of running and maintaining it. Many of us neglect to think these costs through before we spend hundreds or even thousands of dollars. Yet, as Margaret says, "You can go buy another can of beans, if you don't like the brand you bought. But you can't go buy another washer. You don't want to compromise quality on a large ticket item as you might on something small."

Where to Begin

Once you have a good sense of what you need and want in an appliance, it's time to *LOOK* before you leap and do your homework. One place to begin research is at your computer, if you have one. Many online sites are now available with specific, up-to-the-minute information on appliances. A sort of *Consumer Reports* for the 1990s, sites include product specifications and ratings as well as general guidelines. You can find tips or buy a used appliance via computer. There's even a place to submit ideas for features you'd like to see added to appliances in the future. (See page 263 for a list of online addresses.)

Consumer Reports is still the granddaddy when it comes to research, however. Reading its recommendations, ratings, and repair histories will give you solid general information. You can find the magazine in any library—as well as online these days. In addition, check the Resources section at the end of this book for other good consumer guides.

The second step is to shop around and compare prices. Call or visit a wide range of stores, from department stores to warehouse clubs to large chain appliance stores. Start checking local newspaper advertisements. Ann Brewer checks prices herself, but she also relies on her closest friends. "I ask if they are satisfied. I try never to put them on the spot by asking what they paid. If they offer to say the price they paid, then I try to compare."

One piece of "research" that is easy to forget: Before you go to the store, take out your yardstick and measure the space available for an appliance in your home. There's nothing more frustrating and costly than paying a lot for an item that's too big or too small.

The Brand-Name Game

You may be like most of us and shop for appliances according to brand names. Once you know the whole story behind those names, you might reconsider. Many big appliance companies make more than one brand, which they price differently. Often the *only* difference between a company's brands is the price—and the name. In other words you're paying extra for a name you might recognize a little more than the company's "other" brands. Perhaps you're paying more for a few more cosmetic features. The *manufacturing* and *quality* are identical. Let's take a look at some of our favorite brand names:

- *Frigidaire* also makes Gibson, Kelvinator, Tappan, and White-Westinghouse.

- *General Electric* also makes Hotpoint and RCA.

- *Matsushita* also makes Panasonic, Prism, and Quasar.

- *Maytag* also makes Admiral, Hardwick, Magic Chef, Jenn-Air, Montgomery Ward, and Norge.

- *Philips* also makes Magnavox.

- *Sears'* appliances are made by General Electric, Whirlpool, and others.

- *Whirlpool* also makes KitchenAid, Roper, and Estate.

The reason behind this confusing appliance family tree is industry consolidation. Over the last several decades, companies have bought up other companies' brand names. The company that now owns your favorite brand-name appliance might not be the same company that made it 25 years ago.

Companies sell similar models at prices that may vary by hundreds of dollars. Recently we compared two brand-name refrigerators. Both were made by the same company, but one was $1,689.87 while the other—virtually identical—was $1,349.97. If you bought the first one you'd essentially be spending $340 for a little silver-plated name. Is it worth it?

Margaret doesn't think it is: "A brand name is not that important to me. I bought a brand name and it didn't last. You cannot look at a washing machine and say that this washer is going to last me 25 years because it lasted my mother 25 years."

Gadgets and Gizmos

In appliances, as in cars, try to buy the simplest possible appliance to meet your family's needs. The more features you pay for, the more you'll pay in repairs too—not to mention the higher cost of running a more complicated appliance. Recently, Carol bought a clothes dryer close to the bottom of the line, but with the features she wanted: fluff, low heat, high heat, and a timer. She says, "If you get all the extra features, nine times out of ten you don't need them or use them."

On the other hand, when Maxine had to replace her refrigerator not too long ago, she says, "Maybe I went a little too cheap. I thought 'Oh, I'm not going to live too long.' Our old one had been good for when we had a family. It was 22 years old. But it was too large for me. Now, with this new one, I think I should have bought a better one, another step up or two. There's no light in the freezer."

If a certain "bell and whistle" is something you really want, then it's not a waste of money. The trick is to *LISTEN* to yourself beforehand so you don't wind up paying for extras without really thinking about them one way or another. Later in this chapter we'll describe the various features for each appliance.

BEARDSTOWN TALES

My worst purchase was an electric lawn mower. My friend had purchased one in Jacksonville, and it worked perfectly for her small yard. I listened to her and decided, that's the lawn mower for me. It was light, easy to push. The mower was delivered in pieces in a large box. My son put it together. I needed a long electrical cord and an outside hot plug. I have a large yard, which meant purchasing more cord. My grandson offered to help and he ran over the cord. I put an ad in the newspaper to sell it and received one bid. The gentleman said it was too light. It's still sitting in my garage. Any buyers? The moral is, just because something works for your friend, STOP and consider if it's what you really need.

MAXINE THOMAS

How Much Is It?

Many consumers assume that the prices they see in the stores are final, especially when the sticker includes an official-sounding term such as "Manufacturers Suggested Retail Price" or "List Price." A standard price in appliances is a myth: *There is no such thing.* Appliances are similar to cars in the huge markups they command. The retailer pays the manufacturer a price for a certain appliance. He puts a price tag on it that can be anywhere from 40 percent and up on top of the manufacturer's price. All you have to do is ask if there is a better price for the appliance you're interested in. More often than not, the salesperson will quote you a lower price than the one marked on the floor model. Occasionally, only a store owner or manager can authorize on-the-spot discounts. If in doubt, ask to be waited on by the top person.

Ask the dealer about discounts on purchasing a floor model or even an appliance that has been relegated to a damaged-goods area. Who cares if there's a small scratch on the side of a stove when it's going to have cabinets on either side of it anyway?

Comparison shopping is essential when it comes to saving money on appliances. A few phone calls and a few minutes can save you much more than a few dollars. Ann Corley priced stoves at different stores and found a $200 difference between one store and the next. "My husband wanted the stove right away," Ann says. "I thought we could do better and we did." Ann came out ahead because she practiced *STOP, LOOK,* and *LISTEN.*

Ann takes her time when shopping for big-ticket items. Ann has been looking for a VCR. She did her homework and decided she wants one with four heads, stereo, and VCR Plus. She knows roughly the price she will pay. She knows which brand she'd prefer. By being patient and precise, she can afford to wait until she finds the right VCR at the right price. When she walks into the store and says, "I'll take it," she won't be making an impulse buy.

Where you shop can make a difference in how much you spend on an appliance. These days, there are more and more choices available, from the local mom-and-pop shop on Main Street, to huge discount stores and warehouse clubs, to mail-order catalogues and online services. Here again, because the profit margin on appliances can be as high as 500 percent, you are likely to find a vast range of prices on the same item depending on where you buy it. There's no one best place. You probably need to rethink where to buy each time you have to buy an appliance.

Another suggestion is to frequent the "We Can't Be Beat"

stores, which claim they will not be undersold by any competitor. Be sure to get a written guarantee or an advertisement with prices from both the store that claims it will not be undersold and the store in which you find a better price.

Energy

You'd probably never buy a car without considering how much it would cost to drive it. When choosing an appliance it's equally worthwhile to consider its energy efficiency. What you pay the day you buy an appliance is only part of its total cost. How much it costs to operate it can add up to even more than the original purchase price. To save the most money and get the best deal, you need to compare the life-cycle costs of different models.

Say you're in a store looking at two different refrigerators. They're both $750, which is what you've budgeted to spend. If you look carefully at each model's yearly energy consumption—clearly marked on the bright yellow EnergyGuide labels—you will notice there's a difference of $25 a year in fuel efficiency. Over an average appliance life span of 20 years, that's $500 more. This means that if you bought the appliance with the higher fuel consumption costs, you would really be spending $1,250 on a refrigerator, although you wouldn't so much as glance at a model with a price tag like that in the store.

Sometimes, it's cheaper in the long run to pay more up-front for an appliance that will run more efficiently over its lifetime. At the very least, check and compare each model's EnergyGuide label for a rough estimate. (See our annotated label on page 73 for an explanation of how to read them.)

To get an even more accurate cost comparison, use a formula that takes into account not only the appliance's energy consumption but your own local energy cost, or how much you pay for electricity or gas. We've provided a worksheet for you to use on page 79.

First collect the following information:

- The price of each model.

- Each model's annual energy cost, calculated by taking your cost of energy (example: $.11 per kilowatt-hour or $.66 per therm) and multiplying it by the model's annual energy consumption in kilowatt hours or therms (found on the yellow EnergyGuide label).

- The appliance's estimated lifetime (provided in the table on page 79).

- The appliance's discount factor to compensate for inflation and investment rates (provided in the table on page 79).

Now plug those numbers into this formula:

- Purchase price + (annual energy cost x lifetime x discount factor) = life-cycle cost.

Once you have each model's life-cycle cost, you are ready to make an informed decision.

Service Contracts and Extended Warranties

It's hard to buy anything without being asked if you want an extended warranty or extended service contract. Like insurance policies that cover the period after the original manufacturer's warranty on an appliance expires, they may be sold by the store, the manufacturer, or a third-party company called an administrator. The salesperson will try to make you think they are worthwhile—he or she receives as much as 15 to 20 percent commission on each extended warranty sold. He or she may refer to an extension plan, a date-of-purchase plan, a major component program, a replacement program, a comprehensive program, or a deductible plan, but they're all variations of the same basic theme: overpriced, unnecessary insurance for appliances.

Whoever sells an extended warranty is making from 40 to 300 percent profit. A consumer standards organization estimates that retailers spend as little as four cents on service for every dollar they charge for extended warranty premiums. These contracts are often way out of proportion in expense to the amount the consumer spends on the actual appliance.

One study shows that only one out of five new appliances will need a repair within the time covered by an extended warranty. They either break down within the first few weeks or months, while

ENERGY GUIDE LABEL

This is how to read the yellow label you should always see affixed to a new appliance.

Name of appliance, company, and model number.

Kind of appliance and its size or capacity

The estimated average cost to operate this model for one year.

Clothes Washer
Capacity: Standard

Whirlpool Corporation
Models:27B4190(3B)

ENERGYGUIDE

Estimates on the scale are based on a national average electric rate of 8.24¢ per kilowatt hour and a natural gas rate of 60.54¢ per therm.

Only standard size washers are used in the scale.

Electric Water Heater

Model with lowest energy cost	$68	Model with highest energy cost
$22	THIS ▼ MODEL	$150

Gas Water Heater

Model with lowest energy cost	$28	Model with highest energy cost
$10	THIS ▼ MODEL	$55

Estimated yearly energy cost

Your cost will vary depending on your local energy rate and how you use the product. This energy cost is based on U.S. Government standard tests.

How much will this model cost you to run yearly?

with an electric water heater

Loads of clothes per week		2	4	6	8	12
Estimated yearly $ cost shown below						
Cost per kilowatt hour	2¢	$5	$9	$13	$17	$25
	4¢	$9	$17	$25	$34	$50
	6¢	$13	$25	$38	$50	$75
	8¢	$17	$34	$50	$67	$100
	10¢	$21	$42	$62	$83	$124
	12¢	$25	$50	$75	$100	$149

with a gas water heater

Loads of clothes per week		2	4	6	8	12
Estimated yearly $ cost shown below						
Cost per therm (100 cubic feet)	10¢	$3	$6	$8	$11	$16
	20¢	$4	$7	$11	$14	$21
	30¢	$5	$9	$13	$18	$26
	40¢	$6	$11	$16	$21	$31
	50¢	$6	$12	$18	$24	$36
	60¢	$7	$14	$21	$28	$42

Ask your salesperson or local utility for the energy rate (cost per kilowatt hour or therm) in your area, and for estimated costs if you have a propane or oil water heater.

Important Removal of this label before consumer purchase is a violation of federal law (42 U.S.C. 6302)

(Part No. 3361376)

This line shows how this model compares to other brands of similar size made by different companies and the range of operating costs from lowest to highest.

The chart helps you calculate your operating costs based on your local utility rates.

still covered by the manufacturer, or they last until years after the extended warranty has expired. In addition, the average repair bill in the unlikely event that an appliance does need service is far less than the total cost of the warranty premiums.

Carol McCombs, who works in insurance, has a strong opinion regarding extended warranties. She would absolutely not buy one when she recently purchased a new dryer. Her logic is that to pay $50 a year for an extended warranty on a dryer that will probably last five years without any problems is $250 she'd rather have invested. The $250 she saved on not paying for a warranty would be enough to pay for repairs.

Ann Corley agrees that if a product is new, you don't need an extended warranty. When she bought a mixer, the salesperson asked her if she wanted "insurance." "I thought it was so ridiculous to buy insurance on a mixer," Ann says.

Betty thinks most warranties are only making money for the store that's selling them. To prove her point, she shares a story about a lawn tractor with a mower that she and her husband bought in Peoria.

"The salesman talked Bob into a three-year warranty, promising that they would come out anytime the blades needed to be changed, anytime the oil needed to be changed, whenever service checks were needed. All we had to do was call and they would come. We have six acres in sand, so we figured cutting it might be very hard on the blades and they probably would have to be serviced often. They were to check it out every year, do whatever it needed.

"First time he called, we were told we were out of that service area. We're 45 miles from Peoria and 45 miles from Springfield. We bought it in Peoria, but they said we had to go through the Springfield service area. Bob called on April 19 for the spring service. They came April 29 which was 10 days later. They didn't have any parts with them. They used our phone to order spark plugs and an oil filter and said they'd be back May 6. Another week passed. They didn't come. The next week they called and said they couldn't find the spark plugs. They had to back order them but they would try to be there by May 25. I think it was July before they finally came. Instead of having them come every time we wanted, they told Bob he would have to change the oil and different things that the salesman had told us this warranty covered."

Shopping Tips

Besides avoiding extended warranties, there are specific things to keep in mind when shopping for appliances. Here is a summary:

Refrigerators

- Buy only as big a refrigerator as your family really needs. Each cubic foot costs about $50. If you buy a larger capacity than you need, you're wasting money on two fronts: the original price and the energy cost. To calculate how much space your family needs, figure a base of twelve cubic feet for two persons and then add two cubic feet per additional family member.

- In general, models with freezers on the top, as opposed to side-by-side or bottom freezers are hundreds of dollars less expensive and they use far less energy.

- Think twice about ice makers. They add $200 to the cost and $50 to annual energy usage. They are the most likely component to break. They also steal space from the freezer (the cubic footage is measured before the ice maker is installed). So if you make your own ice, you are saving at least $300.

- According to *Consumer Reports*, adjustable crispers, which are supposed to prevent produce from drying out, don't work any better than plain produce bins. On the other hand, adjustable meat-keepers are worthwhile for keeping meat cooler than the rest of your food. Look for separate temperature controls to be sure you're really getting value for your money.

- Try to buy either in January or February, when most major appliances go on sale, or in the summer, when most breakdowns occur. Stores are likely to offer sales then in order to attract business at the height of refrigerator-buying time.

Gas or Electric Ranges

- Look for gas ranges with an automatic spark ignition system instead of a pilot light. They are 30 percent more energy efficient and yet usually don't cost any more up-front.

- October is National Kitchen and Bath Month. Buy a range then during widespread sales and promotions, and you'll likely save up to 20 percent. Or try late summer, since manufacturers introduce new models in the spring.

- The cleaner you keep an oven, the more energy-efficient it is. Burned-on food makes the oven work harder to maintain its temperature. It's worth looking for features that make it easier to keep your oven clean. These include sealed burners, a glass or porcelain back guard, a rim around the cooktop surface, and porcelain drip pans on a gas range. On an electric model, look for smooth-top burners as opposed to coiled burners.

- A self-cleaning oven is more expensive to buy, but it is cheaper to operate because it has extra insulation. Also, since a cleaner oven is more energy-efficient, it might be a good bet if you won't clean your oven often yourself.

- Gas ranges are usually less expensive to run but more expensive to buy.

- If power outages are a potential problem, gas is a better bet.

Washing Machines

- Standard wash cycles include regular, permanent press, and delicate. You'll pay more for extra cycles such as a pre-wash cycle or a heavy wash cycle. Are you sure you need them? Will your clothes come out any cleaner?

- In general, top-loading machines are much less expensive than front-loaders. Although front-loaders do use less water, if you wash mostly with cold water, you won't save enough money on water consumption to justify the extra up-front expense. Plus, front-loaders reportedly break down more often.

- One feature that usually is worth paying a bit more for in a washing machine is a larger capacity. That's because using fewer but larger loads costs less in energy and water. If you have more than two people in your family, you'll want to consider a 15-pound capacity machine.

- When you can't wash a full load, it can save money to be able to adjust the water fill level. Although some machines come with four water levels or are continuously adjustable, three levels are all most consumers need.

- Although machines come with a number of wash/spin speeds, few people need any more than two speeds.

- Extra gadgets on washing machines include electronic touch-pads instead of manual controls, bleach and fabric-softener dispensers, alternate agitators for delicates, small baskets for very small loads, childproof locks, and a recycling feature that allows you to reuse water in the next wash.

Dishwashers

- Dishwashers all work basically the same way. Extra cycles and features, such as the pot scrubber, heavy duty, or plate warmer, are added to the machine to increase the price. You'll pay $100 or more for five or six wash cycles instead of the two or three you really need. Look for a regular wash cycle, a rinse cycle, and a hold cycle.

- How well a dishwasher cleans does vary, however. Quality performance is even more important than in other major appliances. In the case of dishwashers, the higher the price, in general the better the quality. A good strategy is to buy a dishwasher of the best quality but with the fewest cycles and temperature or water pressure settings. Pay for quality, not extras.

- Other features include filtering systems, special racks and utensil baskets, and dispensers.

- Be sure you have a way to turn off the heat-dry part of the cycle. You can save money by letting your dishes air-dry.

- Dishwashers come with either electronic or manual controls. Of course, the manual control models are less expensive. How much do you care whether you have to push a knob instead of to touching a keypad? Is it worth $100?

Clothes Dryers

- It's almost always cheaper in the long run to buy a gas rather than an electric dryer. The initial price will be about $50 higher, but you'll make up the difference in operating costs within the first year.

- There are two main sizes in dryers: compact and standard. The compact models use less energy per load but dry fewer clothes at a time. Unless you live alone or lack of space is an issue, you're probably better off with a full-size dryer.

- The dryer works in one of three ways. A timed drying process is controlled by a timer which you set. An auto-temperature process is controlled by a device that monitors the temperature of the clothes and stops the machine automatically once a certain preset temperature is reached. An auto-moisture process is controlled by a sensor that measures the moisture of the clothes and ends the drying cycle automatically when the clothes are dry enough.

- An automatic shutoff feature will save you energy costs as well as prevent your clothes from excess wear.

- Extras include end-of-cycle buzzers and interior and panel lights. Dryers are among the simpler appliances. The basic models work very well. Nowhere does it make more sense to skip the fancy extra features and save yourself a lot of money.

Air Conditioners

- The single most cost-saving factor in air-conditioners is buying the right size for the space you want to cool. Whether it's too big or too small, you'll waste money. Too big, and it will shut off before it has dehumidified the room enough. Too small, and it won't be powerful enough to cool the room adequately.

- To find out precisely how large a unit you need, you can call your local utility company. If you tell them how many square feet you have, where your windows face, and a few other facts, they will recommend the number of BTUs you need. Try ordering a worksheet from Consumers Union to calculate it yourself. (See the Resources section on page 263.) Don't rely on a salesperson to tell you what size you need.

WORSHEET
COMPARING LIFE-CYCLE COSTS OF APPLIANCES

Use this worksheet to compare appliances you are considering buying. Heating and cooling units won't fit into this worksheet.

MODEL   PRICE   + (ENERGY COST x EST. LIFETIME x DISCOUNT) = LIFE-CYCLE COST

_____ _____ + (_____ x _____ x _____) = _____

_____ _____ + (_____ x _____ x _____) = _____

_____ _____ + (_____ x _____ x _____) = _____

_____ _____ + (_____ x _____ x _____) = _____

_____ _____ + (_____ x _____ x _____) = _____

_____ _____ + (_____ x _____ x _____) = _____

_____ _____ + (_____ x _____ x _____) = _____

_____ _____ + (_____ x _____ x _____) = _____

Life-Cycle Cost Factors

APPLIANCE	ESTIMATED LIFETIME (YEARS)	DISCOUNT FACTOR (%)
Air-conditioner	15	0.81
Dishwasher	12	0.84
Refrigerator	20	0.76
Washing machine	18	0.78
Water heater	13	0.83

- Before you buy an air-conditioner, ask yourself how often you will use it. Then ask yourself how much you pay for electricity. If you live in an area that's hot only a few months a year and your utility bills are fairly high, you may want to consider the most energy-efficient air conditioner you can find. If you live in an area with relatively low electric rates, you may want to buy the least expensive model.

- It's no surprise that the best time to buy air conditioners is in the fall.

Repair or Replace?

Many of us tend to hang onto our appliances as long as they're in good operating order. When Elsie moved into her mobile home, she took her refrigerator, washer, and dryer with her from her former home. She's had her dryer since 1973. "I've had my washer a long time, too." Elsie says.

When an appliance breaks down, how do you decide whether to have it repaired or buy a new one? It helps to know about how long your appliance is supposed to last (see page 79 for estimates) and to price a new one. Carol's dryer conked out when it was 10 years old. "I asked, 'Is it worth it to spend that much money repairing something when it doesn't cost that much more to buy something new and start fresh again?' " She decided to buy a new one for about $279 rather than risk repeated repair bills of $80 to $100.

If the cost of repair is more than 40 to 50 percent the cost of replacement, you probably should buy a new appliance. If it's less, then you need to find out how expensive the problem will be to fix, how likely the problem is to recur, and how much more life remains in your appliance.

Some common problems include the following in descending order of expense within each appliance category:

- *Refrigerators*. Compressor, ice maker, door gaskets.

- *Ranges*. Gas valve, thermostat, igniter.

- *Washing machines*. Transmission, drive motor, water pump, drive belt.

CONSUMER COMPLAINT
LETTER TO A
MANUFACTURER

Date

Manufacturer
Address
City, State, Zip Code

RE: Malfunctioning FVH-2512 video cassette recorder

Dear Customer Service Representative:

I purchased a [brand] video cassette recorder, Model FVH-2512 from [name of store] on December 15, 1995. (Copy of original receipt is enclosed.) At the end of March 1996—a little over three months after we had purchased the video cassette recorder—it ceased functioning as a recorder. It would play videos but it could not tape television programs.

In April I contacted your company. A representative told me to take the VCR to the nearest authorized service shop, which was [name of repair store]. The repair person checked out the VCR and informed us that it would cost $110 in labor to repair and that labor was no longer covered under our warranty.

As you can see from the enclosed copy of my original receipt, I paid $148.98 for the VCR. Clearly, to spend $110 to have a product less than six months old repaired is unreasonable.

Therefore, I would like you to replace or repair my VCR. As a longtime fan of your products, I must say this is the first time I've been so disappointed. I'm sure you would like to provide customer satisfaction.

I can be reached at [telephone number].

I look forward to hearing from you at your earliest convenience.

Sincerely,

Your name

- *Dryers*. Heating element, door switch, drive belt.

- *Dishwashers*. Motor, water valve.

Another thing to consider is whether the latest models of the appliance you need repaired or replaced are substantially improved. A new refrigerator is 50 percent more energy efficient than one from 1980. You'd probably quickly make up the difference in cost between repairing an older one and replacing it with a model that costs less to run.

The same is true of new dishwashers, which are more energy efficient and use less water than older models. Washing machines now offer larger capacities, better cleaning, and use less water. Sealed gas burners and easier to clean surfaces on electric ranges mean you don't have to use as much energy.

Read your owner's manual to do your own troubleshooting before you call a repair person. You can also try calling the manufacturer's 800 number for free help. If that doesn't fix your problem, get a recommendation from the manufacturer or a trusted neighbor or friend for an appropriate repair service.

When you call, ask whether they will come out to look at the appliance free of charge or whether they start billing you immediately. Look for places that ask you a lot of information over the phone and that have common parts in stock. That way, if you opt for a repair, you'll have saved time and therefore money.

If you are unhappy with a product, complain. It can save you hundreds of dollars. We have a friend whose family bought a new VCR. It had a three-month labor warranty. Right after the three months were up, the VCR would not record. The husband took it to an authorized service center because the parts were still covered under warranty. But the repair person said it would cost $110 in labor alone to fix this particular model. They had paid $148 for the VCR, so they could not justify spending that much to repair it.

The wife decided to try a two-prong approach. First, she wrote a letter to the manager of the store where they had purchased the VCR (and a large color television set). She simultaneously wrote directly to the VCR manufacturer's customer service representative, explaining the problem and exactly what she wanted to happen. (See page 82 for a sample Consumer Complaint Letter to a Manufacturer.) She's still waiting to hear from the store manager—so that store has lost her family's future business. But the manufacturer called her within a few days of receipt of her letter. The customer service representative apologized and explained that they had never had problems with that model before. He faxed her an authorization to have the VCR repaired free of charge that very day. Bottom line: She spent a total of 15 minutes to save $110. Not a bad rate of return!

Getting Down to Brass Tacks

1. Don't pay for extra features you don't need or want.

2. Consider operating and maintenance costs when you choose an appliance.

3. Avoid buying extended warranties.

CHAPTER FIVE

THE INSURED LIFE

No matter how much coverage you think you need, you can save money on every kind of insurance by paying attention to discounts and deductibles.

THE OTHER DAY A FRIEND TOLD US THAT SHE FINALLY sat down to add up how much she was spending on automobile insurance. She drives a car, her teenaged daughter drives a car, and her husband drives a car. They have a fourth car her husband uses to deliver the drums he rents and repairs. The total annual bill was $3,900. She was shocked. But she didn't let it bother her for long. She immediately picked up her phone and called her insurance company to find out if there was any way to reduce their premiums. The agent asked her a few questions, and within two minutes she had $400 knocked off the total. If she invests that $400 every year, in 10 years she'll have a very nice retirement nest egg. Yet she won't have to sacrifice a single part of her current lifestyle, get a new job, or inherit any money. She just had to be aware and ask the right questions. She had to STOP, LOOK, and LISTEN.

Everyone has a different level of comfort when it comes to insurance coverage. Like everything else you spend money on, you need to weigh how much you'd like to feel protected for tomorrow against how much you can realistically afford in premiums without undue sacrifice today. "We spend so much money on insurance—vehicle insurance, home owner's insurance, life

STOP!

Consider that the reasons you buy insurance may include:

1. *To protect yourself against unexpected cash outlays. Spending $100 a year is more predictable than suddenly having to pay $20,000.*

2. *To provide for your dependents if you die.*

3. *To minimize taxes on your estate.*

4. *For peace of mind.*

5. *Because the government or a lender requires it.*

6. *As a way to force retirement savings.*

insurance," Ann Brewer says. "It seems we are always having an insurance premium due. Can't afford it, but can't afford to be without it!"

Remember that insurance is meant to keep you from financial disaster. It's too costly to use as protection from relatively small financial demands. Much of the cost of insurance covers the company's administrative costs. Every time you file a claim, it costs them hundreds of dollars to process. Don't pay huge premiums for the convenience of not paying for minor items.

As Hazel says, "I think almost all of us are insurance-poor." Be sure that if you do have a catastrophe, you will not be ruined. Refer to your Spending and Personal Priority pyramids so you keep insurance spending in perspective as part of your big picture.

Shopping for Insurance

STOP and consider how much peace of mind you need. Balance is the Beardstown way. Betty carries some life insurance, "but not an exorbitant amount." She thinks many people are overinsured, especially senior citizens who lived through the Depression. We know plenty of younger families who are buying unnecessary insurance, too. Often it's because they believe that if they have enough insurance it will guarantee that nothing bad will ever happen. But no amount of life insurance will prevent us from dying. At the same time, being uninsured because you're afraid to pay the premiums is no solution either. We need to remain calm and reasonable when thinking about insurance.

What exactly are you buying insurance for? Do you have life insurance? Is it for your children's support and education in case you die? What if your kids are grown? Are you still carrying life insurance? Why? Some kinds of insurance are legally required, such as home owner's insurance when you obtain a mortgage and personal injury protection in states with no-fault car insurance laws. But do you need insurance for minor events that you can easily cover out of your savings?

Whatever kind of insurance you decide you need, you can save money on its cost by considering several strategies. These include weighing your deductibles, checking umbrella policies, and asking for discounts.

We suggest you read this chapter and then take out all your insurance policies. Go over them with a fine-tooth comb, write down any questions that come up, and call your insurance agents. Don't give up until you've saved yourself some of your own money!

Deductibles

Your deductible is the amount you pay on an insurance claim before the insurance company starts reimbursing you. There is a simple rule for saving money on insurance: The higher your deductible, the lower your premium. So it makes sense to take the highest deductible you can manage without being a nervous wreck.

There are two reasons you get a discount when you have a high deductible. First, it lowers the cost to the insurance company when it does pay a claim. Second, it guarantees that you'll think long and hard before getting repairs, since much of the work will be done out of your pocket.

How much will you save? The difference on a premium with a $1,000 deductible instead of a $100 deductible is at least 25 percent, often more. Say your annual home owner's insurance costs $800 with the lower deductible. Raising it to a higher one could save you $200 in one year. If you invest that $200 in an interest-bearing account, pretty soon you'll have made up the difference in the deductible amounts anyway.

Carol, who works for an insurance agency in Beardstown, is our resident advisor on insurance questions. Even if some of us don't buy our insurance from her company, we always ask her advice. Her best money-saving strategy when it comes to insurance is to assess whether you can afford a high deductible to be able to pay a lower premium. You have to know yourself well before you decide. Carol comments, "It depends on your situation. If I wrecked my car and had to scrape up enough money for a down payment, I'd be in trouble. If I pay little by little and keep full coverage on my car, either they'd repair my car or give me enough money for a down payment to buy another car. If something happens to your car, and you have enough money to just go out and buy one, no problem. You should always raise your deductibles."

The more liquid assets you have available in case of an emergency, the higher you can afford to make your deductible. Betty has steadily increased her auto insurance deductible as she has become more financially solvent. She says, "At one time we had no deductible, then a $50 deductible, then $100. Today we have a $250, and we're paying a smaller premium for having a larger deductible."

Carol cautions you need to be careful about *automatically* slashing deductibles, however. If you're only going to save a tiny amount, it may not be worthwhile. Carol explains, "Sometimes on car insurance, there's only a $15 difference between a $250 and a $500 deductible. That $15 or $30 a year isn't worth the extra $250 that you would have to pay if you had a claim. I'd rather put out the $30 a year and have the chance of having a smaller out-of-pocket expense if I had a claim."

BEARDSTOWN TALES

On the farms, we carry liability and we carry insurance on our bins. If you lose a bin, you have to build a new bin. We even carry liability as part of the farm insurance. Because even if trespassers get injured, they might sue you. So, I do carry insurance where I would be endangered. We do not have crop insurance. We feel if we've lost the crop, we've lost the crop. We feel we can afford to lose that 20 percent rather than maintaining insurance on it. Since we don't have debts, we don't need it.

SHIRLEY GROSS

How to Buy Policies

There are quite a few ways to buy insurance. You can use an independent agent, an insurance company with agents, or a direct-response company that sells via toll-free phone numbers. You can buy all your insurance through one company or each policy through a different company. You can buy group insurance or have an individual plan. Although we can't tell you which is the best plan for you and your circumstances, we can tell you this: Shopping around for insurance can save you hundreds of dollars or more.

"The premiums easily can vary as much as 20 percent a year for the same coverage in various companies," says Buffy. "If you get into the wrong policy and overpay 20 percent a year for five years, that's a big loss." Shopping for lower insurance rates should be an ongoing process.

Because the insurance industry is heavily regulated by the states, there's not so much difference between one company and another—as long as their ratings are similar. That makes it easy to shop around for the best price.

Maxine always had "everything with one broker because it's cheaper that way and they give you a better bargain." Carnell's whole farm is on one policy. It includes their vehicles, house, farm, and liability. She says it's cost-effective. However, it's not *necessarily* cheaper to get all your insurance from one place. You can't assume anything, which is why you need to LOOK before you leap.

Insurance Agents

One of the most important steps you can take toward saving money on your insurance coverage is to form a relationship with an agent you know and trust. Be leery of door-to-door agents, or agents you have never heard of. Often, they sell policies with fine print that is not in your best interest, and generally not a good value.

A good agent will sit down with you and fully explain the coverage he or she is proposing and why you need to consider it. He or she will not push you, but rather explain the pros and cons of each type of policy. We suggest you weigh the quality of service you receive from an insurance agent as well as the cost of individual policies. It might be worth paying slightly more to get trustworthy and efficient service.

If you don't trust your current agent or are not satisfied that the answers to your questions make sense, start shopping for a new agent. Choose your agent as you would a lawyer, accountant, or doctor, as their advice will only be tested when you truly need it—in a claims situation. Agents with industry designations such as CIC, LUTCF, CLU, and CPCU are good places to start.

Some agents are paid by one company and sell policies just from that company. Allstate, for example, sells its insurance that way. Other agents, called independent agents, represent a number of companies and are free to pick and choose among policies. There's no guarantee that you'll get a better deal from one or the other, so it pays to shop around.

Discounts

Insurance carriers usually have a standard rate, and then they offer discounts. Very few people don't qualify for at least some of these discounts, which vary from company to company, subject only to state regulations. You may already know about some obvious ones, such as nonsmoker's or good-driver's discounts. But did you know that you may be eligible for an insurance discount if you have an alarm system, carpool to work, take a defensive driving course, or just turn a certain age?

Insurance works because thousands of consumers pool their money and their risk. People who are less likely to withdraw money from the pool get a discount, while those with poor track records pay more. That way, if you are a good risk, you aren't subsidizing those who are poor risks.

Ann Corley has been savvy about asking for discounts. "I get a discount for safe driving, because I haven't had an accident since 1971, and then it wasn't my fault," she says. "I use seat belts, have air bags, and get a senior-citizen discount which helps to reduce my premium. My insurance agent said they could reduce the premium on my car, if I drove it less than 7,500 miles per year. I received a refund check for $32."

Wouldn't you love to be paid $32 for making one phone call? Think of buying insurance the way you approach buying a car: you'd never just accept the sticker price the dealer offered, right?

Get into the habit of asking each insurance carrier, "What discounts do you offer? How can I lower my rates?" Carol says any good agent will automatically do this for you, but it's always a good idea to double-check.

Tell the agent to look at several companies. Be especially careful to ask for quotes from different companies based on the same deductibles, or you'll be comparing apples to oranges. "You have to compare similar terms and conditions," Carol cautions. "You don't want to ask for a quote on insurance for a 1989 Chevy. You've got to be more specific."

Now let's take a closer look at specific types of insurance, including life, car, and home owner's.

Life Insurance

It's easy to spend a large percentage of your income on life insurance. But it's not always the wisest use of your money. As we wrote in our last book, you may not need much life insurance if you fall into one of the following categories:

- You are not married and have no children or others to support.

- You have grown children who can take care of themselves financially.

- You are married but do not work.

- You are a college student.

- You are married and retired, with adequate Social Security, pension, and savings to support your spouse in the event of your death.

But you do need to carry life insurance (although how much you need to purchase will vary according to individual circumstances) if any of the following applies to you:

- You are married and have dependent children.

- You are not married but you support or help support someone.

- Your estate is over $600,000 and there will be estate tax.

- You are married and have no children, but your spouse does not work.

- You are married and you both work, but your spouse would not be able to live in the style to which he or she has become accustomed if you were to die.

Carnell has changed her insurance coverage over time. "When we were younger, we had insurance to cover our risk or for the debt we owed on the farm. We had insurance for our young children who needed to be looked after. When those things were no longer a consideration, we dropped that insurance."

Shirley says she doesn't need life insurance because she has no more obligations or debt. "If my house wasn't paid off and my children had to live at home," she says, "then maybe I would need life insurance. Don't buy something you don't need."

Carol says you should determine what you really need versus what you have bought in life insurance. Insurance agents know how to appeal to your emotions, your sense of guilt, your insecurity, and your love of family. They know how to present you with dazzling charts and graphs that seem to prove, rather dramatically, that you can't afford not to buy as much as possible. Just look at how much your policy will be worth in 20 years! They also make hefty commissions on your premiums. In fact, often the whole first year you pay for some types of life insurance, you're paying your agent's fee. So the first thing to do when considering life insurance is to take what an agent says with a grain of salt.

Before you speak to an agent, it's wise to calculate your insurance needs on your own. It's really not that complicated. You just need to find out the amount of money necessary to fill the gap between your lost income and whatever other sources of support your family may receive. (Fill out the Life Insurance Worksheet on page 93 for an estimate.)

One of the things that makes life insurance so confusing is that it may serve more than one purpose. Most of us think of it as a death benefit. Just as fire insurance pays you if you have a fire, traditional life insurance pays your heirs if you die. But insurance companies have devised numerous variations on a basic life insurance policy, including tax benefits and forced savings. Before you spend a lot of time and money with insurance agents, be sure you understand

WORKSHEET

LIFE INSURANCE

What You Need		*What You Have Now*	
Immediate expenses	_____	Cash and savings	_____
Federal estate taxes	_____	Equity in real estate	_____
State inheritance taxes	_____	Securities	_____
		IRA and Keogh plans	_____
Probate costs	_____	Employer savings plans	_____
Funeral costs	_____	Lump-sum pension benefits	_____
Uninsured medical costs	_____	Current life insurance	_____
Family expense fund	_____	Other assets	_____
Emergency fund	_____	TOTAL ASSETS	_____
Child-care expenses	_____		
Education fund	_____	*Extra Insurance Needed* (Total needs minus total assets)	
Repayment of debts	_____	TOTAL NEEDS	_____
TOTAL NEEDS	_____	TOTAL ASSETS	_____
		ADDITIONAL INSURANCE	_____

what you're getting and what you really need. There are three basic types of life insurance: *term, whole,* and *universal.*

Term Life Insurance

Term life insurance is the least expensive and most straight-forward option. It provides a predetermined death benefit for a set period, or term, of your policy. After the term is up, you can renew your coverage but at a higher premium rate. Term insurance is good when you are young and your income may be on the lower side. For a reasonable amount, you can protect your family without undue strain on your budget. It's the bread and butter of life insurance—a straightforward risk sharing. The older you are, the more it costs.

Whole Life Insurance

For a higher price, you can buy whole life or straight life, also known as cash-value life insurance. These policies do double duty: They provide death benefits and serve as investment instruments. You pay a premium that doesn't change and is set according to your age at the time you purchase the policy. The older you are, the higher the premium. The other big difference between this and term insurance is that the company pools your premium payments into a savings fund and invests a portion of it on your behalf. These earnings are tax-deferred. Gradually the cash value of your policy increases through your own contributions and the company's earnings on its investments. If you want, you can surrender the policy before you die and walk away with the cash it's worth. Or you can borrow against the value of the policy without paying taxes and without canceling your coverage.

You can't figure out if whole life is worth the investment unless you split the two parts in two and compare them to other alternatives. This can be complicated, but it is definitely worth your time if you're considering anything but a small policy.

Universal Life Insurance

Universal life is a more flexible form of a cash-value policy. You can adjust the premiums as well as the amount of the death benefit during your lifetime. You can decide how much of the premium is going toward life insurance and how much is going toward accumulating cash. You can change *when* you pay the premium, too. This flexibility may come at a price. While you can change your premiums, by the same token, the company can change your coverage. If interest rates go down, for example, the company will likely increase your premiums if you want to maintain your previous amount of coverage.

Cash-value insurance that combines savings, estate planning, and traditional insurance may seem convenient, but it can be significantly more expensive than doing all three things separately. For every $1,000 of coverage, you pay from $15 to $35 for whole life—and as little as $3 for term insurance. You may well be able to reap a greater return for your investment through a noninsurance investment program. It's worth spending a few hours of comparison shopping to save a few thousand dollars.

Take a Proactive Approach

Buying life insurance without understanding exactly the benefits you're getting is wasting money. Yet many of us aren't assertive enough when it comes to trying to compare insurance policies. Often, we buy life insurance from neighbors or golf partners or business acquaintances. We don't ask tough enough questions. After all, who wants to dwell on death? Ruth admits when her husband got home from the service, he took out an insurance policy from a distant cousin who had an insurance office across the street.

If you take a more proactive approach, you should save a lot of money. Keep in mind that although many insurance agents are trustworthy, it is in their own best interest to sell you a more expensive policy. Some may subtly put down cheaper term insurance, for example, by referring to it as "temporary" or Grade B or some such. You need to try to ignore any disparaging remarks and base your decision on facts. If you feel an agent is purposefully pushing you towards a higher-cost policy without good reason, find another agent you can trust.

Start asking questions and keep asking questions. Ask your agent to show you the *interest-adjusted net cost index* of various policies you are considering. This figure is the result of a formula which state insurance departments force insurance companies to place on their illustrations to help consumers compare policies, but it is only relevant and useful if you're comparing the same type of policy.

Here's the important point: A 20-year term policy may have a higher initial net cost index rating than a 10-year term, but maybe the 20-year policy better serves your needs. The lower the index, the better the deal in general. If you're thinking of buying term, ask whether it's automatically renewable or not. Try to find one that is renewable until you're around 65. After that, your life insurance needs may be close to zero. Ask what the policy is going to cost in five, 10, or 20 years. If a policy is bargain-basement priced for only the first few years, it's not a true bargain.

If you want to buy cash-value insurance, you can reduce its cost by going directly through an insurance company. Because these "no-load" companies don't pay agents' commissions, they can be as much as 20 percent cheaper. Your policy accumulates cash value the first year instead of paying out to the agent. For example, if you buy a regular whole life policy with a $2,000 premium, after the first year your policy would be worth nothing. If you bought the same policy directly from an agentless insurance company, after the first year your policy probably would be worth $1,700.

Call your insurance company to inquire whether it offers any no-load policies. Or call the National Insurance Consumer Organization for recommendations of companies that sell over the phone. Another option is to buy life insurance through your credit union or savings bank. One of the best deals of all is to purchase group insurance, often offered as part of your benefits package through your employer. The rates tend to be lower, and sometimes you avoid medical exams. If your employer doesn't offer group insurance, check with your union, alumni association, professional organization, or credit card issuer.

Riders

Life insurance policies, like new cars, come with a host of options. Called riders, these are features you can add on to your policy if you're willing to add on to your premium cost. They add value to your coverage only if they fill a need based on your individual situation. Be especially careful to ask your agent to explain the following riders and purchase them only if they make sense: waiver of premium, accidental death benefit, cost-of-living riders, guaranteed insurability riders, revertible or re-entry term rider, and joint life annual renewable term rider.

Ratings

Insurance companies invest your premiums in real estate, the stock market, and other vehicles. Some companies are better at this than others. Several independent agencies, including

Moody's, Standard & Poor's, and A. M. Best, rate insurance companies by how conservative they are—how much cash they have to cover future liabilities. When you invest in an insurance policy, you may be betting on a company being here 30 or 40 years from now. It's worth checking out the rating of any company you're considering. (See the Resources section on page 265 for ratings information.)

Car Insurance

The time to think about car insurance is *before* you buy a car. You need to add in the cost of your insurance to figure out how much you're paying for a particular car. That's because insurance rates are based in part on safety statistics, repair costs, and how likely a car is to be stolen or vandalized. Of course, rates are also based on where you live, what sex you are, and your age. Those are things you don't have much control over!

What kind of car you choose *is* up to you. Imagine you're pining for a dandy little sports car with a price tag of $20,000. Then you look at a sturdy station wagon. It's also $20,000, so you decide you might as well go for the sports car. But what if the sports car cost you $10,000 more? Would you still buy it? All other things being equal, that sports car might cost $2,000 a year more than the station wagon to insure. If you drive the car for five years, you'll be spending $10,000 for the privilege. Yet you would not have considered spending $10,000 more in the first place. To find out how a prospective car "rates" in terms of insurance, call one of the services or hotlines listed in the Resources section on page 264.

Car insurance is broken down into different categories, and each state requires different types of coverage. Once you've met your state requirements, which you can find out by calling your state insurance department (see the Resources section on page 264), you can begin to whittle away excess coverage. You need to understand these terms in order to think intelligently about each category:

- *Bodily Injury Liability.* This covers injuries to another person or persons if you are held liable for an accident.

- *Property Damage Liability.* This covers damage to someone else's property if you are held liable for an accident. Property may be defined as a car, a lawn, a house, a store, etc.

- *Uninsured and Underinsured Motorist.* If you are involved in an accident with a driver who has no or insufficient insurance, this coverage pays for injuries, including pain and suffering, you and any of your passengers suffer. It applies only if the other driver is at fault.

- *Medical Expenses or Medical Payments.* Pays medical and funeral expenses incurred in any accident involving a car, whether you were driving, riding a bicycle, walking, or a passenger. It applies regardless of who was at fault.

- *Personal Injury Protection.* In states with no-fault insurance laws, this kind of coverage is now mandatory. It covers medical expenses and some liability, no matter who was at fault. States with no-fault insurance include Colorado, Connecticut, Florida, Hawaii, Kansas, Kentucky, Massachusetts, Michigan, Minnesota, New Jersey, New York, North Dakota, Pennsylvania, and Utah (and the U.S. territory of Puerto Rico).

- *Collision.* This pays for the cost of car repairs or replacement in the event of an accident. If you don't have loan payments, it's usually not required by state law.

- *Comprehensive.* If your car is stolen or is damaged by theft, vandalism, or forces of nature (earthquakes, hurricanes, floods), this insurance covers it. It can be costly if you drive a thief-attractive car.

- *Other.* You can obtain extra coverage for additional items such as towing, labor, rental cars, and built-in camper equipment.

The first place to look to reduce your costs is in the collision and comprehensive coverages, which often account for a third of your premium. Collision can be one of the most expensive parts of car insurance, depending on your vehicle and deductibles. By asking for your deductible to be raised from $200 to $500, you can save from 15 to 30 percent.

Once your car is seven to 10 years old, you might consider canceling collision altogether, suggests Ann Brewer. She period-

WORKSHEET

CAR INSURANCE

AMOUNT OF PREMIUMS FROM EACH COMPANY

COVERAGE	COMPANY 1	COMPANY 2	COMPANY 3
Bodily injury liability			
Property damage liability			
Uninsured motorist			
Underinsured motorist			
Medical payments			
Personal injury protection			
Collision			
$100 deductible			
$250 deductible			
$500 deductible			
$1,000 deductible			
Comprehensive			
No deductible			
$50 deductible			
$100 deductible			
$250 deductible			
$500 deductible			
Membership fees			
SUBTOTAL A			
DISCOUNTS			
SUBTOTAL B			

SUBTOTAL A MINUS SUBTOTAL B EQUALS YOUR TOTAL PREMIUM

_____ _____ _____

ically checks her insurance premium to see if it warrants a change and drops collision when her cars get older. "We feel in our situation it doesn't pay to carry it."

DOLLARS AND SENSE

CAR INSURANCE DISCOUNTS

Be sure to ask whether you qualify for a discount on your insurance premium if you:

- *Have more than one car.*
- *Have had no accidents or moving violations.*
- *Are over 50 years old.*
- *Have taken a driver training course.*
- *Have an antitheft device.*
- *Have a low annual mileage.*
- *Have automatic seat belts.*
- *Have air bags.*
- *Have antilock brakes.*
- *Are a student with good grades.*
- *Are a nonsmoker.*
- *Have auto and home owner policies from the same insurance company.*
- *Have children who are college students living away from home with no car.*
- *Pay a lump-sum premium payment.*

She's right. It's silly to spend as much insuring an old car as a new one—unless, of course, you happen to own an antique! Once your collision coverage costs 10 percent or more of the car's resale value, or the resale value is less than $1,000, consider dropping collision insurance—only if doing so won't cause you economic hardship should your car be totaled in an unforeseen accident. (Look up the market value of your car in the National Automobile Dealer's Association price book, found in most libraries.)

The next place to check for savings is medical coverage. Very often there's overlap between your health insurance policy and what you're paying to cover medical costs in the event of a car accident. Also, few states require medical coverage. Read the fine print in both policies carefully to see if you can drop something.

Liability coverage is one place it's not wise to skimp on coverage. To buy the amount experts recommend—$100,000 per person and $300,000 per accident—doesn't cost much more than buying less. And it ensures a lot more peace of mind. Buffy is a positive thinker so she says, "I take as high a deductible as I can stand in relation to the reduced premium. I would recommend a $250 deductible because there are a lot of bad drivers and a lot of people driving without insurance."

Home Owner's Insurance

Ann Corley used to get upset every time she got her home owner's insurance bill because it had gone up. Ann says, "Carol explained to me that you get more coverage because the cost of labor and materials to rebuild goes up and homes appreciate." Well, not every home. Maxine says, "One time, I received my insurance bill and was surprised to see how high it was for my home's location. My agent told me that at times companies raise the rates, which is something you must watch for. My agent refigured my coverage at a lower cost."

Which just goes to show, if you are serious about saving money, you can't assume anything, including what home owner's insurance does and does not cover.

What Does It Cover?

The most basic home owner's insurance offers financial protection for your home and the contents of your home in the event of damage from fire, lightning, smoke, hail, explosion, vandalism, vehicles, riots, theft, burglary, and glass breakage. It also covers your liability in case anyone is hurt while on your property or even off your property if you somehow were responsible. In addition, there is coverage up to a certain percentage of the total insurance policy for such extra expenses as staying in a hotel or renting temporary shelter, or for damage to other buildings on your property such as a garage or storage shed. In certain states, home owner's insurance even covers theft of your possessions from a hotel, car, or boat.

It will not cover earthquake or flood damage. For those situations, you need to purchase endorsements or special separate policies. You can also buy upgrades to regular home owner's insurance which will then cover you for falling-object damage, roof collapse, electrical surges, frozen pipes, or damaged trees, or for historical, unique, or otherwise very valuable homes.

There are a few things you cannot buy insurance for at any cost.

These include nuclear meltdown, power failures, normal wear and tear, damaging your own property, intentionally hurting someone in your home, or pets. Luckily, damage from these occurrences is rare.

Replacement Value versus Market Value

In life insurance, you can choose either term or cash value. In car insurance, you have a choice between carrying liability and collision or just liability. When it comes to home insurance, there is a similar broad choice: replacement value or market value coverage. Replacement value means that should your house be destroyed, the insurance company will cover the cost of replacing or rebuilding it. Market value means that should your house be destroyed, the insurance company will pay you however much it thinks you could have sold the house for before it was damaged, or the amount of the policy coverage.

A market value premium is less expensive than a replacement value policy. But, Carol points out, if something does happen to your house, you're not going to get nearly as much as you would with a replacement policy. Which kind you buy depends on your attitude. The whole point with home owner's insurance is to figure out how important your specific house is to you. Maybe you feel, "If anything happened, I would want to live in a house that's just like this." Then you would definitely want to buy replacement value insurance. If you think, "If this house burns, I'll just move someplace else," then don't spend the money for an expensive replacement cost policy. Get a cheaper policy. You've got to weigh what you want and why.

Carol explains that if all you care is that your house is rebuilt, then a fire policy will cover you, "but it might not be what you expect. Say you have hardwood flooring with the wide five-inch walnut baseboard. They're not going to put that back. They're going to put this inch-and-a half casing with some varnish."

Insurance companies figure a replacement cost on your house based on certain rules. They measure the square footage. Is there a basement? How many bathrooms? Is there central air? Is there an attached garage? They take all this information and come up with a replacement cost. Then, most companies write your policy at 100 percent of replacement cost. "When I first started working six years ago, you could write 80 percent of replacements costs. They've raised it to a higher percent," Carol says. "You pay more, but you're better off to have a better policy. You don't have that many catastrophic losses. But if your house ever burned and you didn't have enough coverage, then you'd be upset. When you stop to think that you can get $100,000 worth of coverage for $300 to $400, you're not spending that much money to protect a lot."

More Tips on Home Insurance

Like car owners, home owners can take advantage of discounts on their insurance premiums. Check with your carrier to see whether any of these circumstances can save you money:

- You don't smoke.

- You installed smoke detectors, fire extinguishers, and fire resistant-doors.

- You have a security alarm system.

- You have an automatic emergency phone-dialing system.

- You buy your car or life insurance from the same company.

- Your house is new.

- You have been a customer for many years.

- You are over 50 and/or retired.

You'll be better off financially if you raise your deductible on home owner's insurance than with almost any other kind. Most claims are so high that you can get away with a fairly high deductible. Raising it from $100 to $500, for example, will save you around 25 percent on your premium.

Videotape or photograph your possessions to avoid lengthy arguments with claim adjusters should a catastrophe occur. A visual inventory will ensure a fairer, more timely insurance payment. Go room by room, including valuables such as jewelry or silver hidden inside drawers and other furniture. Don't forget to go into the attic and basement, the garage, the patio, and anywhere else you have possessions worth reimbursement. When you're done, store the tape or photos somewhere safe—but not at home!

Getting Down to Brass Tacks

1. Insure yourself only against catastrophes and financial ruin, not mere financial inconvenience.

2. Find an agent you can trust and ask for annual reviews of your policies.

3. Take as a high a deductible as you can afford to pay out of pocket should you have a claim.

CHAPTER SIX

UTILIZE YOUR UTILITIES

You can save even when dealing with a monopoly: electricity, gas, and water bills.

BETTY AND BOB BOUGHT THEIR HOME in Beardstown in 1960. On three sides of the house were large elm trees, which helped to keep them cool in the summer. When the trees became diseased and had to be cut down, they immediately noticed a 20 percent increase in their cooling bills. Later they had the whole house re-insulated and they installed siding. They soon noticed a decrease in both their cooling and their heating bills.

Utilities are big money eaters. For every dollar you spend on utilities, the Department of Energy says 46 percent goes toward heating and cooling systems, 15 percent for heating water, 15 percent for running refrigerators and freezers, and 24 percent for lighting, cooking, and other appliances. Because utilities are invisible, it may seem more difficult to focus on saving money on them. That's where using both types of your pyramids is helpful. We doubt many of you put utilities anywhere near the top of your Personal Priority Pyramid, yet utilities are probably fairly high up on your Spending Pyramid. Once you have a graphic illustration of how much of your income is spent on those utilities, you'll be more motivated to reduce those bills the way Betty did.

We think you'll be surprised by the hundreds of dollars you can save through a few major improvements. One family in California, for example, spent $276 on home improvements which reduced their annual utility bill by $579.93, resulting in a total savings of $303.93 in one year. It also pays to make those small but numerous changes in your energy use. They can be as simple as switching from hot water to cold water for certain washes or letting dishes air dry. Yet the savings from these changes add up faster than you can count the extra change in your pocket.

STOP!

Consider that the reasons you spend on utilities may include:

1. *To stay warm enough.*
2. *To stay cool enough.*
3. *For better health.*
4. *To make your home look nicer.*
5. *To save time.*
6. *For cleanliness.*

Utilities are the biggest percentage of Sylvia's current spending. She says her gas, electricity, and water bills, while "not exorbitant," are at the top of her pyramid. Considering that her husband and son worked for the Central Illinois Public Service Company, this seems oddly fitting. Unfortunately, Sylvia doesn't receive any sort of discount from the utility company she's helping to support. Still, because they make up her largest expense, it pays for Sylvia to try to reduce her utility bills. How?

It may seem as if it's impossible to save on utilities. You can't haggle, shop around, raise deductibles, or use any of the other methods we've described in previous chapters. Even if you could reduce your use of electricity or gas or water, it would only save a few pennies here and there, right? Wrong! *STOP, LOOK,* and *LISTEN.*

Dealing with Utility Companies

It's all too easy to think of utility companies as enemies. Month after month you write out checks for big amounts to some anonymous office. But actually, the people who staff those offices can be extremely helpful allies in your quest for saving money. We recommend you give your utility company a call (the number is always printed on your monthly bill). If you say you're interested in reducing your energy spending, chances are you'll receive lots of great information. And it's usually free or costs very little. Some companies provide rebates or subsidies if you buy certain energy-saving appliances or lightbulbs, for example. Others have comprehensive energy-saving programs. We know a family in California who received a zero-interest loan from the utility company to install insulation in their attic. The payments were added to their monthly utility bill and spread out over a few years.

Energy Audit

Carnell has saved a lot by dealing directly with her utility company. She received a special reduced rate for converting her whole house and farm to electricity. She also took advantage of one of the best services the companies offer: an energy audit.

When you request an energy audit, your local utility company sends a qualified conservation expert to your home to do a complete energy inspection. The person checks how efficiently your furnace works, how much caulking and weather stripping you might need, whether you have the right size air conditioner. After the review, you receive an individualized recommendation of energy-saving measures, how much each will cost, and how much they will save you on your annual bill.

Schedule an energy audit immediately, if you've never had one done on your current home.

Billing Options

Another question to ask your local utility company is whether they offer any special billing options. Sometimes you qualify for lower rates if you use electricity at certain times of the day that are considered "off-peak." Wouldn't it be worthwhile to run your dishwasher at night if it meant you saved a few dollars a month? Carnell and her husband save quite a bit by taking advantage of off-peak billing for their hog farm. "We've had contracts with the utility company," says Carnell, "where if we don't use any electricity for things such as grinding feed for the hog operation during peak hours, we get a special rate. At the end of each year, the amount is readjusted for the following year."

Many people on fixed incomes like the option of paying their utility bills on an average-use basis. Instead of having your meter read every month and paying a lot in the winter and less in the spring and fall, for instance, you pay whatever the company calculates is an average amount for what you use all year. This option makes it easier to budget for utility costs. Maxine is on what she calls an "equalizer" plan. She says, "I pay the same every month. It's worth it to me to know that my bill's going to be $89 every month. Otherwise it might be $159 some months. Maybe a particular month I wouldn't want to spend that much."

It's a good idea to read all the inserts that come tucked inside your utility bills. That's where all kinds of offers like those we've described often show up.

Heating and Cooling

Keeping ourselves comfortable—warm in winter and cool in summer—accounts for the biggest portion of our utility spending. So, given our pyramid approach, it makes sense to concentrate your effort in this area. Now, some people are not that interested in saving money on heating and cooling. They'd rather not spend energy trying to save on energy. Shirley feels that it's most economical to set her thermostat where she is comfortable summer or winter and then leave it alone. If you *are* willing to spend a little time and energy, however, you can realize great savings. Some of these measures, such as adding insulation, are fairly substantial. But they are one-time-only expenditures that reward you with years of savings. Many of us have been happy with improvements we've made.

Insulation

Start with the outside of your house and work in. It really pays to think smart about insulation. The average house loses as much heat as a well-insulated house would if it had a hole three feet by three feet punched in the side. So the single most important improvement to make is insulation. A well-insulated house, with storm windows, fireplace dampers, attic ventilation caulking, and weather stripping will cost up to a third less to heat and cool. Insulation is rated by number according to its thickness and energy efficiency—the higher the number, the thicker and more energy-efficient the insulation. For ceilings, R-30 is preferable. R-19 is good for floors, and R-12 is okay for outside walls.

Ruth says one of the best purchases she ever made was insulation. "We had a furnace with a stoker. After we had insulation blown into the house, my husband had to use ony half as much coal. That was a wise choice for us. We were really pleased."

KEEP THE HEAT IN

Sixty percent of the energy used to heat your home escapes through the walls, ceilings, and floor—parts of your house that can be insulated. Insulating your attic, for example, can cut 20 to 35 percent from your heating bill.

The effectiveness of insulation is described by its "R-value," a measurement of its resistance to the flow of heat. The higher the R-value, the less heat your insulation will allow out of your house. R-values usually range from 9 to 30. Window manufacturers assign R-values to windows to indicate their ability to keep in heat. Windows allow 12 times more heat to escape from your home than ordinary walls.

Five factors determine a window's R-value:

- The glazing material (e.g. glass, plastic, treated glass).
- The number of layers of glass.
- The size of the air space between the layers of glass.
- The conductivity (thermal resistance of the conductance of the frame and spacer materials).
- The tightness of the installation; the presence of air leaks.

Make sure that R-values set by the manufacturer are set based on current standards of American Society of Heating, Refrigeration, and Air-Conditioning Engineers (ASHRAE) and are calculated for the entire window including the frame and not just for the center of the glass. When you compare windows, make sure R-values correspond to the same style and size of window.

"Our house is insulated somewhat," Carol says, "but when they put our new siding on, they'll put a backer board which insulates even more." Carol's mom, Elsie, moved into a mobile home a few years ago. She had it insulated and put a roof over it so it actually looks like a little house. She also upgraded a window and got a new unit for both air-conditioning and heating, all of which has helped her cut down on her utility bills.

Heat Pumps

A heat pump, which is placed outside your house, can be a great boon in your cost-reduction program. An air-conditioning unit, it also provides heat. In winter, a valve reverses its function and fans the hot coils in the air conditioner into the house. Although the initial expense can run into thousands of dollars, heat pumps can reduce both heating and cooling bills by 40 percent. Ann Corley, who has always been very conscious of energy efficiency and utility bills, installed an electric heat pump. She says it's very cost-efficient.

If you do opt for a heat pump, you will maximize your investment by paying attention to certain things you might not think of doing when you have only a regular furnace:

- Keep the thermostat on a constant setting and don't close off unused rooms. (This may seem illogical, but it works.)

- Be sure the heat pump is not blocked by shrubs, flowers, or weeds.

- Every few weeks, hose it down to get rid of dust, dirt, leaves, and grass.

- Avoid stacking anything against the pump or covering it with anything.

Furnaces

As your primary source of heat, your furnace is an important unit to consider. Just by having it tuned up, you can increase its efficiency by at least 5 percent. Carol bought a new energy-saving furnace last year and immediately noticed a big difference in her utility bills. "We had electric baseboard heat," she says. "There was a furnace in the basement that was used strictly for the central air, but it had gone kaput. We decided to take it out and put a regular furnace in and then get the central air. We did that all in one purchase. Now we use our gas furnace to heat our whole house and we save a lot on our utility bills. It really does save energy."

Ann Corley discovered another great trick to get the most out of her furnace. "I've had a little trouble with my furnace," she explains. "My son thought the air was too dry in my house, and I had noticed it too. I had a lot of static electricity, and the furnace repair man said that it was because of the dryness. I plan to get a humidifier installed on my furnace and lower the thermostat. This will put moisture in the air and it will feel warmer than it actually is. Over time the humidifier will pay for itself in lower heat bills, and my house will be more comfortable."

Thermostats

Sometimes we fall into the habit of keeping our thermostats at the same setting for years. Maybe we've changed, have bigger or smaller families, or bigger or smaller bodies. All that is bound to affect our own comfort zones. Time to *LISTEN* to yourself. Whether it's hot or cold outside, being a little experimental with your thermostat can be financially rewarding. Raising the temperature two degrees cuts cooling costs by 5 percent. Lowering the setting by just one degree cuts heating costs by 5 percent. That means that if you wear a sweater in the winter and set your thermostat to 68 degrees instead of your usual 72 degrees, you'll save 20 percent on your utility bill. Which is nothing to sneeze at—as long as you don't wind up sneezing yourself.

Water, Water, Everywhere

Every time you wash a load of clothes, take a bath, or run your dishwasher, you're using hot water—gallons of it. In fact, the average family uses 600 gallons of heated water each week. Hot water conservation can cut your bill by 20 percent. What do we mean by conservation? We aren't suggesting you forego the pleasures of a nice hot shower or wear dirty clothes. There are much less severe ways to reduce your use of hot water.

Start at the source, with your hot water heater. Do you know how it works? It continually heats up the water to a preset temperature, whether you're using that water or not. In other words, when you're gone for the day and when you're sleeping, you're still paying for your hot water heater to produce hot water. If you install a timer, you can control when the heater works and save as much as 35 percent. You can have it produce hot water only during cheaper, off-peak hours, for instance. You don't need it to work around the clock in order to have plenty of hot water.

BEARDSTOWN TALES

Several years ago we bought storm windows for our house in Beardstown. A salesman came and he had a small sample window. Everything seemed great. Because we were so inexperienced, we didn't realize that many of these companies just hire jobbers to install the windows. They don't really know much about storm windows. When they put them on, I had to sign that they completed their job. Well, when Bob came home and looked around, there was already a piece of metal stripping falling off. It was a very poor job. It looked like it was a good product and it was. Those windows are still up today, but had they been installed properly, we would have been much happier. We determined from then on, we were better off using local people whom we knew.

BETTY SINNOCK

Check to see what temperature it was set at when it was first installed. Usually, it's set to heat water to 140 degrees. By simply lowering that setting to 125 degrees, you'll still have hot enough water for 2 to 10 percent less money. It's also a great safety precaution to prevent accidental scalding, an especially appealing bonus if you have small children in the house.

There is a simple maintenance chore that only takes about 20 minutes—yet most people have no idea how to do it or that it even needs to be done. Every three months or so, turn off the power to the water heater at the circuit breaker. Look for a cap at the bottom of the heater. Unscrew it and attach a garden hose. Then drain the water that collects on the bottom of the tank, which contains sediment and mineral deposits. There: You just saved 10 percent of your annual hot water bill.

Betty and her husband went further in moving their water bill to a lower spot on their Spending Pyramid. The house they bought in 1989 had a furnace and hot water heater in a garage at the opposite end from two bathrooms. Betty says each time they used hot water in those bathrooms, they wasted a lot of water while the tap ran until the water got hot. Last year, they installed a new hot water heater and a furnace with an air conditioner near the center of the house, underneath in a crawl space. They are now paying much less on their propane bills.

COOL FACTS ABOUT EFFICIENT HOME DESIGN

Here are some pointers on how to keep your home cool and save money through energy efficiency.

- Dull, dark-colored home exteriors absorb 70 percent to 90 percent of the radiant energy from the sun that strikes the home's surfaces.

- About a third of the unwanted heat that builds up in your home comes in through the roof. Even white asphalt and fiberglass shingles absorb 70 percent of the solar radiation.

- A radiant barrier can reduce heat that comes through your ceiling by about 25 percent.

- Roughly 40 percent of the unwanted heat that builds up in your home comes in through windows.

- Shading your home can reduce indoor temperatures by as much as 20°F (11°C).

- A grass-covered lawn is usually 10°F (60°C) cooler than bare ground in the summer.

- A properly installed awning can reduce heat gain up to 65 percent on southern windows and 77 percent on eastern windows.

- Ventilated attics are about 30°F (16°C) cooler than unventilated attics.

- Opening windows at the lowest and highest points in your house creates breezes.

- Compact fluorescent lamps emit 90 percent less heat for the same amount of light.

Cutting Costs from Top to Bottom

Every room in your house offers opportunities to cut your energy use and save more money. The following tips cover your whole house, from your attic to your basement:

Attic

- In the evening in summer, open your windows and turn on an attic fan, which will draw in cool night air. In the daytime, turn the fan off, and close the windows and curtains. You'll be amazed at how cool your house will stay for a fraction of the cost of running an air conditioner.

- Plug up any holes from pipes or ducts in the floor of your attic.
- Keep your attic ventilated, both winter and summer, to control heat in the summer and moisture in the winter.

Bedroom

- An air conditioner with clean filter and coils uses 5 percent less energy than a dirty, clogged one.
- Remove window air conditioners in the winter, or buy special covers to prevent heat loss.
- Don't forget to caulk and weather-strip windows here, too. Lined drapes or curtains will help hold heat as well.

Bathroom

- To reduce water flow by up to 50 percent—without sacrificing spray power—install a plastic or metal water restrictor that fits behind the shower head.
- Showers usually use less water than baths. Very shallow baths, however, use less water than showers. Pick your personal preference.

Kitchen

- Don't overuse kitchen vents or you'll waste electricity. Turn off vents once you've finished working in the kitchen.
- Keep your freezer three-fourths full for maximum efficiency. Any more will prevent the flow of air and any less will waste energy.
- Let your dishes air dry in the dishwasher rack after the wash cycle.
- Run only full loads in your dishwasher.
- Use a microwave or toaster oven when possible to save 50 percent of cooking costs compared to using a regular full-sized oven.
- Every few months, clean the condenser coils on the back of or underneath your refrigerator. Dust and dirt that collect there

make the appliance work harder. (Try putting your refrigerator on rolling casters to make this task easier.)

- Keep the refrigerator door open as briefly as possible. Also, check the gasket around the door to make sure the seal is air tight by placing a dollar bill in the doorway and then closing the door. If it slides out easily, you should replace the gasket.

Living/Dining Room

- When you're not using it, close the flue in your fireplace to save 8 percent of your house's heat.

- Use compact fluorescent lightbulbs to reduce electricity costs by 75 percent. They also reduce your air-conditioning costs because they give off less heat. A room with three compact fluorescent bulbs instead of three regular 100-watt bulbs will reduce an air conditioner's energy output by 12 percent.

Basement

- Try doing more cold-water washes. Often cold water does just as good a job, especially for rinsing.

- Run only full loads of wash.

- If it's convenient to do all your laundry at one time, you'll save money. That's because a dryer is more efficient once it's heated up.

- Keep your dryer's lint filter clean for optimal operation.

- Wash and dry similar weight clothes together.

Getting Down to Brass Tacks

1. Have an energy audit done on your home to save hundreds of dollars a year on heating and cooling costs.

2. Ask your utility company about any cost-reduction programs it may offer, such as off-hour rates or load management.

3. Be conscious of how you use electricity, heat, and water every day in each room of your house.

CHAPTER SEVEN

BANK ON THIS

*There may be no such thing as free money,
but that doesn't mean you should spend a
fortune on banking.*

IT'S A GOOD IDEA TO EVALUATE YOUR NEEDS and wants when
you choose a bank the same way you do when you shop for a car.
STOP, LOOK, and *LISTEN.* By trying to match the right bank
and the right kind of account with your banking style you will
save money. How much? Several surveys have shown that fees
and interest rates can vary by more than $200 a year from bank
to bank. That means if you choose the most reasonable bank, you
could save $2,000 in 10 years—simply by *doing your homework.*
That's not a bad rate of return for an investment of a few hours
of your time.

It used to be that it was most cost-effective to do all your
banking at one place, preferably a local one, because your relationship with bank management was important. But as new types
of banking have entered the field and it's become more competitive, it may be worth rethinking how and where you bank.

Nearly half of the Beardstown Ladies are either bank employees or on the board of directors of a bank, so we have plenty to
say when it comes to how to choose a financial institution. We
live in a small town (population 6,000), and we like to support
our local banks as much as possible—especially the ones we work
at. We have two banks, one savings and loan association, and
one credit union. So we have many choices about which financial institution we want to use for what service.

STOP!

Consider that the reasons you choose a bank may include:

1. *Interest income on savings and checking.*
2. *Checking.*
3. *Charge cards.*
4. *Friendly service.*
5. *Convenient location.*
7. *Loans.*
8. *Credit references.*
9. *Brokerage services.*
10. *Foreign cash exchange.*
11. *Business loans and letters of credit.*

We shop around for the best deals in town. Service charges and interest rates may vary from bank to bank. We don't hesitate to invest our money in the bank that is offering the highest rate of interest. Carol says that when her bank lowered the interest that they were paying on Christmas club savings accounts she checked with the other places in town and found out that the credit union was paying 1 percent higher. It does make a difference. We want to earn the most that we can on our hard-earned money.

Maybe Carol inherited her business attitude from her mother. Elsie says, "We dealt with one bank for a long time. We would borrow for our farm operations and when we were given a better rate at the other bank, we opened an account for that purpose. We continued banking at both banks."

Choosing a Bank

First, look through several months of your bank statements. Refer to your calendar or appointment book. Think about your day-to-day routine. Then ask yourself the following questions:

- What's your average balance?
- How many checks do you write per month?
- How many deposits do you make per month?
- Do you use automatic payroll deposits?
- Do you use ATMs (automated teller machines)? If so, how often?
- How often do you go inside the bank?
- Do you live in the city, the suburbs, or the country?
- Do you travel a lot?

Now that you have this information at your fingertips, you

can compare it against different prospective bank accounts. If you often dip below the minimum no-fee balance, you aren't going to save the fee in such an account. If you write many checks each month, you probably will do well to find a free checking account. If you find ATMs the height of convenience, be sure you're not being charged a hefty fee every time you use one. If you carefully think about your personal banking needs and *STOP* and consider, you may save money.

Checking Accounts

Next it's time to *LOOK* before you leap. For example, some banks offer no-fee checking accounts in exchange for a required minimum balance, but watch out! The service charge might be quite large if you fail to keep the minimum balance in the account. You need to *LISTEN* to yourself. Would it be difficult to maintain the balance?

Today regular savings accounts are not earning a very high rate of interest. Many checking accounts don't charge service fees if you keep a minimum balance as low as $100 and a $5 monthly fee if the balance falls below $100. If you have money in a regular savings account earning 2 percent, doesn't it make sense to transfer $100, which would only earn $2, to the checking account, to save $60 in service fees?

Carnell and her husband Willard have a checking account with no service charge as long as they maintain a certain balance. They avoid the fees and they earn a little interest on their money at the same time.

Most banks offer these interest-earning checking accounts, called NOW, Super NOW, Money Market accounts, or something similar. They require minimum balances, which may range from $1,000 to $25,000, and the interest paid varies according to the amount in the account. Some accounts have limits on the number of checks that can be written each month, although you may be able to write more checks than the limit for an additional fee per check. It pays to find out what is available in your area.

Many banks offer checking accounts with very small fees for every transaction (as low as 10 cents). This works well if you write less than 10 or 12 checks a month. A variation more and more banks seem to be making is a no-fee, no-statement, no-checks checking account. The bank keeps your records and canceled checks on file, of course, but saves the expense of monthly mailings to you. Called a truncated account, it works fine for some people. Others like to have some kind of a record of checks. Margaret chose an account with a small fee so that she can get a statement every month. She also receives an electronic page of her canceled checks.

Another way you can save money on checking is to buy your checks as inexpensively as possible. Many people assume that they must order their checks from their bank. Banks typically charge $15 to $25 per 200 checks. You can cut that amount in half or more by using non-bank checks. These are often advertised in the backs of magazines with coupons. Don't let your bank convince you that you must buy checks from them. (We've listed some suppliers in the Resources section on page 267.)

The banks in our area also offer club accounts for people who like to buy package deals. For a monthly fee, you receive a laundry list of bank services, including accidental life insurance, at no charge. You need to consider realistically how many of these services you would use before you can figure out whether or not such an account is worthwhile. The bank has priced the account to make a profit; how much profit they make depends on how frequently you use the available services.

We hear more and more about the convenience of banking from your home via a phone system, a television, or a personal computer. You may transfer funds, check your accounts, and even pay bills. Before you pay for such convenience, be sure you consider the cost and whether the same service is available elsewhere for less. We live in a very competitive environment where both services and fees vary greatly. Once more we say, *LOOK* before you leap.

Automated Teller Machines

Some people think automated teller machines, or ATMs, are the greatest new invention since sliced bread. Imagine: Now we never have to run out of cash on weekends, holidays, at night, or

CHOOSING THE RIGHT ACCOUNT

Because they think they may need it one day, many people leave too much money in a checking account that's not earning anything for them. We used to say, put it in savings—but today, savings are so low, it's kind of a joke. If you have a large enough amount of money, you should probably check into either the money markets, a NOW account, or one or more certificates of deposit.

	INTEREST	WITHDRAWAL LIMITS	FEES	MINIMUM BALANCE
REGULAR CHECKING	NO	YES	NO	YES
INTEREST BEARING CHECKING (NOW)	YES	YES	NO	YES
MONEY MARKET DEPOSIT (MMDA)	YES	YES	YES	YES
SAVINGS	YES	NO	YES	YES
CERTIFICATES OF DEPOSIT	YES	NO	YES	YES

on trips—even when we're out of the country! They surely can't be beat when it comes to convenience. We know a few people who haven't seen the inside of a bank, let alone the end of a long line, in years.

ATMs were introduced by banks to reduce the expense of bank tellers' time and to make bank services available 24 hours a day. To attract people to these new machines, they offered free service. Well, that's changed in many cases. The banks have to make a profit, and now that so many people love their ATMs, the banks figure they can charge them for it.

The lesson is to use ATMs wisely and well. You need to find out whether or not your bank is charging you for ATM transactions, and if so, how much. Next, try to use only your bank's ATMs. Change banks if the ATMs aren't located conveniently enough. When you do use another bank's machine, try to find out if you're being charged. If you are, cancel the transaction and find another ATM.

Be especially wary in beach and resort locations, and in casinos or on cruise ships. Knowing you are on vacation and likely to be in need of more cash than usual, banks often charge more for ATM use in such places. One couple we know ran out of cash on vacation in the Bahamas. The most convenient ATM—the only ATM—happened to be in a casino. Though they never gambled, they wound up making a trip to the ATM about every other day. Unbeknownst to them, each time they withdrew cash they were charged an additional four dollars. That's expensive convenience.

Overdraft Protection

Banks charge some of their highest fees when an account is overdrawn. Betty, who works in a bank, says that some customers continue to write checks after their accounts are overdrawn and their charges build up to an astronomical amount. It's an expensive way to use—or abuse—your checking account. Think about it: You don't really want such charges making up a big part of your pyramid, do you? Most banks offer overdraft protection, which you must apply for in the same way as you would a pre-approved loan. You are approved for a certain limit, and as long as you do not exceed that limit, you may overdraw your account for a minimal fee, which is less than the charge for a Not Sufficient Funds (NSF) check. There is an interest charge on the balance you owe which is less than the current charge for a personal loan. You pay for this service only when you use it.

An alternate plan if you have both a checking account and a regular savings account is to sign up for an automatic transfer of funds. Then, if you overdraw your checking account, the money is transferred from your savings account in increments of $50 to $100. Again, the transfer fee is much less than the NSF charge you would incur without this protection.

We urge you not to write bad checks in the first place, of course. Instead, if you don't have the money to pay for something, ask those involved if they would make arrangements for a different payment schedule.

WHAT TO ASK ABOUT BANK ACCOUNTS

If you want to compare banks and be a smart consumer, ask the following questions:

Checking Account

- Is there a minimum-balance requirement?
- How is it calculated? The lowest balance of the month or the average daily balance?
- What is the penalty for going below the minimum balance?
- What fees are there?
- What is the bank's policy on clearing checks for deposits?
- What is the charge for overdrafts?
- Is there any advantage to having other accounts with this bank?
- If I take out a loan or buy a certificate of deposit, will the bank eliminate any checking account fees?

Savings Account

- How does the bank calculate interest?
- How often does the bank compound interest? Daily, monthly, quarterly, or annually?
- How often is your account updated with earned interest?
- What is the annual percentage yield?
- How much will $100 earn in one year?
- What is the periodic payment rate?

"Free" Services

Remember that in the chapter on buying a house we mentioned getting the seller to throw in appliances or drapes or some other object you could use? You can apply the same principle to banking. But you need to make sure you're not being charged for the "freebies" some banks throw in when you open an account. You also need to consider whether the offer is for something you really use or need. As always, ask lots of questions before you open an account just to receive a gift.

Ann Brewer says her bank gives seniors free checking and free checks. "Sometimes it's not so bad getting old!" she adds. Other Ladies have obtained credit card protection, savings on rental cars, and upgrades on rental cars.

Direct Deposit

If you receive a regular paycheck, the single smartest move you can make is to have direct deposit. Instead of having your check mailed or given to you in person, the funds are deposited directly by your employer in an account you designate. This saves you time, guarantees that you never lose a check, and most important, your money starts earning interest for you sooner. If your bank doesn't offer this option, switch banks.

Service Charges

If you see anything on your bank statement labeled "service charge" or "service fee," be sure to find out what it's for. Banks are at liberty to charge whatever they want for whatever they offer. Although each individual fee may seem minor, they add up—the cost of items is from $1 (for night deposits) to $25 (for overdrafts). Don't be nickeled and dimed into losing money. The only way to protest is to either ask to have the charge removed or switch banks. Here are the kinds of things you may be charged for:

- Per-check charge.

- Stop-payment orders.

- ATM withdrawals.

- Using a different bank's ATM.

- Balance inquiries by telephone.

- Using a bank teller.

- Depositing an NSF check from a third party.

- Writing an NSF check of your own.

- Asking for rolls of coins or packages of bills.

- Night deposits.

- An inactive or dormant account.

- Closing an account within a certain time period after opening it.

Credit Cards

It seems as if most everyone takes credit cards for granted and assumes it would be impossible to live without them. That's exactly what we've been trying to say in this book: Don't assume anything when it comes to how you spend your money. *STOP* and consider. Check your Spending and Personal Priority pyramids. See how the two fit together. It amazes us how many people would have to put credit card debt at the top of their Spending Pyramid. Think about it first. Then decide whether you really need a credit card or not. If you don't, you've automatically avoided one of the biggest financial pitfalls Americans fall into.

Sylvia, Hazel, and Ruth have never owned credit cards. Ruth says "I feel like my credit's good and it is. When my husband was ill, the bank called and told me that if I needed any money, they'd be glad to send it. I just don't need credit cards."

There are some good reasons to own credit cards. Carnell, for instance, likes their convenience. "You're paying for things with one check instead of a few. Rather than carry cash, use a credit card," she says. Doris and Margaret use credit cards because they travel so much and find them helpful for making hotel reservations. Some credit cards provide consumer protection. In the event you buy a defective product or feel you've been cheated, you can usually get the charge removed. Other cards offer protection when you rent a car by covering the collision insurance for you.

Carol is the first to admit the danger of not paying down her balance. "Right now they're nearly paid off," she says. "My husband thinks it's ridiculous to pay the high interest rates, and it is. He'd just as soon cut them all up."

Although we haven't gone so far as to cut up our credit cards, most of us do pay them off before any interest accumulates, so they don't wind up costing us anything extra. Ann Brewer has a MasterCard and pays it off monthly, as do both Doris and Carnell.

BEARDSTOWN TALES

You have to know yourself well enough to know whether you are capable of using cards this Beardstown way.

Of course, none of us lives in a perfect world. The point is to do the best we can. Although Betty agrees that the ideal thing would be to be able to pay everything off at the end of the month, she's not always able to do that. "When I'm not able to pay the whole balance, I always pay more than the minimum due to get it paid off as quickly as possible." Otherwise, credit card debt would soon climb to the top of her Spending Pyramid—and Betty would much rather see her retirement fund up there.

If you find yourself paying more than $100 a year in credit card interest, take a look at your spending habits. You either need to cut back or find another place to borrow money (like a home equity loan) that isn't so expensive.

Annual Fees and Interest Rates

When you opt for owning credit cards, you usually have two very basic choices: a high-interest card with no annual fee, or a low-interest card with an annual fee. It all comes back to assessing your own needs and then finding a good match. If you honestly think you can pay off your balance every month, then it doesn't matter how high the interest rate is—you'll never have to pay it. So it makes sense to shop for a credit card that you can use for "free"—without being charged any sort of annual fee or service charge. Annual fees can be anywhere from $15 to $100. If you know perfectly well that your typical style is to carry a fairly regular, large balance, then you would benefit more from searching for the absolute lowest interest rate, or annual percentage rate, as it is more accurately called. It will be worth the annual fee because you will save much more than that in interest.

If you really want to save money using credit cards, you can search out low-rate cards with no annual fees. How low an APR are we talking about? While the average credit card APR is 18 percent, some cards are currently offering APRs as low as 8.5 percent—and no annual fees. That's an amazing rate, and they are few and far between, but they are available. Check the Resources section on page 267 for more information on how to track down these bargain cards. If you think it's not worth the time, think about saving almost $200 a year: That's the potential difference in interest charges if you carry an average $2,000 credit card balance.

A word of caution. It's easier to get stuck with spending more than you bargained for on a credit card than probably any other consumer product. The fine print in those tiny credit card agreement brochures is hard to read, much less understand. It's common practice for companies to offer extremely low introductory interest rates, called "teaser" rates, only to increase them after a few months of lulling you into a false sense of economy. Credit card companies have been known to charge penalties when a customer charges above a certain amount on competitors' cards or for not using part of a credit line. The bottom line is LOOK at the fine print, and be especially wary of language regarding billing cycles, grace periods, and interest rates.

There is one other strategy for reducing credit card costs: Talk directly to your credit card company. Though one of the simplest tools, most people don't take advantage of negotiation, either out of ignorance, reluctance, or the "never get around to it" factor. Call your credit card company's customer service representative. Say you want the card for free, or you need a lower interest rate. If you've been a good customer, odds are you'll get it, just for asking!

In addition to considering annual fees and interest rates, you probably will want to compare credit limits. Some of the cheapest credit cards extend only low credit lines. If you need a higher one, you may want to shop around. Margaret pays an annual fee for her

SAFE DEPOSIT BOXES

Banks charge from $25 to $200 for a safe deposit box, so clearly it's worth it to *STOP*, *LOOK*, and *LISTEN* before you rent one.

What should you put in them?

- Birth certificates.

- Marriage certificates.

- Rarely worn, expensive jewelry.

- Divorce papers.

- List of insurance companies and policy numbers.

- Photographs and/or videotapes of personal property in your home.

- Real estate titles and abstracts.

- Titles to automobiles, boats, trucks, etc.

What should stay out of them?

- Original copies of wills; insurance policies. (Your heirs need immediate access.)

- Passports. (They are irreplaceable.)

- Photographs; baseball cards; or stamp collections. (Safe deposit boxes do not have adequate climate control for preservation.)

Visa Gold Card with a $5,000 limit. When she was getting ready to go to Hawaii, her husband thought she might need more than a $300 credit limit for emergencies as she traveled.

Special Cards

The credit card industry has become so competitive, it tries to lure customers with more than convenience. Almost every day we get a new pitch in the mail from a card company offering everything from free airline miles to the kitchen sink—or at least a toaster. If you're comparing cards and everything else is equal, only then should you look at the extra bells and whistles. Some are more worthwhile than others and some wind up costing you money in the end. Many of these so-called bonuses are services you'll probably never need or else already have.

Some of the special options you may get with a credit card include:

- *Airline Frequent Flier Miles.* This is one of the more valuable deals. For every dollar you charge, you earn a mile toward a flight. If you charge a lot, you may benefit. You usually need 25,000 miles or more to take even one free flight. Also, most of these frequent flier cards have high annual fees—$50 to $75. So if it takes you a few years to charge enough for a flight, your total annual fees might cost more than the flight. A couple in New Jersey has found a good way to take advantage of their frequent flier credit card. They use it to buy absolutely everything, including their groceries, gasoline, doctor, and dental bills—even a car. But they pay off the balance each month, avoiding high interest rates. They've racked up enough miles in a year to go to Spain.

- *Purchase Protection.* This is like getting extra insurance for whatever you buy with your credit card. Theoretically, it means you'll be reimbursed if purchases are damaged, broken, lost, or stolen within a specified time period. It won't cost you anything but a lot of time spent dealing with paperwork should you ever want to actually file a claim.

- *Rental Car Collision Damage Waivers.* When you rent a car, this covers you if the car is damaged or stolen. Rental car companies charge $8 to $15 a day for collision damage waivers, so if you travel and rent cars frequently, you stand to save a substantial amount. In fact, take a minute right now to check your current card for this extra. If you don't have it, ask for it.

- *Travel Accident Insurance.* This accidental death insurance for air travel is almost like getting nothing for nothing. Chances are it won't cost you a cent—and you'll never be in an air crash, given today's statistics.

- *Price Protection.* A variation on the big chain stores that advertise their prices can't be beat, this guarantees that you'll be reimbursed if you find a lower price for something you've already charged. You have to ask yourself, how likely is this? How often would you take advantage of it?

- *Emergency Roadside Help*. Who needs it? If you belong to AAA already, not you. Most of us have this coverage through our auto insurance policies.

- *Lost Luggage Assistance*. Again, this is extraneous help because the airlines are obligated to take care of any luggage they lose.

- *Rebates*. This is a variation on the frequent flier cards. Instead of miles, every dollar you charge earns some sort of rebate. It can take the form of cash—usually about 1 percent of what you spend—or rebates of up to 5 percent on gasoline or cars or other purchases. Before you opt for such a card, carefully look at your spending and charging style to make sure it's worth it.

One additional "perk" you may be "offered" for a fee is credit card insurance to pay your bills in the event you are disabled or unable to work. Then there is insurance against lost or stolen cards. We discuss this in more depth in the following section.

Credit Card Insurance

We Ladies have saved money by being sensible about credit card insurance. When Elsie received a call from a man trying to sell her credit card insurance, she replied, "I don't even use my credit cards." He said, "You have them, you should have them insured." I said, "Well, I don't want to be bothered." Indeed, it would have been a complete waste. Betty explains, "I don't think it's necessary. You're only liable for the first $50 on your card as long as you notify them. I think they have a racket. My husband's retired. I'm planning to retire this year. We don't have that much of a balance. We keep getting these calls for disability credit card insurance when you're not able to work. I think the only reason is that they're looking to make a dollar. They talk to people as if they're doing them a favor, and most people who pay for it never use it."

You're also very likely covered for any credit card loss through other sources. There is an automatic protection against excessive charges if your credit card is stolen. Technically, your home owner's insurance will cover credit loss up to a limit shown on your policy. You should find out if it's on your policy. *LOOK* before you leap.

No matter what, credit card insurance is one expense you can forgo safely and still feel perfectly secure.

Debit Cards

A debit card is a relatively new wrinkle in money. Debit cards, which look like credit cards or ATM cards, allow you to pay for purchases using money in your checking account—without writing a check. You can insert your debit card into a machine at a grocery store, for example, and the amount is automatically deducted from your account. Or you can "charge" purchases without using a credit card: Wherever they take credit cards, they'll accept debit cards and process them in the same machines used for credit cards.

At first glance, this variation on the money theme may seem like the perfect way to get the convenience of a credit card without the sacrifice of paying high interest rates. If you don't pay your credit card balance off each month, a debit card may seem especially appealing. But, like so many things, there are pros and cons. The good news, as we said, is that you avoid running up huge credit card interest payments. The bad news is that debit cards may have annual fees; you may be charged each time you use one; you may have a limit on how much you can spend using your card; and, perhaps the worst news of all, you are more vulnerable to unauthorized use of a debit card than of a credit card or check. Should a thief steal your card, for example, you are responsible for up to $500 starting two days after it's been stolen. If for some reason you don't notify the bank within two months, you are liable for an unlimited amount.

No-Bank Banking

With the growth of discount brokers like Schwab and full-service brokers like Merrill Lynch, many consumers now have access to bank-like accounts at brokerage firms. They may offer more competitive rates, the opportunity to switch money from a money market account to checking, and other benefits. While we certainly don't want to put banks out of business, these non-bank alternatives are interesting enough for you to explore and compare.

Getting Down To Brass Tacks

1. Shop around for the best financial institutions as you would any consumer purchase.

2. Don't leave unnecessarily high balances in non-interest-bearing checking accounts.

3. If you must use credit cards, pay off the balance every month.

CHAPTER EIGHT

TAX BREAKS FOR ORDINARY PEOPLE

~

Up to a third of your income goes to Washington. Here are some secrets that the rich already know.

TAXES ARE BASED ON YOUR INCOME, *not* on how much money you have. The government has been adding to and refining the tax system for decades. As a result, it's filled with twists and turns. It's possible to pay far less than you do now and still be paying your fair share. It's just a matter of looking at your options.

The top of Buffy's Spending Pyramid is her income tax. It's her biggest expense because she's managed to get everything else, including her house and cars, paid off. So how does she try to save on her income tax? Her main tax reduction strategy was to realize that her business was buying many assets that were depreciable. "Other than my IRA, that's one of the only legal tax shelters I can use," says Buffy.

Buffy uses the Spending Pyramid approach: realizing what's on top of your pyramid and then figuring out how to keep those costs to a minimum by practicing *LOOK* before you leap. For Buffy, it's by looking at her real estate investments. For Carnell, it's staying up-to-date on what part of her hog business may be tax-deductible. She points out that her best tax savings strategy changes with each year's new tax laws.

"At one time," says Carnell, "we bought feed handling equipment and were allowed an investment credit on a percentage of the cost. Another time, we utilized tax advantages when we used solar heating in a new building. In general, it pays to be informed, to keep good records, and to take advantage of things that are allowed. We always pay taxes, but we don't want to pay more than we should."

STOP!

Consider that the reasons you pay taxes may include:

1. *To be a good citizen.*
2. *To avoid penalties.*
3. *To get a big refund once a year.*
4. *To force yourself to save money.*
5. *To pay for public services.*
6. *To support your government.*

None of us thinks you should pay more than is required. We cannot imagine that any reader would put income tax at the top of a Personal Priority Pyramid either. This chapter will describe some good general tax planning, how to make the most of your allowable deductions, whether or not you need to pay an accountant, how to avoid a tax audit, and the best tax-sheltered retirement investments.

Tax Planning Strategy

One of the biggest tax mistakes more people than we'd care to admit make is having too much tax withheld from their paychecks. They think it's a way of forcing themselves to save and they like getting large refund checks. You can probably guess what we have to say about that! Why let the government have the use of all that money for a whole year, when you could be earning interest on it for yourself? Instead of withholding more than you need to, we think it's better to have less withheld and then deposit the difference into some sort of interest-bearing account or investment. This single change, because of the magic of compound interest, could mean you wind up with a lot more money. For example, say each year you receive a refund of $2,500. If you had $2,000 less withheld and invested the difference in an investment that yields 8 percent, in 20 years you'd have $9,853. If you did that each year for 20 years, you'd end up with $108,019, quite a nice nest egg.

Shirley also likes to pay her income tax on a quarterly basis now that she is not on a salary. "I don't have withholding, so I have to pay estimated tax on my income. I try to pay enough so I don't have a penalty at the end of the year. The government takes enough of my money away."

She also suggests buying municipal bonds as a good tax-saving strategy because you do not have to pay federal and/or state taxes on them. Sometimes you don't have to pay city taxes either. These can be complicated investments, however, so be sure to do your homework before you purchase them.

Retirement Plans

The beauty of the many tax-deferred retirement savings plans now available is that you are making your money do double duty. Doris, for example, has a school pension fund that's automatically deducted from her paycheck. "I never see that money," she says. She's smart—not only is she saving relatively painlessly for her retirement, she's sheltering that portion of her salary from taxation. Several Ladies use their annuities to shelter taxes.

As we said in our last book, IRAs and Keoghs are wonderful instruments. The money you deposit in them each year can be subtracted from your adjusted gross income at tax time. For every $1,000 you deposit, the government, in effect, kicks in a few hundred dollars—the amount you would have had to pay in taxes on that money.

"You don't have to pay taxes until you withdraw the money," Buffy explains, "But by that time I figure I'll be slowing down and in a lower tax bracket, so I'll not only have the interest earned, but I will have succeeded in paying lower taxes on that money. What this says to me is, there is no free lunch but there is a subsidized lunch. All the rest is gravy."

If you compare investments, one taxable and the other tax-deferred, you'll see what she means. An investor in the 28 percent tax bracket invests $2,000 each year in two vehicles with a 10 percent return. One is taxed and the other is tax-deferred. After 20 years, the tax-deferred investment is worth $126,005. The ordinary investment, which has been taxed each year for those 20 years, is worth $84,272.

401(k) Plans

The benefits of 401(k) plans include:

- They provide retirement funds.

- You get to contribute part of your income *before it's taxed*.

- The money is invested to accrue interest which is *tax-deferred*.

- Your 401(k) contribution is automatically deducted from your paycheck.

The plans let employees have part of their salaries set aside in special funds earmarked for them and not taxed until they withdraw the money at retirement time. You decide how much you want to put into your 401(k), where you want the money invested, and it's automatically deducted from your paycheck. Another great feature is that most companies add to or even match your contribution. Now think about that for a minute. You're saving for your retirement without having to lift a finger, reducing your current income tax, and getting extra money from your employer. It's almost too good to be true. Betty is proof that it really works. She has a 401(k) through the bank where she works. The bank matches what she contributes up to a maximum of 6 percent. "I take full advantage of it," Betty says, "with 10 percent of my salary going straight from my paycheck into that plan."

You need to keep in mind that 401(k) plans are definitely for retirement savings only. To remind people, the government says you can't touch the money until you're 59 1/2. If you do withdraw it before then, it will be taxed like regular income plus you'll be charged an extra 10 percent of the total as a penalty. There are some exceptions. In case of retirement, death, disability, or economic hardship, all or part of the money may be withdrawn.

Individual Retirement Accounts

Individual Retirement Accounts (IRAs) were an instant success when the government first introduced them in 1981 to encourage Americans to save more. Anyone who earned a living could contribute 10 percent of his or her income—up to $2,000 each year—into a special account through a bank, brokerage, or mutual fund. Not only would the contribution be deducted from taxable income, the interest earned would be tax-deferred. Since 1986, deductions for IRA contributions have been limited to the following:

- Workers without other pension plans.

- Married couples with less than $50,000 annual income.

- Single people who earn less than $35,000.

If you make more than the above amounts or if you or your spouse qualify for any company pension plan, you can't deduct your IRA contribution from your taxable income. However, you can contribute to your IRA and the interest earned is tax-deferred, but the tax laws keep changing. There's even been talk of getting rid of some of the penalties and taxes for withdrawing IRA money before age 59 1/2 under certain conditions. To take advantage of any retirement savings plan, you need to keep up with the changing rules.

Even if the original contribution isn't deductible, your investment earnings are still protected from taxation as long as the money is kept in the IRA. Any tax on the interest earned is deferred until you withdraw from the IRA. That difference can be worthwhile if the IRA is kept for 20 or 30 years. All those years your taxes are postponed, your extra money is earning compound interest.

Annuities

Annuities come in all sorts of shapes and sizes, but they each offer tax-deferred income for the future. Usually sold by life insurance companies, annuities are like policies you buy to provide yourself with income after you retire. You pay into an annuity while you're working, and then you're guaranteed a monthly income for a certain period of time, or, more commonly, for the rest of your life.

The way you pay into an annuity or the way you receive your annuity payments are what makes them so varied. Three main types are *immediate*, *deferred variable*, and *deferred fixed-rate* annuities. There is no limit on how much you can contribute to an annuity and the tax advantage is a definite plus. But keep in mind that the fees and early withdrawal penalties that insurance companies may charge can really add up. So an annuity is a better choice for someone who is relatively young and can keep building a retirement nest egg for a long time.

Keogh Plans

Keogh plans are for the self-employed. There are three different types of Keogh plans. To set up a Keogh you have to first decide what type of investment you want to fund. Then go straight to that vehicle for a Keogh application form: banks for certificates of deposit; insurance companies for annuities; mutual fund companies for mutual funds. Keoghs require an annual tax return called Form 5500. If you hold a Keogh, you must be on the lookout for frequent changes in the federal regulations on retirement plans.

After you've completed the application form, return it to the same institution. For more information on setting up Keoghs and other related retirement plans, you can call the Internal Revenue Service at 800-829-3676 and ask for Publication 560, *Retirement Plans for the Self-Employed.*

Simplified Employee Pension Plans

Simplified Employee Pension plans, or SEPs, aren't as well-known as Keoghs, although they've been in existence since 1978. SEPs are not only simple, they're more flexible because they're administered like IRAs, yet they allow tax-deductible contributions of much more than the $2,000 IRA limit—about 15 percent of your net income (up to $30,000 when combined with other plans).

SARSEP stands for Salary Reduction Simplified Employee Pension Plan. These are voluntary programs in which an employee voluntarily has a salary deduction. The difference is then put into a pension plan that can be invested. The employee winds up with less taxable income and a tax-sheltered retirement plan.

Of course, everyone's situation is different. You will want to *LOOK* before you leap by checking with an accountant, financial planner, or employee benefits representative to decide which plan is right for you.

Whether to Use an Accountant

Deciding whether or not to do your own tax returns or to hire a professional tax preparer can be a tricky choice. You need to weigh the amount you will save by doing it yourself against how much a professional may be able to save you beyond his fee. You should also factor into the equation the value of your time. No one has ever claimed that filling out a tax form is simple or quick. The IRS itself states, "We try to create forms and instructions that can be easily understood. Often this is difficult to do because our tax laws are very complex. For some people with income mostly from wages, filling in the forms is easy. For others who have their own business, pensions, stocks, rental income, or other investments, it is more difficult."

How do you decide? Again, it comes back to knowing yourself and what you want and what you're capable of doing. *LISTEN* to yourself. Maybe you don't believe anyone else would pay as much attention to detail as you do and therefore wouldn't save you as much money. Perhaps you enjoy the challenge of math, or on the other hand maybe you've always assumed it was too complicated. If you actually read the IRS tax form instructions, you may be surprised to find that you understand a lot more than you thought you did. The IRS also offers plenty of free help, from hundreds of publications on specific forms, to telephone lines and recorded tax information, to videotapes and large-print forms, to offices where you can go in person for assistance. If you're older, disabled, non-English-speaking, or have a low income, there are special programs to help you do your tax return. To estimate how long it will take you to prepare it yourself, the IRS even provides average preparation times for each kind of form in the front of any tax form instruction booklet.

If you have a relatively simple financial situation, you may want to try doing it yourself like Maxine and Shirley. Maxine worked in a bank so she's good with numbers. Technically she and Shirley both get a little help: Maxine's son happens to be an accountant, while Shirley's daughter is a former H&R Block tax preparer.

Shirley explains, "We work on it together. It usually takes a couple of afternoons or evenings. Suzy goes over what I should be paying. When you have farm income, it isn't always the same and it isn't always regular. I have to re-evaluate my income tax peri-odically and if necessary add to my estimated tax or maybe reduce it, trying to keep it in line."

If you opt for using a professional, you still have to spend time keeping good records and gathering documentation. That's why Carol chooses to do it herself. "My husband has folders for all our records. He's very organized," says Carol, "more organized than I am. Every bill we have goes into a folder during the year. At the end of the year, all the information we need is in the fold-ers. It's really not that difficult."

BEARDSTOWN TALES

Farming is not a simple situation when it comes to tax returns. Ever since I was married, back in 1937, our tax returns have been trusted to tax preparers. When the gentleman who always took care of our returns passed away, a firm in Springfield was recommended. A young man from Kansas City was assigned to us. That was back in 1960, and I am still with him. I pay everything by checks and keep daily records of all farm and personal transac-tions by using a Farm Record Accounting System put out by the Department of Agriculture. My CPA keeps copies of all my returns. Paying out the money for his services sure gives me piece of mind. It costs, but I feel he is very reliable and well acquainted with our operations. He would take care of my auditing if it were ever needed.

ELSIE SCHEER

Carol adds one more reason for not using a tax firm. "Today many tax preparers market the idea 'Get your tax refund right away.' You have to pay $60 to $70 to get an instant tax refund. It is ridiculous. The tax preparation service is just giv-ing you a loan. The people who want refunds that fast are paying an extra fee to get their money. I don't know if a lot of people realize that, or they're just anxious to get the money. They would be money ahead if they waited."

Again, we say STOP and con-sider. Those who have more complicated returns may want professional help. But you may be able to find low-cost tax ser-vices or get special customized information that could save you money in the long run. Carnell uses the services of the Farm Business Farm Management Association. It has a contract with the University of Illinois to provide specialized farm information. Members are sent information comparing their individual business to businesses in their peer group (no names, of course). Thus Carnell and her husband know just where they stand, comparatively, in their industry.

How to Get the Most from Your Accountant

If you decide to use an accountant, there are ways to get the most benefit from the fee you pay. Start with the fee. How will you be charged? Big national chains usually charge by the number of forms you need filled out. Certified public accountants usually charge by the hour. Do you get what you pay for? Not necessarily. Fees can vary widely, anywhere from $50 to $3,500. If you have a relatively straightforward return, it's probably overkill to employ a high-priced CPA. By the same token, if you have large investments and need expert financial and tax planning, an experienced CPA or tax attorney might be your better bet.

Doing taxes is more of an art than a science. Give the same information on one household to 10 different tax preparers and no doubt you'll get 10 different tax calculations. Look for a professional with at least five years of experience. Ask for references and recommendations from trusted colleagues in your field. A farmer needs someone with experience doing farm returns, while a newspaper reporter has completely different needs. Next, check to see how up-to-date the person is on new tax laws. The one thing we know is that they change every year. A good tax preparer will attend seminars, read special publications, and make it his or her business to stay current. Try to line up the person you want to use before January 1. During the interview, get a sense of how well matched the two of you are: Do you want someone to be ultra-conservative or as aggressive as possible when it comes to finding loopholes and deductions?

Once you're happy with your choice, it's only the beginning. Keep as careful track of records as you possibly can to save your tax preparer's time, and therefore, your money. You can experiment to find the system that works best for you, whether it's a series of file folders or envelopes for each expense category, a computer system, or a coded checking account. Whatever you do, avoid the dumping-everything-into-a-shoebox system. It will cost you money.

When tax time rolls around, you should be prepared to bring the following information to your tax adviser:

- Your earnings, including salary, dividends, interest, income or loss from partnerships, subchapter S corporations, and tax shelters; pension amounts including Social Security, Veterans Administration, Civil Service, etc.; withdrawals from IRAs or other retirement plans.

- Estimated tax payments you've already made, including the dates and amounts.

- Copies of your tax returns from the last few years, if this is the first year this person is doing your taxes.

- Investment information, including any securities you have sold, stock transfer taxes, commissions, dates of sale, original costs, and copies of brokerage statements.

- A list of tax-deductible expenses, including medical items, interest, taxes, contributions, and business expenses. If in doubt about a specific item, bring a record anyway.

- Any paperwork regarding real estate transactions, including escrows, closing statements, and improvement costs.

Itemized Deductions

You no doubt would like to have more tax savings strategies to bring your taxes even lower down on your pyramid. Itemized deductions can help you get there. These are the nitty-gritty of tax saving. It's the area where you have the best chance to come up with a previously overlooked way of saving. Sometimes it just takes more careful review of the tax form instructions and tax guides you might have bought. Other times it means looking more creatively at your date book, checkbook, and credit card statements.

Maxine says, "Of course, I itemize and I always have. I don't keep as complete records as my son who passed away. My goodness, he'd go to a restaurant and always ask for his receipts. He used to embarrass us. He sure could itemize every little penny. When tax time came around, he was ready."

Those "pennies" can add up to many dollars if you're really

detail-oriented. As a first pass, go through your checkbook and credit card statements and check off every possible item you think might be deductible. Then go through your calendar for the year, looking for business expenses, travel, entertainment costs, charity events. Are any of them related to your business? Did you give a dinner party for potential clients? Have you attended a fund-raiser for a non-profit organization?

"Keep track of your receipts," Carol suggests, "when you donate to your church and different charities. Our church gives us a statement at the end of the year telling us how much we've donated. Save your receipts and keep track of things like that."

We can't tell you what to itemize. We can only urge you to scour your spending records for legitimate deductions. To inspire your search, here is a list of deductions that people often overlook:

- Alimony, in certain cases.
- Appraisal costs on property donated to charity.
- Business gifts up to $25 per recipient.
- Cellular phone depreciation.
- Cleaning and laundering costs of uniforms and costumes.

BEARDSTOWN TALES

Once, about 32 years ago, our tax return was audited. They had a question regarding my husband's travel expenses. He worked on the river as a deckhand on a boat, and he would have to board it wherever it was on the date he was due back. He took a bus, train, or taxi to get to the boat. Same when he was to come home. We deducted the amount of his expenses. Our son, who was five, had an eye injury the night before our scheduled audit. He had to have eye surgery that same evening. I stayed with him at the hospital all night and my husband came back to Beardstown to pick up our two-year-old from her grandmother's. My husband came to Jacksonville the next morning to relieve me so I could gather my tax papers up and go to the local post office to meet with the tax auditor. What a night! I was tired and worried sick about it. But we had all the receipts, so it was no problem and all the expenses were allowed. Talk about being relieved!

ANN BREWER

- Contact lenses (only if you pay an insurance premium to cover their cost).

- Fees charged for early withdrawal of certain savings plans.

- Home computer depreciation if used for business purposes.

- Lead paint removal.

- Legal and professional fees.

- Mortgage pre-payment penalty fees.

- Prescription contraceptives (if you pay an insurance premium to cover their cost).

- Safe deposit box fees in certain cases.

- Subscriptions to publications used for education or business.

- Substance abuse treatment.

- Tax preparer's fees.

- Tools used for work if they wear out within one year.

- Transportation for medical care.

- Worthless securities.

How to Avoid an Audit

It's almost a cliché how much everyone lives in dread of being audited. "We were always very apprehensive of that," admits Carnell. Yet the likelihood is extremely rare: Less than 1 percent of tax returns are questioned each year. Not only that, there can be advantages. Though Carnell is one of the unlucky few who have had to undergo tax audits, each time it has resulted in a refund to her and her husband.

Anyway, you *can't* really avoid an audit, anymore than you can avoid paying taxes. What you *can* do is be prepared in the event your return is flagged. How? By keeping meticulous records, and by taking Shirley's advice: "Be honest. If you're honest, then you don't have to worry if you're going to be audited." Shirley speaks from experience.

"The IRS agent spent two days at my kitchen table. The only

mistake I had made was including some income with my divi-dends that I should have put as farm income. But it didn't make any difference. When we ended up, there was no change. The government paid his salary for two whole days plus the time that he must have spent in his office. They didn't make any money off of that audit."

It's much more likely that you are not taking advantage of as many deductions as you're entitled to than it is that you will be audited. Don't let fear of audits prevent you from claiming what is rightfully yours, even if it seems to be such a large amount that you're sure it will be like turning on a neon sign for the IRS. The IRS computers are programmed to look for patterns, not specific dollar amounts. It looks for the proportion of deductions to income and how that figure compares with other returns from people with similar incomes. The tax law says a small-business owner, for example, can deduct $17,500 in depreciable business expenses, such as computers and furniture. Many small-business owners are not comfortable claiming such a large amount for fear of an audit. Their fear is costing them a lot of unnecessary taxes.

It's Never Too Late

We have one last suggestion that you may not have consid-ered for saving money on taxes. Don't assume once you mail off your return that's the end of it forever. If you realize a new tax-saving strategy, you can file an *amended return* for the past three years. For instance, maybe your brother married a CPA last spring. At a family gathering, she tells you about a deduction you hadn't realized you could take. You can file an amended return and retroactively take the new deduction. Often, the tax laws change and are applicable retroactively to previous years as well. The IRS will not send you the extra money automatically. It's up to you to file an amended return to get your money back. The only way to find out about these possibilities is to keep your eyes open and keep doing your homework. That's right, to *STOP*, *LOOK*, and *LISTEN*.

Getting Down to Brass Tacks

1. Don't have too much income tax withheld from your paycheck.

2. Shelter as much as you can in retirement plans.

3. Keep scouring your spending for itemized deductions.

CHAPTER NINE

FIRST-CLASS TRAVEL AT HALF THE PRICE

Did you take a vacation last year? How much did you spend?

TRAVEL DEFINITELY IS A BUSINESS OF SUPPLY and demand. When a flight is out of seats, an airline can't add more. When a plane flies with an empty seat, that's money the airline is forced to lose. The smartest way to save money on travel is to be as flexible as possible. Then you will be able to take advantage of the supply and demand.

This is a travel tale of two families, the McSorleys and the McDuffs. They each wanted a Caribbean vacation for as little as possible. Friends recommended an island where the McSorleys could camp out. They booked reservations for themselves and their two children over the Christmas vacation, feeling smug about spending so much less than they would on a condominium or hotel.

Unfortunately, the trip was a disaster. Ms. McSorley hates to camp. She found the accommodations far too rustic for her taste. The beach was extremely buggy. The tents leaked and it rained every night. They ate out at expensive island restaurants to console themselves for sleeping in tents while they were on vacation. Their airfare was the highest of the year because they traveled during the peak Christmas rush. The bottom line was that they spent a lot of money and didn't get a good return.

If only they had practiced STOP, LOOK, and LISTEN, they might have saved money and salvaged their vacation. They would have *stopped* to consider: Did they really enjoy camping? Would they be comfortable enough? What would they do if it rained? How would they deal with food? They would have *looked* before they leaped by researching the place instead of just relying on friends; checking on the airfares that time of year and whether there was another time they could go that would be cheaper. They would have *listened* to themselves. They knew they were used to nice hotels. Maybe they could have gone off-season, stayed at a place they were more familiar with, and spent the same amount in the end.

STOP!

Consider that the reasons you spend money on travel may include:

1. *Business.*
2. *Pleasure.*
3. *Health.*
4. *Family obligations.*
5. *Convenience.*
6. *Education.*

The McDuffs decided to go away during the March break, when fares would be substantially lower. They got several books out of the library to narrow down a Caribbean destination. After getting very high quotes from some travel agents, they began calling resorts themselves. One of these calls turned up a fantastic unadvertised package deal. The resort had a special that included airfare and two rooms—one without a view but the children didn't care—plus all water sports equipment and instruction. It seemed too good to be true, so the McDuffs checked an online travel forum to find out more about the resort. It received top grades from everyone. They also asked careful questions about the relationship of the beach to their rooms, how quiet it was, the quality of the snorkeling, what weather to expect. A meal plan could be part of the package but they calculated they'd be better off having breakfast in their rooms, picnicking on the beach, and exploring native restaurants for dinner. The total cost of their splendid week in the sun was about half what the McSorleys spent for their vacation.

Here, There, and Everywhere

During the past several years, we've been traveling more than ever before in our lives. We go all over the country talking about our investment club. One thing we've learned is that the price of travel can vary more than any other area of consumer spending. Geography affects travel prices almost as much as it does housing costs. According to the *Wall Street Journal*, for example, the average hotel room costs a high of $228 in New York to a low of $93 in Phoenix. Daily car rental rates average $66 in New York and $32 in Miami.

In addition to geography, timing affects how much you pay for travel. Depending on time of day, time of week, and time of year, everything from the price of a flight to the price of a resort vacation can vary by as much as 50 percent or more. How far in advance you make your travel arrangements also determines what you pay. Sometimes it's less expensive to go at the last minute; other times it's much more economical to make plans as far ahead of time as possible.

Finally, nearly every part of travel includes discount arrangements and a wide range of service levels. Do you want first-class, business-class, coach, or no-frills seats on the plane? Superior deluxe, limited-service first-class, or moderate tourist class rooms at the inn? Are you going though a consolidator for bucket seats? Have you checked the off-rack hotel rates? It almost sounds like a foreign language, doesn't it?

When it comes to airfares and hotel rates, the price structures can be very confusing. You may not always be able to choose your location or plan your timing to be the most cost-effective. Still, it's probably easier to save money on travel than on anything else if you *STOP, LOOK,* and *LISTEN.* You need to be informed and to ask the right questions. What is it you hope to get out of a given trip? What should you ask travel agents, hotel clerks, and other travel service employees before you go? Travel costs can add up quickly, so you stand to save large amounts—hundreds of dollars or more on one trip.

As in choosing cars or appliances, it comes back to figuring out what your personal priorities are and then matching your travel plans to those preferences for the lowest possible cost. Perhaps you want to travel extensively but don't care about having a private bathroom everywhere you go. You'd be happy to walk down a hall to bathe and thereby save $40 a night or $560 during two weeks in London. Or perhaps you prefer to go to a few select places where you indulge in very extravagant service and luxurious suites. Maybe you have a choice of commuter flights and could save $60 by getting home exactly two hours later. Why not? On the other hand, when you put your nine-year-old child on a cross-country flight, you are willing to pay $100 more for a nonstop flight—and for your peace of mind.

HIGH SEASON, LOW SEASON

When considering a family vacation, don't overlook the contrarian approach. You can slash the cost of a trip by thinking the opposite of most people. Instead of going to a ski resort for a winter vacation, try one in August. You'll get a beautiful mountain setting, indoor/outdoor swimming pool, miles of hiking and biking trails, delicious restaurants, crystal-clear air, gorgeous sunsets—all for about half the price of staying there in winter. The same principle applies to island resorts that call winter high season. If you're looking for a bargain in the winter, try places that cater to a summer crowd.

Most of us have always practiced *STOP, LOOK,* and *LISTEN* before we travel. Ruth has a very definite sense of her travel priorities. She says, "Cousins have invited me to California and to Florida. Rather than spend a thousand dollars to fly there, I'd rather take that money and see a lot more. There are so many other shorter trips, places in Illinois that I really enjoy."

Doris does like to fly when she travels. She's been to Florida, Hawaii, and to Europe several times. How does she afford these trips? "We just try to live like we do at home," she says. "We don't go first-class when we fly." For shorter trips, she drives "because more of us can go and it's cheaper. If it's a great distance, I'd rather fly."

Betty and her husband enjoy traveling quite a bit, but they don't feel a need to stay in the most expensive hotels. Other parts of travel are much more important to them. "There are a lot of things you can enjoy without spending a great deal of money. When our daughters were younger, we went tent camping. We took our own groceries with us. So it was very seldom that we were stopping in restaurants. We saved that way," Betty says. Now that their children are grown, they continue to spend conservatively on travel but get a maximum amount of fun from a trip. "One vacation, we went out to Yellowstone and stayed in a motel. Every day we took a different side trip, enjoying nature and the wildlife. To us, that was better than going to a four-star restaurant."

In the rest of this chapter, we'll talk about how to save in the three areas of travel that people spend the most on: airplanes, rental cars, and accommodations.

Travel by Air

Airfares change as often as the weather. Instead of telling you specifically how to fly for less, we will give you general guidelines to follow. The first key is to understand how airlines deal with seats. It's not as if on any given flight, on any given day, there are a certain number of seats priced at certain amounts, which are sold until the flight is full. Instead, seats are considered "inventory." The airlines constantly update this inventory by adjusting each seat's price according to how many seats have been sold in each price category. That's why when you call to inquire about a fare, the person will say, "That price is subject to availability." You wouldn't dream of buying a car for its advertised sticker price. You should be able to avoid buying a full-fare airline ticket too.

Next, you need to decide how to buy a ticket. You have three basic choices:

1. Travel Agents

Using a travel agent is probably the most convenient method. Whether or not it's the cheapest depends on a few factors. Travel agents earn money through commissions from airlines, generally about 10 percent of each fare. If they want to keep you as a good customer, it's to their advantage to search for the best possible fare for you on any airline. If they have the right type of computer system, they can indeed get you the best fare. It really does take a computer to sort through the labyrinth of airfares, codes, and discounts. So the first question to ask a potential travel agent is whether or not they use a computerized "low-fare search program." This type of electronic system works nonstop to check for price adjustments on the seat you have booked. If it finds that an airline has released a new block of lower-priced seats or that a cancellation has released a seat on your flight, it automatically retickets you at the new lower amount.

2. Airlines

If you can't find a reliable travel agent, you might consider calling the airlines directly. They all have 800 numbers, so you don't spend any money on the actual phone call. Before you call, start keeping an eye out for advertised sales—sometimes known as "fare wars"—which usually begin about six weeks before peak travel times. Ask if there is a discount for traveling midweek, staying over a Saturday, or booking a certain number of days in advance. Also ask whether tickets are non-refundable; often the sale-priced seats are non-refundable or refundable for a fee. Sometimes you can ask the airline to make your reservation but hold off on paying for the ticket for a few days.

To fly any of the new start-up or no-frills airlines, you have to call yourself since they don't work with travel agents. That's one way they keep their costs down. They also have fewer flight attendants, no movies, and maybe only beverage service. But on many flights you'll save as much as half the regular cost. See a list of regular, budget, and foreign airlines on page 155.

In this computer age, more and more services are accessible online. If you have a computer, you may be able to take advantage of the last-minute discounts from individual airlines. Recently, some airlines have started using sites on the Internet to offer reduced prices on thousands of seats that otherwise are unsold. These fares can be 70 percent lower than fares you would be quoted if you called the airline's regular 800 number or asked a travel agent.

3. Consolidators

These are brokers that buy airline tickets in bulk and then pass the resulting discounts on to consumers. They are sort of like the Wal-Marts of the airline industry. Wholesale consolidators sell only to travel agents, but many consolidators sell directly to individuals. Savings, which consolidators are able to get because they buy in such volume, range from 25 to 75 percent. Seats sold by consolidators are on major airlines, as opposed to charter flights. But you may be confused because often the same company will handle both charters and consolidators. If you see an ad in the back of your newspaper for extraordinarily low airfares, be sure to ask whether these are for charter or regularly scheduled flights.

As long as you shop carefully, buying tickets from consolidators is usually a good bet. The few possible disadvantages are less choice in airlines, inconvenient schedules, more indirect travel, or slow ticket delivery. Also, many consolidators don't accept credit cards.

Frequent Fliers

Using frequent-flier miles to travel can seem almost like flying for free. When you join an airline's frequent-flier program, you "earn" miles you can apply toward future trips. A typical coach round trip ticket for a U.S. flight "costs" about 25,000 miles. You usually earn a mile of credit for each mile you've flown on a given airline. These days, you don't ever have to leave the ground to earn those miles. Non-airline businesses buy frequent-flier miles from airlines to distribute to customers as added attractions. So if you play your cards right, you don't have to be a frequent flier to fly free. You can earn frequent-flier miles through long-distance telephone carriers, credit cards, rental car companies, hotel chains, restaurants, and specialty chain stores.

Here are some ways to make the most of frequent-flier mileage:

- Go ahead and join as many programs as possible. There's no charge, so it can't hurt and it may help.

- Enroll all your family members—children can earn miles too.

- Check each program periodically to see whether you need to use your miles by a certain date.

- Before you "spend" your frequent-flier mileage, check to make sure there's not a low fare for which you will collect even more miles to use when the fares go back up if you pay for it with money now.

AIRLINE FREQUENT-FLIER PROGRAMS

How many miles each airline requires to be credited to your account to fly to three locations—one domestic, one Caribbean, and one European:

ALL FLIGHTS OUT OF NEW YORK	ST. PAUL	CARIBBEAN	PARIS
American Airlines Advantage 800-433-7300	25,000	30,000	40,000
Continental OnePass 800-525-0280	25,000	35,000	50,000
TWA 800-221-2000	20,000	20,000	35,000/50,000
Delta 800-221-1212	25,000	25,000	50,000
USAir 800-428-4322	25,000	40,000	40,000
United Air 800-241-6522	25,000	50,000	50,000

- If you travel on business, ask your company whether it will reimburse you for flights you book using your own frequent-flier mileage.

More Ways to Save Money on Flying

- *Be flexible.* Many major urban centers have more than one airport. If you're willing to fly into Washington's National instead of Dulles, for instance, you may be able to save money. By the same token, sometimes departing from New York's LaGuardia is cheaper than from JFK, even though you wind up in the same place.

AIRLINES

LOW-FARE AMERICAN AIRLINES

American Trans Air 800-225-2995

Carnival 800-437-2110

Kiwi 800-538-5494

MarkAir 800-627-5247

Reno Air 800-736-6247

Tower 800-221-2500

ValuJet 800-825-8538

FOREIGN AIRLINES

ACES* 800-846-2237 (Colombian)

Air Canada 800-776-3000

Balair 800-322-5247 (Swiss)

Canadian International
800-426-7000

Condor 800-524-6975 (German)

Eva* 800-695-1188 (Taiwanese)

El Al 800-223-6700 (Israeli)

Martinair 800-366-4655 (Dutch)

Polynesian 800-592-7100

Virgin Atlantic* 800-862-8621

MAJOR AMERICAN AIRLINES

Alaska Airlines 800-426-0333

America West 800-235-9292

American Airlines 800-433-7300

Continental 800-441-1135

Delta 800-221-1212

Hawaiian Airlines 800-367-5320

Midwest Express 800-452-2022

Northwest 800-225-2525

Southwest 800-435-9792

TWA 800-221-2500

United 800-241-6522

USAir 800-428-4322

*Comfort bargains

- *Be even more flexible*. We know a Massachusetts family with grandparents who live on the eastern border of Indiana, exactly halfway between Dayton, Ohio, and Indianapolis. The grandparents don't care at which airport they pick them up. So they fly into whichever one is the least expensive, which varies from time to time. If possible, be flexible about your destination.

- *Be even MORE flexible*. If your schedule permits you to hop on a plane whenever the mood happens to hit you, you are a good candidate for flying as a courier. This involves accompanying baggage such as business papers on flights around the world. You call a courier agency and tell them where you'd like to go.

They check to see whether there is a need for a courier and if so, sell you a ticket for as little as $100 for a round-trip to Europe. Of course, you have to travel alone and take only carry-on luggage. See the Resources section on page 270 for one courier service we recommend.

- *Ask about special discounts for children, students, seniors, or military.*

- *Emergency fares are often available for attending funerals or to visit a critically ill family member.* Be sure to inquire when you make your travel arrangements and ask exactly what sort of proof you'll need to qualify for these "bereavement" rates.

- *Throw away a ticket.* We're not kidding! Believe it or not, sometimes it's cheaper to buy two round-trip tickets instead of one. How? Suppose you need to fly from Chicago to Los Angeles on a Monday and return on a Thursday. A regular round-trip coach seat between Chicago and Los Angeles costs $800. A discounted-fare ticket that requires a Saturday night stay costs $300. So you'd buy two round-trip tickets for a total of $600, use half of each one, and still save $200. We told you it takes a computer to figure out airfares!

> **Ticket #1**
>
> Chicago to Los Angeles
>
> > Leave **Monday**
> >
> > Stay over a Saturday night
>
> Los Angeles to Chicago
>
> > Leave Sunday
>
> Throw away the second half of this ticket.

Ticket #2

Chicago to Los Angeles

   Leave Friday

   Stay over a Saturday night

Los Angeles to Chicago

   Leave **Thursday**

Throw away the first half of this ticket.

- *Travel light.* It's almost always less expensive to ship heavy items separately than to pay surplus baggage charges at the airport. We've seen people paying hundreds of dollars at the baggage check-in counter when they tried to bring what looked like a kitchen sink on the plane.

Rental Cars

Now, for the fun part: What kind of car do you want to rent? Do you have a lot of luggage? A lot of children? Do you need a station wagon, child's seat, or luggage rack? One way or another, you'll be paying for the car's fuel, so consider fuel economy in your choice. If you're driving in a congested city, you might very well opt for a small, maneuverable car. If you're spending lots of time in it during your trip, you might prefer a larger, more luxurious model. For those who don't care about prestige or style, there is the option of renting older cars through one of the rock-bottom companies such as Rent-A-Wreck. (See page 271 for a more complete list.)

Ann Corley's husband had a different set of criteria when it came to car rentals. He would try out types of cars he was interested in purchasing by renting them first whenever they traveled. That way, they could drive it a while to see if they liked it, before investing in a new car.

In general, a good rule of thumb is to request a slightly smaller model than your ideal size. That's because companies run out of the smaller cars faster and then are forced to give you a larger car at the same rate—so you might get a free upgrade.

Rental car companies, like airlines, are constantly revising their rates according to supply and demand. Agents may not have the most up-to-date information, or their information may differ from what you think you should be getting. The best way to get the best rate is to keep asking for it, right up to the very last minute before you accept the keys to a car. If you've seen a special discount advertised in the newspaper, say so. If the agent claims not to know anything about such a rate, refer to the promotion's code, usually displayed in tiny print within the ad, either below the rate or in the rental terms and conditions. The computer at the rental car counter may suddenly have a new promotional rate.

You also need to mention any organizations you belong to that could possibly entitle you to further discounts. These might include airline frequent-flier programs, automobile clubs, senior citizen, professional associations, and corporate memberships.

Ask about daily rates versus weekly rates or weekend rates, should that apply to you. Compare carefully. Sometimes, it's less expensive to rent the same car twice. What do we mean by that? Say you need a car from Friday to Tuesday. You rent it on Friday and are charged the regular daily rate, $30, through Tuesday. Your total is $150. But if the company offers a special weekend rate of $40 for Friday to Sunday, you're better off taking that and then renting the car for an extra two days, Monday and Tuesday. Your total will be $100, for a savings of $50.

You can't rely on the rental car employees to fill you in on all these nooks and crannies. You can't even assume that when an

BEARDSTOWN TALES

I was born and raised on a farm and lived on a farm until I graduated from high school. I've lived three-quarters of a century and I never thought I'd get to fly in a big airplane. I've had chances to go in a little one, but I couldn't take that. Phil Donahue will always have a tender spot in my heart because I got to fly to New York to be on his show. We saw New York City at Christmas time. It was a fabulous experience for this little country girl.

RUTH HUSTON

employee quotes you two different prices for a compact car and an economy car, he's talking about two different cars. Always ask exactly what kind of car—the make and model—an agent is describing. It's a good idea to have a calculator handy whenever you're so much as considering renting a car.

Once you've gotten a satisfactory rate for the right model, your cost-saving strategy is only half over. Have you seen a rental car agreement lately? There's more fine print in one of them than there are lawn geese in Beardstown. This is where those notorious "extra charges" are hidden away. When you're on vacation, the last thing you'll want to spend time doing is reading all that fine print. So we did it for you. These are the important points to watch out for when renting a car. (We still don't know what the "wizard number" is on a rental car document, but if anyone asks you if you want one, we bet it's safe to say no.)

- *Unlimited free mileage.* Although you usually save money by taking this option, it can be a misnomer if the rental car company then does set a limit on how many free miles you are allowed to drive. To avoid unpleasant surprises, be sure to ask exactly how unlimited the miles are and how much any extra miles will cost. Also, if you don't need many miles because you'll be driving so little, a rate with a set number of miles might turn out to be a better deal for you.

- *Collision Damage Insurance.* Otherwise known as CDW—along with LDW (Loss Damage Waiver), PEP (Personal Effects Protection), ALI (Additional Liability Insurance)—and PAI (Personal Accident Insurance)—it's almost always unnecessary. Anyone who has either automobile or home owner's insurance or a credit card is most certainly already covered for all these overpriced insurance options. And they're just that: completely optional. Don't let an aggressive agent in a crowded airport try to convince you otherwise.

- *Additional drivers.* If anyone else will be driving the car, you may be charged as much as $5 to $25 a day for each addition. If you know you will need to share driving the car, comparison-shop first. Some companies don't charge extra for spouses, for instance.

- *Drivers under 25 years.* Many companies either won't let anyone under this age rent or else they charge a fee—$15 to $20 per day—for the privilege. Check first.

- *Refueling fee.* No matter what, try to return the rental car with a full gas tank. You'll pay up to double the price of gas at the company's refueling station. Some companies give you the option of paying a small, onetime fee to be able to return the car without a full tank of gas. This may be worthwhile if you think you'll be pressed for time before returning the vehicle, or if you're using the car in an unfamiliar city.

- *Geographic rules.* The cheaper companies may limit what state you may drive their cars in. If you will be crossing over into another state, inquire whether that's acceptable or not.

- *Drop-off charges.* One-way rentals usually cost more money than returning a car to the same place you picked it up.

- *Cancellation fees.* This is a relatively new wrinkle in rental charges. It's also an expensive one. When you reserve a rental car with a credit card, you may be subject to a cancellation charge of $50 to $100. Before you provide your credit card number, think twice about how likely it is you may need to cancel.

Lodging

We've noticed that no matter how much people are willing to fly or drive for budget rates, when it comes to hotels they usually don't want to compromise on quality. They figure they've worked hard all year, they're on vacation, and they want to splurge and pamper themselves. So given a choice between a deluxe hotel and a tourist hotel, there's a tendency to go deluxe, no matter how much more it costs. But what does "deluxe" really mean in the language of hotels? What does the extra money buy you?

Sometimes, it buys a great view, a large lobby, or a more spacious room. Sometimes, it buys extra-special service, a choice of on-site restaurants, or conference rooms. As with everything else, the way to spend smart money on lodging is to STOP, LOOK, and LISTEN. Instead of being swept away in a fantasy vacation mode, try to think clearly about how much you want to spend. Say, for example, you're driving for several days to reach your final vacation destination. You plan to stop at a motel each night on your way. Is it worth spending $50 more to get a place with a pool if you won't have time to swim? If all you need is a clean, comfortable bed to sleep in, why spend a lot of extra money on extras you won't ever use? On the other hand, if you are staying with your family at a resort for a week and it's your only vacation of the year, you might want the most luxurious accommodations you can afford. You might want to rent two large, separate rooms, get a nice view, and have a refrigerator so you don't have to eat out for every meal.

The other thing to keep in mind is that one hotel's "budget" priced room could be another's idea of a "deluxe" room. Even the big national chains, such as Holiday Inn or Best Western, vary tremendously from one location to another. You can't count on a brand name in hotels. More reliable are numerous rating systems, from AAA guides to Michelin to something called the *Official Hotel Guide*. This is used mostly by travel industry professionals rather than by the average consumer. Most hotel or tour ads that advertise a certain "grade" are referring to their rating in the *Official Hotel Guide*. Here are the descriptions used in descending order:

- Superior Deluxe

- Deluxe

- Moderate Deluxe

- Superior First Class

- First Class

- Limited-Service First Class

- Moderate First Class

- Superior Tourist Class

- Tourist Class

- Moderate Tourist Class

What do they mean? Well, according to the *Guide*, Superior Deluxe is "an exclusive and expensive luxury hotel, often palatial, offering the highest standards of service, accommodations, and facilities. Elegant and luxurious public rooms. A prestige address. Establishments in this category are among the world's top hotels."

We're guessing that if you're reading this book, you might be less interested in locating a superior deluxe hotel. How about Moderate Tourist Class? "Low-budget operations, often quite old and may not be well-kept. Should only be used in a pinch if no other accommodations are available. Clients should always be cautioned what to expect." The *Hotel Guide* is obviously a bit prejudiced. It doesn't really deal with the lowest-priced places, such as Motel 6. Yet if you're simply driving to reach another place, these motels can be perfectly adequate and save you money that you'll then be able to spend elsewhere. They have comfortable beds, clean bathrooms, a color TV, and a telephone. They're budget-priced because they don't have fancy lobbies, conference rooms, room service, or porters. The rock-bottom priced motels definitely have smaller bedrooms, starting at 100 square feet. But the "regular" budget chains, such as Comfort Inn, La Quinta, and Courtyard by Marriott, offer as much spaciousness as more costly hotels. Remember, you can always ask to see a room before you check in. If you feel too claustrophobic, you can pass.

You do run a slight risk when you don't make advance reservations. Betty explains that when she and her husband go on

BEARDSTOWN TALES

We usually dealt with this one company for cruise ships. After one or two trips with them, you could get very reasonable rates. One person could even almost go free. Whenever there was a bargain, they would send us an announcement. They knew we loved to travel. Sometimes if someone had canceled, they would give me a call and offer a good price. No high pressure. Just "someone canceled, we're going here, do you want to go?" One time I went to the Caribbean that way. It was a last-minute thing and we got a good deal. I loved it.

MAXINE THOMAS

vacation, they don't like to reserve rooms ahead of time. "If we're in our own car, we don't want to be held to a strict time that we have to be in a certain place at a certain time. We tend to try to start looking fairly early so we're not out there at 10 at night trying to get a hotel room. But once, we were down in St. Louis and we couldn't find a hotel. We drove all night looking for a vacancy and ended up at home the next morning."

Once you know the general type of establishment you're interested in—assuming there are rooms available and you don't have Betty's luck—the next step is to get the best possible room rate. Here again, there is no *one* rate for any hotel room in the world. Just as airlines price seats differently according to supply and demand, time of week or year, and many other variables, hotels may have up to 20 different prices for the same room. We feel we can safely say that under no circumstances should you ever pay the first rate a reservation clerk quotes to you. That is what is called the "rack" rate and it is almost always an artificially inflated amount, similar to the sticker price on a new car. You need to work with the hotel to whittle it down to a more acceptable rate.

It's better to contact a specific hotel or motel directly than to call a chain's toll-free central reservation number. The operators at the other end of those 800 numbers can only quote you a computerized price. You will have better luck dealing with the individual hotel to get the best rate. No doubt, you'll more than make up for the cost of the phone call by saving on the cost of your room.

Start by simply asking whether the first quoted price is the best available price. Often, you'll immediately be offered 5 to 10 percent less, just by asking.

Now, make your way down the following list of possible special discounts:

- *Corporate rate.* You don't have to be traveling on business for this rate. If you are employed by a company or have a business card, you usually qualify.

- *Senior citizen rate.* Betty says that because she's over 55, and belongs to AARP, she tends to ask for that discount—it's almost always honored.

- *Convention rate.* If you're in a town that's holding a big convention, there may be a special rate for attendees, or for anyone in town then.

- *Weekend rate.* This one applies especially to hotels which cater to business people during the week. Rates can drop by as much as 50 percent on weekends, when the rooms would otherwise go empty.

- *Automobile club rate.* Do you belong to AAA? Mention it for a 10 percent discount at many hotels.

- *Super-saver or special discount rate.* This is a vague price that some clerks may be authorized to offer should they suspect that otherwise you're going to balk and walk.

- *Government rate.* For military personnel, government agency employees, or government contractors, up to 50 percent off is available.

- *Shareholder rate.* Do you happen to own stock in a company such as Disney? You are entitled to terrific discounts when you book a room at a Disney resort. Same with Marriott and other publicly-held travel companies.

- *Hotel membership rate.* If there is a club attached to a hotel, you can get discounts by joining.

- *Preferred rate.* This is another rate that is left up to the discretion of the management. If no other rate seems to apply, you can always ask for this one.

- *Frequent-flier rate.* Many airlines have formed partnerships with hotel chains as part of their frequent-flier programs.

- *Emergency situation rate.* Like bereavement airfares, these rates apply to those traveling due to family illness or funerals, as well as to those stranded by fire, earthquakes, hurricanes, or other natural disasters. Ask if the hotel offers such a "Good Samaritan" rate.

- *Long-term stay rate.* If you're going to be staying for more than a few nights, ask about discounts.

- *Package rate.* Especially popular at resort destinations, these rates may include breakfast and/or recreational opportunities, or be called "family package" rates.

Finally, don't be shy about asking for extras if you can't get a room rate reduction. You may remember our farmer friend and his wife from Indiana, who we described in our last book. They recently visited their son and daughter-in-law on the East Coast, and stayed at a motel they had been to on previous trips. When they checked in, they noticed that the rates had gone up substantially. Our friend got a AAA discount, but still wasn't satisfied. So he said, "Now breakfast is included at that price, right?" The desk clerk politely answered no, it wasn't. Our friend said, "Well, I think it should be." With that, the clerk handed him coupons good for free breakfast for the entire three-day visit.

We've said it before, and we'll keep saying it: It never hurts to ask.

Half-Price Hotels

Remember airline consolidators? Well, there are hotel consolidators too. They are companies that buy up blocks of rooms at hotels around the country at hugely discounted rates. You pay a small fee to "buy" a room from a consolidator at 30 to 65 percent off regular rates. The advantage of using a consolidator is that you get the lowest possible price. A few disadvantages include: You can't book through a travel agent; your credit card payment is nonrefundable; you're not always able to get the exact hotel for the exact dates you want. Some consolidators have more hotels in certain regions of the country, while others offer rental car or restaurant discounts. If you travel regularly, it may be worth the fee to join one of these half-price programs. See page 270 of the Resources section for a sampling.

Tours and Packages

These days there are tours tailor-made for every taste and budget. Although saving money isn't the only reason to choose a tour, it's one of the best reasons. You can save hundreds of dollars on the cost of a vacation by going with a packaged tour.

What the package includes varies a lot. A basic package offers a combination of transportation—either air, train, or motor vehicle—and lodging for a set price, usually to one destination such as an island resort. Sometimes a rental car or a book of coupons is thrown in. Escorted tours are at the opposite end of the package spectrum. They often involve everything but tips and taxes. This means you pay for travel, hotels, meals, and sightseeing. You also travel with a group, which is why some people shy away from tours. If you're with a compatible group, Doris and Maxine have found, it can be an advantage. They've both covered many miles on group tours. Here's what Doris says in favor of tours:

"Not only do I get a special rate, I take advantage of all the walking tours. A travel group gets you into places that you wouldn't ordinarily get into. They've scouted the area to find out what events are coming up. When we went to Alaska, we took a helicopter ride up to Kotzebue and walked on the glacier. When we were in Europe, we got into a lot of museums and places of interest that we would never have had access to if we hadn't been with a tour group. Every place we went, they had a guide who would tell us all the history. You learn much more than if you're traveling on your own."

You can take advantage of the cost savings a tour provides but maintain your independence as a tourist if you prefer. There are tours in which you fly to a location en masse but then are left on your own for sightseeing. Sometimes it's worthwhile to pay for a whole package and then just toss the sightseeing or meal portions, if you'd rather be alone. To calculate the cost of a tour and to compare different tours, you can use the following method:

1. Find out the least expensive round-trip airfare for your destination, should you purchase it separately.

2. Subtract that figure from the total cost of the tour. (If the airfare alone is *more* than the tour package, you already know you have a pretty good deal.)

3. Divide the difference by the number of nights you'd be spending in a hotel. (Don't count overnight travel, for example.)

Sometimes, it's easier to compare the financial cost of a trip than the amount of pleasure you would derive. Maxine has almost made a second career out of chaperoning student tours. She saves

WHAT TO LOOK FOR IN PACKAGED TOURS

Here's what to check for when you read a tour brochure:

- *Length of tour.* It's the number of *nights*, not days, that are important. A ten-day, nine-night trip means you'll be traveling for two out of those ten days.

- *Air transportation.* Does the price include flights from wherever you live?

- *Ground transportation.* Does the tour take care of travel to and from airports, from one city to another?

- *Accommodations.* Read this section very carefully. Is the hotel described as four-star or two-star? Deluxe or tourist? If you have any doubt whatsoever, have your agent check.

- *Meals.* Are they all included? Is it a full breakfast or a continental breakfast? What do those terms mean in the countries you'll be traveling through?

- *Sightseeing.* Are tours included? Are guides included? For every stop or only some? Do you have to make the arrangements yourself once you get there, or is there a guide to accompany you throughout the tour?

- *Size.* How large a group will you be traveling with?

- *Frequency.* The more often a company runs tours, the better the chances that it is a reputable and successful firm.

a lot of money because the trips are subsidized and the group receives student discounts. When you listen to Maxine describe these travels, you suspect that she gets more out of them than saving money. "There is a teacher at the high school near here who takes the senior class on a trip each year. They are required to earn their own money. They cannot get it from grandma and grandpa or their mom and dad. My friend Katherine and I have taken three trips with him now: one to Tahiti, Australia, and New Zealand; one to England; and one to the Holy Land and Egypt. We gained so much knowledge from the teacher's lecture on what the students were to expect the next day.

"At night our job was to paste tape across the girls' rooms so the boys would stay out. We checked to make sure everyone was in. We were responsible to see that they were doing what they were supposed to do. They were fine young people. Of course, they're harder trips because you carry your own luggage. Our rooms weren't always fancy, but they were comfortable."

If you're half as adventurous as Maxine is, you may be a good candidate for some more offbeat lodging possibilities. Read on.

Alternative Accommodations

- *Hostels*. These offer dormitory-style rooms in buildings which range from converted bunkers to Italian villas. Family rooms sometimes are available. Although hostels are dirt cheap, you only have use of your bed during nighttime hours. During the day, you have to depart.

- *Bed-and-Breakfast*. This is like staying in someone's private home. In fact, you *are* staying in someone's private home! If you are the friendly type, you might enjoy getting to know your hosts. The money you save might make you feel even friendlier.

- *Home exchange*. If you live in a location that might be desirable to others, this may be an option. There are organizations you can list your home with, or you may be able to do it informally with friends and relatives. Don't count yourself out because you think your home isn't fancy enough, either. If a family with children who live in a big city want to visit relatives in the country, they might love the chance to stay in your quaint farmhouse. By the same token, if you have an apartment close to all the Broadway musicals, maybe the country family would appreciate its convenience.

- *College campuses*. If you want to feel young again, go back to school. You'll feel wealthier too when you've saved a lot on lodging by staying on campus. Many colleges and universities rent out dormitory rooms (when school is not in session, of course) to travelers. There are also organized travel programs, such as Elderhostel, that use college campuses to house participants. Maxine was very pleased with her Elderhostel trip.

- *Retreats*. There are all sorts of retreat centers, from Zen to Catholic to just plain serene. You don't have to participate in a center's spiritual life in order to stay at one. They're often in particularly beautiful locations too and are very inexpensive. We know a family of four who once spent a week in the Caribbean at a Club Med type of resort. It cost about $2,000 for lodging and meals. One day, they were strolling along the beach when they noticed a small sign for a yoga retreat. It turned out they could rent rooms there, including all the vegetarian food they could eat, for $30 a night. They didn't have to do yoga and they'd be right on the same pristine, white sand beach as at the high-priced resort for about 75 percent less. Can you guess what their vacation plans for next year are going to be?

For specific organizations and resources on all of the above, see page 268.

Getting Down To Brass Tacks

1. Take advantage
of the airlines' computerized
inventory system to get the
lowest-priced seats.

2. Avoid unnecessary insurance and
waivers when renting cars. Check
your own insurance policies and credit cards first.

3. Always ask for a discount when
making hotel reservations.

CHAPTER TEN

HOW TO LOVE YOUR CHILDREN FOR LESS

The most expensive budget line of all. How to cut costs on everything from preschool to college.

A SINGLE MOTHER WE KNOW IN CONNECTICUT has two young children. The children attended a small, private school, which they loved. After she was widowed, she thought it was important to keep them there. In order to do that, she found a full-time job. She had to pay a baby-sitter to pick up the children from school, drive them home, and fix them dinner. Some days she had to pay the sitter for before-school care as well. She was spending $10,000 a year on tuition and $13,000 a year on extra child care—an amount that equaled half her income. She hated her job, never saw her children, and was slowly going broke. When asked why she didn't send them to a public school around the corner, she said, "Because they really like the private school." These children are five and seven.

Finally this mother realized, after several conversations with some wise older friends, that she wasn't doing her children any favors by sending them to a school they probably wouldn't even remember at the price of her own financial and emotional health. By putting them in public school, she was able to quit her horrible job, do freelance work at home, fire the baby-sitter who was becoming unreliable anyway, and reduce her stress and her expenses enormously. And her children? They are happier than ever.

Raising a child is not like buying a house or paying taxes, although it may cost even more. The United States Department of Agriculture estimates that it costs almost a quarter of a million

STOP!

Consider that the reasons you spend money on children may include:

1 Love.
2. Guilt.
3. Safety.
4. Education.
5. Your career.
6. Special needs.
7. Peer pressure.

dollars, or $239,000 adjusted for inflation, to raise one child these days, not even including college. That's quite an outlay of capital. Of course, few parents think about raising children in financial terms. We do "invest" in our children and in their futures but we do so for emotional reasons, not to make a profit. It's our very love for our children that makes it so difficult to think clearly and wisely about how to spend money on them. Situational spending is probably more prevalent when it comes to kids than in any other area of our Spending Pyramid.

Clearly, the case of the single mom was one of "situational" spending: making money decisions based on sheer emotion instead of rational thought. Situational spending is when we keep changing our basic guidelines on how much things are worth, depending on the situation. We make decisions based on love or anger or fear or even fatigue. For this mother, the main emotion was probably guilt, one of the most common emotions behind unnecessary spending on children. If you have children, you know there are times when you feel as if you aren't giving them enough attention. Maybe you just had a new baby, so you shower your first child with gifts.

It's possible you've gone without many comforts, perhaps even necessities, in order to provide them with more. For instance, we all know of parents who don't buy themselves new clothes but who dole out more than $100 for a certain brand of sneaker a child simply must have. Or parents who don't take vacations so they can send their children to camp. As parents, we tend to assume that how much we spend on our kids is how much we care about them. If you think about it for even a second, of course that's not true. How can you put a price on love? Yet some parents never seem to learn that.

How else to explain the birthday party a friend's grandchild was invited to? It was a luncheon held at a country club for 100 people. A professional deejay provided dance music. Party favors, complete with monograms for each guest, were more costly than most of the gifts the children brought. The birthday child was turning seven. What in the world will this child expect next?

Our advice is, before you spend another penny on your child, remember: The amount you spend on your children has nothing at all to do with how much you love them. Then keep that rule in mind as you go about making choices. *STOP*, *LOOK*, and *LISTEN* applies as much to child-rearing as to any other area of spending. There may be times when you wouldn't dream of economizing— when it comes to the safety or well-being of your children. Other times, depending once again on your own values, there may be ways to reduce your child-rearing costs dramatically without sacrificing the quality of your child's life in any way.

Buffy, the only Beardstown Lady with a young child at home, is a good example of this attitude toward spending. "There is one thing I wouldn't skimp on and that is the welfare of my child," Buffy says. She is lucky enough to have found a wonderful family day care provider in Beardstown for her three-year-old son T.J. The woman is worth her weight in gold, according to Buffy. "If she were charging three times as much, it would be worth it to me. I wouldn't go to a cheaper day care." In other areas, she doesn't hesitate to save money, however. "I skimp on clothes all the time. If I saw T.J's size, I would think nothing of getting all of his clothes at a yard sale. It wouldn't bother me at all."

That might sound a little extreme, but is it any less extreme to buy baby designer clothes? A friend of ours was the first in her circle to have a baby. She had three baby showers and received countless designer outfits. Now that her "baby" is about to enter college, she'd give anything to go back in time and exchange those costly togs for equally cute, much less expensive clothes.

Then she would have invested the difference—a few hundred dollars—in a college fund. No use crying over spilt milk!

As your children get older, you can reduce the cost of raising them and provide important lessons in independence and responsibility at the same time. How? By encouraging them to earn some money of their own and to pay for certain luxuries themselves. This seems to be a novel idea to some parents, but we think its time has come again. Back when Maxine's children were young, they all had jobs to do. Her son sold greeting cards out of his bicycle basket and paid for a new bicycle that way. He also carried out groceries to earn money.

"They had their allowance," Maxine says. "If they wanted something special, or if we thought what they wanted was foolish, then they earned it themselves. We were Depression people, my husband and I, so that made a difference in our attitudes."

In this chapter, we'll tell you how you can save money on the cost of children—even though you weren't raised in the Depression.

Child Care

In 1960, when the USDA first started tracking the cost of raising a child, child care was an insignificant portion of the total. Today, child care is one of the biggest child-raising expenses. It makes sense to treat shopping for good quality child care at the most reasonable cost the way you would buying any other major product. That means narrowing down the model, choosing the right options for your family, shopping around, and then comparing costs. There are whole books written on how to choose child care, and we recommend some in the Resources section. But here is a brief summary of the pros and cons of different types. Think carefully about which kind best suits you and your child's needs—and your pocketbook.

	ADVANTAGES	DISADVANTAGES
Day care center	Reliable, always open.	Less flexible hours.
	Affordable.	Less individual attention.
	Long hours.	More exposure to viruses.
	Trained staff.	Can't use if child is sick.
Family day care	Even less expensive.	Not as professional.
	More personal attention.	Usually can't use if child is sick.
	Smaller group.	Less convenient schedule.
In-home care	Most flexible arrangement.	No interaction with others.
	Good for sick children.	Most expensive option.
	Most personal care.	Caretaker can quit or get sick.
Live-in care	Less expensive than non-live-in.	Lack of privacy.
	Even more flexibility.	Lack of training.
	May help with other chores.	Probably only temporary.
Babysitting co-ops	Very inexpensive or low-cost.	Takes more work.
	Built-in quality control.	Can't use for full-time care.

Once you decide which kind of child care you want, there are a few ways to reduce the cost. If you opt for an in-home provider, try to find another family to share the sitter. You'll split the cost in half, and your child may enjoy a pal. Some day care centers provide optional hot meals. If yours does, try not to pay for them. Brown-bagging lunches for children saves as much as brown-bagging lunches for grown-ups! See whether a family day care provider or day care center would reduce your fee in exchange for a few hours of work. This is a great deal if it involves spending time with your child at the center. Finally, sometimes you can get your employer to pay part of your child care costs as one of your employee benefits. Ask if your company has a "cafeteria" plan for benefits. These plans work by deducting the amount of your child care from your salary so that you aren't paying income tax on it.

If you're really lucky, maybe you can bring your child to your office with you—at least for a while. Buffy was able to bring T.J.

to work until he was about a year old. Although she did it because she enjoyed it, she happened to save quite a bit of money too.

As your child grows and your situation changes, you need to periodically re-evaluate your child care arrangement. Whereas you might want a one-on-one provider for your infant, by the time your child is three, you'll probably be looking for more opportunities for him or her to make friends. In that sense, shopping for child care is different than making a onetime investment like a house.

One family in New York had a baby and a preschooler. They hired a mature woman to come to their house four days a week to watch the children while the mother went to her office. Almost all the mom's salary went directly to the child care provider. But it was worth it to these parents while their children were tiny to have such a nurturing, motherly person in their home. As the children grew, the family's needs changed. The mother wanted to work more hours, but couldn't justify it as long as her salary was all going to pay a baby-sitter. They had moved to a much larger house, which meant a larger mortgage as well as extra space. Meanwhile, the children were becoming more involved in social activities, going to dance classes and birthday parties. The obvious solution was to hire a live-in person to watch the children, drive them around, and be available for more hours. Because they provided her room and board, the family reduced their annual child care costs by $12,000.

Let Them Wear Cloth

"Before I had T.J.," says Buffy, "I couldn't spend all the money I made. Now, I think 'I need more money.' I couldn't believe the cost of diapers. You can't reuse them, either." No, and you can't buy secondhand diapers either! But do you necessarily need brand-name diapers? Try the generic store brands, which are usually just as effective, and you can save as much as 40 percent. If you can buy them in bulk by the case, you increase the savings even more. You also make it easier on yourself by not having to run out to get diapers as often. The same is true of any baby product that will be consumed or used frequently, including diaper wipes, diaper liners, baby food, formula, disposable plastic bottle liners. Buy as much as you can store conveniently to save a maximum amount of money.

Another way to cut the cost of diapers—by as much as half—is to use a diaper service instead of using disposables. Although many new parents prefer the convenience of disposables, we can say from experience that it's not one bit harder to diaper your baby with cloth. Often your baby is more comfortable in cloth diapers too—and less prone to rashes.

Baby Equipment

Some of baby's big-ticket items are excellent to buy used or to borrow from friends and relatives. Others you have to be careful about because of safety considerations. Here's a breakdown of the main pieces of equipment you'll need and whether or not to buy them used or new:

- *Cribs*. There are now strict safety standards for cribs, with specific measurements for mattress height and slat spacing, guidelines for raising and lowering the sides, and restrictions on what kind of paint can be used. If you're absolutely sure a secondhand crib meets the most current standards, then go ahead and save your money. Be especially wary of using an older crib that might have lead paint, which your baby will undoubtedly chew on.

- *Car seats*. Required by law, car seats come in a range of models. It's very important that you buy a car seat that meets safety standards. In most cases, that means not purchasing a used car seat because you won't know whether it's been damaged or in an accident. Plus, you won't have the manufacturer's instructions. A car seat which is not properly installed is next to worthless. One option to lower the cost of a car seat may be available in your area. State highway patrol, sheriff, and police departments sometimes lend car seats to low-income families. Other programs let anyone "rent" them for as little as $5. Call your local authorities to check on such offers.

- *Strollers*. There's no reason not to go with a used or hand-me-down stroller, as long as you feel it's sturdy, stable, easy-to-clean, and that you can steer it comfortably. Go ahead and shop for a bargain.

- *High chairs*. High chairs are sometimes okay to buy used. Again, make sure the chair is sturdy, stable, and not painted with lead paint. Check to be sure your child can't slip out of it. Consider, too, how easy it is to get your child in and out of the high chair as well as how easy it is to clean. An antique wooden high chair might look nice, but it may be difficult to clean all the nooks and crannies, and it could be on the flimsy side.

Toys

There's no doubt about it. Today's parents buy their children far more than our parents bought us. The question is are today's kids any better off? Happier? Smarter? Anyone who has ever watched a child play knows the truth of the matter is that they're quite content with very basic playthings. Give a toddler a new toy, and chances are he'll play with the box it comes in! As children get older, they may clamor for all the stuff they see advertised on television, but that doesn't mean you have to give them everything they ask for. Many items turn out to be a passing fancy. If you take a look at the average American home's basement, you'll see what we mean: boxes and boxes of toys that children no longer play with. So our main way to save money when it comes to toys is to buy fewer of them in the first place. *STOP, LOOK*, and *LISTEN*.

When you do buy a toy, try to select the really classic, good quality type rather than the easily breakable, faddish gimmicks. Classic toys are better value in the long run because your child will get more play time out of them and they can be passed on. They are often more creative, too. Good wooden blocks, construction sets, a variety of balls, a few dolls and puppets, some cars, pails, and shovels, an unlimited supply of books—a child really doesn't need a whole lot more.

A good technique for getting more out of the toys you do buy your child is to rotate them. Only have a few out at a time and store the rest. Every week or so, put some away and take out "new" ones. Your child will feel like it's Christmas all over again. A bonus for you is that it will be a lot easier to keep your house picked up!

Buffy explains how she saves money on buying T.J. toys. "You can buy toys that do everything, you can buy videotapes, but children would rather play with you. I try to spend a lot of time playing with my son instead of buying him so many toys," she says. "I think, too, because I'm working, I want to play with him. Not only does it save me money, but it's more fun."

If you want to occasionally provide the "toy of the moment" for your child, why not try used-toy stores? These offer great bargains for those types of toys which kids soon tire of. Yard sales are another good source for children's toys. You can also make it a policy to only buy toys when they go on sale, usually right after Christmas. Otherwise you will pay quite a premium for any toy that has a special brand name or licensed character associated with it.

One family we know belongs to a game club. Every three months, they pack up all the games in the house and rotate them to the next member of the club. This way, they get new games all the time!

A Lesson on Lessons

A neighbor of ours has a nine-year-old daughter. To arrange a play date for her child, the mother needs to refer to a calendar. Monday? No, sorry, violin lesson. Tuesday? Gymnastics, then Brownies. Wednesday? Religious instruction. Thursdays? Swimming lessons. Friday? Pottery classes. By the weekend, the girl's exhausted and has to catch up on homework. Her mom complains about her hectic schedule and all the money she spends on classes, instruments, outfits, and equipment. It doesn't seem to occur to her to eliminate some of these activities. We think a little cutting back would go a long way toward her daughter getting more out of those activities she does keep.

It's easy for parents to get caught up in the excitement of a child's initial enthusiasms. It's also easy to try to force your own enthusiasms onto your child. Add to that the incredible variety of activities offered to today's children, and it makes it doubly difficult to keep from overenrolling and overstimulating them. With kids, you shouldn't push and you can't compare. Just because you wish you had learned piano as a child doesn't mean your daughter wants to. If little Tommy down the block is taking three kinds of lessons a week, it does not mean your child should. Maybe Tommy needs more physical outlets. Maybe your child tires easily and would rather read.

Here are some things to keep in mind when you are considering lessons or classes:

- Keep your perspective. How many lessons or classes does a four-year-old need? A ten-year-old? Set a limit and stick to it.

- Make sure lessons are child-motivated and child-directed. Don't bow to adult peer pressure.

- Think about the reasons for any activity. If it's purely for socialization, schedule more play dates. Encourage free team sports.

- Scout around for low-cost community- or school-based programs.

- Barter your services for lessons for your child. Does the flute teacher need a pet sitter? Would the karate coach like you to design a brochure?

- Ask whether bringing in new students will earn you a discount.

- Check for signs of burnout in your child. Evaluate how much he or she is getting out of each activity.

College

Education can be a major consumer purchase as well as the best investment you'll ever make. Where a person goes to school has a big impact on future career achievement, income-earning potential, and personal satisfaction. For this reason, it pays to spend even more time and attention choosing a college than practically anything else in life. Simply saving money on college tuition is false economy if it's the wrong college in the first place. It's essential to match a student's goals, interests, and abilities with the right institution.

Several of Shirley's grandchildren, for example, went to private colleges. One grandson is attending a relatively inexpensive state school, Southern Illinois University. It happens to have the forestry program he wanted. Shirley's daughter went to MacMurray College, a private school in Jacksonville, because they had certain special education courses she wanted. Shirley never tried to influence where her children or grandchildren went to school, despite the financial responsibility she assumed for their education. "Go to the college that's going to give you what you need," is Shirley's motto.

If you happen to have a child whose first-choice school is an expensive private college, it might seem impossible to "spend smart." Even given that scenario, you do have some options. There are always ways to shave down the cost of college and to lessen the financial burden.

How Much Does College Cost?

The biggest difference in cost is between private and public institutions. In 1995, the average cost of tuition, books, and room and board was $11,522 for private and $2,689 for public, according to the College Board. Harvard cost $28,896, while the State University of New York cost $3,400. That is a substantial difference. You and your child need to consider carefully whether the private school is worth so much extra. Beyond that, however, you need to assess whether that seemingly inexpensive state school is not such a bargain if you live out of state. Or whether the expensive private school is so well-endowed that your financial aid package would more than make up for the high cost.

Sylvia's two grandsons both went to UCLA. As state residents, their tuition was very reasonable and they received a high-quality education in their chosen fields. One grandson majored in graphic arts and for a while illustrated *Spiderman* comic books. Now he has his own comic book company. The other grandson majored in English and now works for Microsoft. Would they have been any more successful or happier if they had gone to Stanford, at twice the expense? We doubt it.

Once you have narrowed down the choice to several schools, you need to figure out how much each one will cost so that you can compare them more accurately from a consumer standpoint. Use the Comparing College Costs Worksheet on page 183. Fill in the tuition and any other fees charged on an annual basis. You'll want to factor in an inflation rate too, since schools almost always increase tuition each year. If there's a possibility it will take your student five years instead of four years to complete the degree requirements, be sure to add the extra year's expense. Include room and board, keeping in mind that where the school is located will affect this amount dramatically. Food, for example, in a large east coast city is a lot more costly than in a small rural town. If your child is renting a room or apartment as opposed to staying in a dormitory, those costs will vary as well. Transportation expenses will also depend on geography. How far away from home is each school? Will your child need to fly home for holidays? Have a car on campus? Next, estimate how much books for all the courses will cost. This budget line might be much higher for a science major than for a history major. Ask the college for help in estimating this expense.

BEARDSTOWN TALES

We didn't have a separate college savings plan. We saved for college via our hog business. We made our business grow enough to take care of paying for college. Our son had his own hog business in high school, so he paid a great deal of his own college expenses. The girls worked too. They also had scholarships. Our son went to the University of Illinois and then to the University of Illinois Medical School. Our oldest daughter went to Illinois State University in Normal because she was interested in teaching special education. Our middle daughter went to Augustana, a private church school in Rock Island, Illinois. She was interested in music. The youngest daughter went to the University of Illinois. They pretty much chose what they wanted to do. After they had finished college, we tallied up how much each of them had spent on college expenses. We gave them all a certain amount of cash to equalize it. Those who went to less expensive schools got a dividend at the end.

CARNELL KORSMEYER

Finally, add any personal expenses such as laundry, fraternity/ sorority dues, extra insurance, telephone, grooming, and fun. Now you are ready to add it all up. We suggest you sit down first! It might seem like an impossibly high figure.

More and more colleges are becoming aware that they may be scaring away potential "customers" with such high costs. One result is that there is more of a sense of market competition among schools. Some innovations have begun slowly sprouting on campuses across the country. A few schools, including Muskingum College and North Carolina Wesleyan College have actually been reducing tuition by as much as

WORKSHEET
COMPARING COLLEGE COSTS

This worksheet will help you fill in all the numbers you need to do a cost comparison of three schools.

	COLLEGE 1	COLLEGE 2	COLLEGE 3
TUITION	_____	_____	_____
FEES	_____	_____	_____
BOOKS/SUPPLIES	_____	_____	_____
ROOM	_____	_____	_____
BOARD	_____	_____	_____
PERSONAL (CLOTHING, TELEPHONE, MEDICAL, LAUNDRY, ENTERTAINMENT)	_____	_____	_____
TRANSPORTATION (COST OF THREE ROUND TRIPS HOME, IF LIVING AT SCHOOL; IF LIVING AT HOME, COST OF TRAVEL TO SCHOOL EACH DAY)	_____	_____	_____
TOTALS	_____	_____	_____

29 percent. Others guarantee a cap of 3 percent on any tuition increases. Clark University in Massachusetts and Lehigh University in Pennsylvania offer qualified undergraduates a year's free tuition toward the cost of an advanced degree. Perhaps the closest thing to a money-back guarantee is to be found at St. John Fisher College in Rochester, New York. Students who keep up a certain grade point average, have a career plan, and complete an internship qualify for partial tuition reimbursement if they can't find a job within six months of graduation.

Besides searching out these fairly unusual gimmicks, you can peruse tried-and-true ways of paying for college such as saving and investing *early*, securing low-interest loans, applying for financial aid, and qualifying for scholarships. We'll look at each of these options in turn.

How to Invest for College

As the Beardstown Ladies, we stress that the most sensible approach is to save as much as you can as soon as you can. How and where you invest will be determined by how many years you have before your child goes to college. The older they are, the less risk you want to assume. The earlier you start, the more choices you will have. "We see a lot of parents putting money into growth mutual funds or in zero coupon bonds, where they know how many years before they need the money and exactly what they're going to get at the end," Betty says.

- *Stocks.* If you have begun investing early enough, this is a terrific choice. By investing regularly in top-notch stocks, you should earn a good return. As your children grow, so will their college fund. There is always risk involved with stock investments, and there is no guarantee that the day the first tuition bill is due will be the right time to liquidate. We suggest you use our first book, *The Beardstown Ladies' Common-Sense Investment Guide* to help you invest wisely and well.

- *Mutual Funds.* If you don't think you can find enough time to invest by yourself in a variety of stocks, you would do well to consider mutual stock funds. By diversifying your portfolio among different companies, you reduce your investment risk. An advantage of mutual funds is that you get the benefit of professional money managers. Also, it's easy to make small, automatic payments into a mutual fund so you are "forcing" yourself to save.

- *Life Insurance.* The advantage of funding college through whole or cash-value life insurance is that your savings are not taxed until you withdraw the money. The disadvantage is that there are often more commissions and fees on life insurance than on mutual funds. In addition, you have to be extra careful that the insurance company has a solid credit rating. Otherwise, your careful savings plan could wind up worth nothing when the insurer defaults.

- *U.S. Savings Bonds.* Many parents like the security of these government-backed Series EE Savings Bonds. Sold in denominations starting at $50, they go up to $10,000. They also offer a tax advantage. Savings bond income is exempt from state or local tax, and you only have to pay federal tax when you cash them in. Not only that, if your income is under $40,000, you may not have to pay any tax on the earned interest if the money is used entirely for education and the bond was purchased after January 1, 1990 by an adult. The bond cannot be in the name of the child. You may get a partial tax break if your income is under a certain amount. Income limitations are set annually. We suggest that you check with your tax preparer to find out whether you are eligible for this tax break.

- *Zero Coupon Bonds.* As Betty mentioned above, these bonds are good for investors who want to know exactly what their investment will be worth at maturity. You buy only the principal amount, and your interest is not paid until maturity. When you buy zero coupon bonds, you are in effect "locking in" an interest rate. Obviously, if you believe that interest rates are going to stay the same or get lower, this is a good move. Otherwise you might be better off investing in more variable interest-rate vehicles. Another consideration is that you must pay income tax on the accrued interest each year even before maturity. Most of the income tax has been paid, however, when you receive the money.

- *Prepaid Tuition Plans.* The newest way to pay for college is also the most controversial. Some states, including Florida and California, have started programs in which people can pay tomorrow's college tuition at today's rates and thus avoid inflationary increases. Although you could wind up saving from $30,000 to $60,000 by buying these tuition "futures," there is one obvious, huge potential problem: Your child might decide not to attend the school you selected when he was knee-high to a grasshopper. Consider, too, the loss of investment return on the money you pay to the college in advance. It still might be a worthwhile option if you live in a state with a topflight university system, such as California. You need to weigh which way you come out ahead.

- *Retirement Plans.* As their name suggests, these plans are meant to be used for retirement. That does not mean, however, that occasionally they can't be used effectively to help defray college costs. For one thing, you usually don't have to include retirement plan funds as part of your assets on financial aid applications. Some plans, such as 401(k)s, are relatively easy to borrow against. You can borrow up to 50 percent of your accumulated total at low interest rates as long as you repay the loan within five years. Be sure to check whether or not there are any penalties for early withdrawal from other types of plans (IRAs, annuities, pension plans).

- *Home Equity.* This can be an excellent option if you have enough equity built up in your home to borrow against. A home equity loan has the added advantage of helping reduce income tax since interest expenses are deductible. You need to weigh the higher home equity interest rate and its tax benefit against a lower-cost student loan to determine which makes more sense for your family.

Financial Aid

By and large, financial aid is determined on the basis of financial need. Given the high cost of college these days, that means almost everyone has some level of financial need. You don't have to be below poverty level to qualify. Unless you feel you can afford to pay complete college costs for all your children without suffering

INVESTING FOR COLLEGE

This chart assumes the cost of one year in a private college is $11,000 and the annual college cost inflation rate is 7 percent. The investment returns are after tax.

ONE YEAR OF COLLEGE WILL COST	YEARS UNTIL YOUR CHILD ENTERS COLLEGE	YOU NEED TO INVEST THIS MUCH ANNUALLY IF YOU RECEIVE		
		5% RETURN	8% RETURN	10% RETURN
$11,770	1	$11,210	$10,898	$10,700
12,594	2	6,143	6,055	5,997
13,476	3	4,275	4,151	4,071
14,419	4	3,345	3,200	3,107
15,428	5	2,792	2,630	2,527
16,508	6	2,427	2,250	2,140
17,664	7	2,169	1,980	1,862
18,900	8	1,979	1,777	1,653
20,223	9	1,834	1,619	1,489
21,639	10	1,720	1,494	1,358
23,153	11	1,629	1,391	1,249
24,774	12	1,556	1,305	1,159
26,509	13	1,497	1,233	1,081
28,364	14	1,147	1,171	1,013
30,350	15	1,406	1,118	955
32,474	16	1,373	1,071	903
34,748	17	1,344	1,029	857
37,179	18	1,321	993	815

any financial hardship whatsoever—including having to sacrifice a retirement fund—you should go ahead and apply.

Financial aid is almost always a combination of loans, grants, work-study, and scholarships. Your need is the difference between how much your family can contribute and how much college will cost. So the crucial information is how your family or parental contribution is calculated. Since 1992, a formula called Federal Methodology Analysis has been required for federal grants, loans, and work-study programs. The formula takes into account your income, your assets (excluding home equity or farms, retirement plans, and life insurance), your age, your marital status, the size of your family, and living expenses, including how many family members are in college.

Once financial aid officers have this somewhat "scientific" amount, they can use their own discretion to factor in individual circumstances. In your financial aid application there is always a section where you can explain compelling reasons why your family might need more aid than sheer number-crunching might indicate. For instance, unusual medical expenses for another child in the family might affect how much financial aid you qualify for. If you are in doubt as to whether or not to disclose certain information, check with the financial aid office of the school where you're applying. You can also ask your high school guidance counselor, or any other college's financial aid office.

It may help and it can't hurt to file your financial aid applications as early as possible. In some cases, aid is based on a first-come, first-served basis. Even if this is not an official policy, it's been shown that, for psychological reasons, officers assign larger amounts earlier in the process than later.

The Offer

After you receive your financial aid offer from a college, you should carefully evaluate it. If it seems low, check to be sure that all the estimated expenses are accurately reflected. Perhaps the college made an error. Also, make sure that all the categories of aid you applied for have been evaluated. If not, find out why. Finally, compare the information taken into account when the aid offer was made to your situation today. No doubt some months have passed since you filled out your application. Have there been changes? Have you been laid off, been demoted, had to move, gotten sick? Be sure to let the financial aid officer know as soon as possible.

In the end, it is the financial aid officer, not a computer, who will determine your offer. Treat the person with as much respect as possible and don't expect miracles. Communicate calmly, and supply as much printed documentation as you can: doctor bills, divorce papers, letters, insurance reports. The officer will weigh all the information presented as fairly as possible. Your job is to ensure the information is complete.

If your child receives a better financial aid offer from school A but really wants to attend school B, don't hesitate to mention this fact to school B. Perhaps the school will increase its financial aid package. You will be in a better negotiating position if your child is an excellent student. One of the best money-saving approaches for college is to encourage academic success at an early age!

Grants

The largest grant program is the federal Pell grant. In 1994-95 it awarded $5.65 billion to lower-income students in amounts ranging from $400 to $2,300. No matter how poor your chances of receiving it, you need to apply anyway because many other grants and loans won't consider you unless you have applied for a Pell grant.

A second federal grant program works a little differently. Called the federal Supplemental Educational Opportunity Grant (SEOG), it is disbursed to college financial aid offices, which then distribute it to students. The total amount in SEOG in 1994-95 was $5.45 million.

Both these grants must be applied for each year. Other grants are available on the state level. Check with your high school guidance counselor for information.

Loans

A federal loan program was created as more middle-income families needed financial help to pay the high cost of college.

Like the Pell and SEOG grants, there are two main types of federal loans, one direct (Stafford) and one administered through individual campuses (Perkins).

Anyone can secure a Stafford loan, regardless of income. These are very attractive loans for a number of reasons. First, the interest rate is far below regular loan rates. You don't need collateral or even a credit rating—the government backs the loan. There is a grace period after a student graduates before repayment begins, and then payments can be stretched out over as much as 10 years. Stafford loans come in two forms, subsidized and unsubsidized. A subsidized loan means the government pays the interest during the time the student is in college and that the origination fee, assessed when the loan is first made, is 5 percent. The origination fee on an unsubsidized loan is 6.5 percent and you have to pay the interest. The total amount you can borrow is $15,125 for undergraduate education.

The federal Perkins Loan Program is similar except that how much loan money colleges offer varies from year to year. The total a student can borrow through a Perkins loan is $15,000. There is a possible bonus to taking out a Perkins loan. Some or all of the loan repayment may be canceled if your child pursues a certain career such as teaching special-needs children, full-time nursing, or working with family service agencies in low-income areas.

BEARDSTOWN TALES

My granddaughter has been searching for colleges. The colleges are interested in her because she was declared the outstanding center on the basketball team. All these colleges have offered to reduce the tuition. But many of them will only let her take 12 hours of school if she plays basketball. In high school she's taking eight academic subjects and making straight As. Her ability is there. Yet she'd end up going to college for five years. So I said, "Jennifer, are you going to college to play basketball for four years or are you going to college to get a degree?" When you add it up, it comes out more expensive to go five years. She finally decided on a state college at Normal, because it's the one school that has the courses she needs. Whether she plays basketball will be up to her.

SHIRLEY GROSS

Other loans not based on need are available at slightly higher interest rates. Most offer generous repayment periods of up to 30 years. They have names that sound like an alphabet soup of acronyms and include the Federal PLUS, Education Resources Institute's TERI, Knight Tuition Payment Plan's ABLE, University Support Services' PLATO, Nellie Mae's EXCEL, and the College Board's Extra Credit. For these loans, you usually do need to demonstrate a good credit history. Toll-free phone numbers for some of these are listed in the Resources section on page 273.

Although in general we don't recommend going into debt, taking out a low-interest loan to pay for college is an exception. Hazel wouldn't hesitate to tell a young college student to borrow money in order to get a good education. When she was younger, her father told her she'd have to earn her own living. "I hope you find a job you like," he told her. "If you don't, you can always come home and we will help you." After she became a nurse, she decided she wanted to switch careers. Hazel went home, took out a $500 bank loan, and went to the University of Illinois to become a laboratory technician. When she finished her education, she started to work for the state for $110 a month. "The average girl then only made about $60. I was able to pay back the loan quickly. It was a good investment," Hazel says.

Scholarships

Every parent dreams of sending their child through college on a full scholarship. Although qualifying for a full scholarship is rare, putting together a package of small amounts is quite possible because scholarships come in many shapes and sizes. They are awarded for many reasons, including academic ability, athletic prowess, ethnic origin, artistic or musical talent, career interest, fraternal organization membership, corporate employment, and such esoteric reasons as having the name Gatling or Pennoyer. There is even one scholarship just for students who don't receive any *other* form of financial help.

Hazel urges families to seek out scholarships. "So many people don't know that there are scholarships that are wasted because people only use half of them. Many scholarships are never used."

Besides the federal government, state governments are the second largest source of scholarships. Private organizations and universities themselves also offer scholarships. If you work for a large company, you might be in a good position to benefit from its scholarship program. For employees' children, corporate scholarships usually are not huge. There is much less competition for them, however, than for the larger federal grants.

There are several directories of college scholarships, which we list on pages 272 to 273. Your high school guidance office and your public library should have them. Always ask each college your child is applying to for special scholarships the school might award. Generally the computerized scholarship search firms are a waste of your time and money. They charge a lot for finding out information that is readily available through your college admissions office.

Other Options

None of the following strategies will work for every family or even for most families. They're worth mentioning, however, because those who can use them will save thousands of dollars.

- *Junior or community colleges.* They cost only hundreds of dollars a year as opposed to thousands. If your child starts out at one of these local schools, lives at home, and then transfers to a more prestigious four-year college, you can save almost half the cost of a college education. In the end your student will still have the degree from the more well-known school.

  Carol makes an interesting point about another advantage to attending a junior college. She says, "If you go to a state school for two years and you drop out, you have nothing. With a junior college, you at least have the Associate degree after two years. If you decide at the end of that two years you want to go on, then you can."

- *Accelerated degree programs.* Your child completes four years of school within three years to save a year's worth of tuition, room, and board. This can be a daunting task, but if your child is exceptionally efficient, bright enough, and motivated, it can be done.

- *College credits.* Another way to reduce the time spent in college paying high tuition and living costs is to take a few college courses while still in high school and living at home.

- *Establish residency.* If your child wants to attend an out-of-state school, consider establishing residency early enough to qualify for in-state tuition. Perhaps there is a relative your student could live with for the last year of high school?

Getting Down To Brass Tacks

1. Try to spend more time with and less money on your children.

2. It's worth the extra effort and research to find child care that fits your family's needs and budget.

3. Start investing for college as early as you can.

CHAPTER ELEVEN

Your Health: Physical and Fiscal

You can be a smart consumer when it comes to health care, too.

We remember when there was only one doctor for an entire family—no specialists, no fancy machines. In some ways, medical care seemed better then.

Studies have shown again and again that there's very little connection between the amount you pay for medical care and the quality of care you'll receive. Perhaps we need to reevaluate our desire to find the most advanced machines, the best surgeon, the most expensive treatments. That's what a young family we knew did.

They lived in a college town and had a three-year-old and a new baby. The woman had an obstetrician, but no general physician. Her husband didn't have a doctor. Their little boy went to the most well-known pediatric group around, the one that most of his parent's friends children used. When it came time to find a doctor for the new baby, the couple realized they had never been really satisfied with their son's pediatricians, who charged about $60 for each well-child visit, yet didn't take very much time with the boy. The woman also knew she needed to find a doctor for herself—she couldn't call the obstetrician when she had the flu. And her husband definitely needed a good doctor now that he was in his thirties.

They decided they needed an old-fashioned family doctor. After interviewing several, they chose one who had gone to a very good medical school, seemed warm and friendly, took a lot of time with each patient, and got to know their entire family. He charged $20 less per visit than the pediatric group. A few years later, when the woman had some mysterious symptoms, he knew enough about her and the family to order only the minimum number of tests before making a diagnosis.

STOP!

Consider that the reasons you pay for health care may include:

1. *Insurance coverage.*
2. *Reputation.*
3. *Location.*
4. *Price.*
5. *Convenience.*
6. *Fear.*

This family made some wise choices for their health and their budget. Instead of staying with the expensive pediatricians for the sake of prestige and reputation, they found a doctor who not only cost less but who met their needs much better. That's true economy.

We value our health so highly it might seem as if it's the one area in which we wouldn't dream of *trying* to economize. No amount of money can make up for being ill or injured. No amount of money seems too much to spend on obtaining good health. We're not suggesting you compromise on your medical care. We're simply saying that a slight adjustment in your *attitude* could save you money. Many of us go to the doctor as if we were going to church. We have so much faith in our doctors, we forget that they are only human. We forget that physicians provide a service and that we pay for their services. When we obtain health care, we are *consumers* making a purchase every bit as much as when we buy a car.

When we talked about how to buy a car, we discussed evaluating your needs and wants before deciding what model and which options you were willing to pay for. Health care is different because everyone wants the same thing: the best possible health. The way to stretch your health care dollars is to think like a consumer. That means finding the best value for your money, asking lots of questions, not taking anything for granted, checking your bills carefully, and negotiating when necessary. No, we don't mean sitting in an examining room half clothed and haggling with a doctor as if you were at a flea market. We mean staying informed, calm, and in control. After all, it's your body and your health.

It can be extra challenging to STOP, LOOK, and LISTEN when you're seeking medical help. You may be anxious the second you step into a doctor's office or a hospital lobby. You may be afraid you're going to miss days of work, have a terrible illness, or need painful tests. If you can try to stay focused on what to ask and what you need to do, you'll be in a better position not to waste money. You'll be able to keep your health in top shape without making medical costs go to the top of your Spending Pyramid.

Let's look at how to reduce spending and maximize savings in the three main components of health care: doctors, hospitals, and medicine.

Doctors

Having your own doctor will end up saving you money in the long run. First of all, if you don't have a doctor, you might use an emergency room for routine treatment. Emergency rooms cost at least twice as much as, if not more than, a scheduled doctor's visit.

In addition, when a physician who is completely new to you first sees you, chances are he or she will want to err on the side of caution and order lots of costly tests to rule out potential problems. A regular doctor becomes familiar with your history. He or she can put new symptoms or problems into perspective. A regular doctor will have a complete picture of your health. All that translates into better preventative care. You probably take care to get tune-ups for your car or to clean your gutters regularly to prevent more extensive damage and repair costs. Having regular physical checkups accomplishes the same thing. Nipping a physical condition in the bud through physical therapy or a lifestyle change is cheaper than having surgery, for instance.

If you're in good health, it's ideal to have one top-notch general practitioner instead of a small village of specialists. If you haven't yet, find a trustworthy reliable internist, family practitioner, or primary care physician. Then you won't pay premium fees for routine exams.

Help Your Doctor, Help Yourself

Once you have a good regular doctor, it's essential to make the most of your office visits. You can do this by preparing ahead of time. It's all too easy to get into an exam, have the doctor take over, and come home without having any of your basic questions answered. That's what we call a waste of money and a waste of time. Write down everything you can think of that is relevant to your visit and your health. If it's a routine checkup, mention any lifestyle changes since your last visit. Have you taken up jogging, gained weight, or traveled out of the country? Say so. Ask whether there are specific things to keep an eye on as you reach new stages of your life.

Here are the five things you should do whenever you visit your doctor:

1. If you're seeing the doctor for an illness, write down all your symptoms and your questions in order of importance. Think about likely questions the doctor may have for you so you don't have to waste precious office time pondering when your headaches first began, for example. Doctors usually look for patterns, so timing and location of symptoms become significant.

2. Take notes during your visit. The more complicated your condition, the harder it is to concentrate and retain information. Write everything down to refer to later. If your illness is making you at all confused or affecting your memory, consider bringing a friend or relative with you to act as a lobbyist and take notes.

3. If the doctor prescribes anything, ask what it is, what it's for, what side effects you may expect, how effective it is for your condition, how long you will need to take it, and how much it costs. Most prescribed medicine goes untaken, so if you don't intend to take it, tell the doctor now, before you pay for it.

4. If tests are ordered, ask how necessary they are, what they will determine, how conclusive they are, if it makes a difference

where you have them performed, and if there are less expensive alternatives.

5. If surgery is recommended, get a second opinion from an independent source (unless, of course, it's emergency surgery for a life-threatening condition). Don't rely on the first doctor's referral to a second doctor. Professional courtesy could interfere with objectivity. Ask the doctor how much practice he or she has in performing this particular operation. Ask whether it can be performed on an outpatient basis or not. Ask whether there is any advantage to waiting for the condition to resolve on its own. Find out if there are options as to where the surgery is done and if the cost varies accordingly. Sometimes doctors have affiliations at more than one hospital.

In general, don't be shy about raising concerns and asking for clarification. Don't let your doctor throw around medical terms or jargon you don't understand. Don't wait for your doctor to read your mind. Work with him or her to get the best possible treatment. If you feel you're being rushed, say, "I'm sorry to take so long, but I feel it's important to have all my questions answered." Most competent physicians will appreciate and respect your attitude.

Your Bill

Many doctors are reluctant to discuss money with patients. Perhaps they feel it spoils their image as being somehow above the realm of mere money, dealing as they do every day with life and death. But there's no reason to avoid having straightforward conversations regarding a doctor's fees. You don't hesitate to ask plumbers and electricians what they're going to charge you before they work on your bathtub or wiring, right? You're even quick to balk at a ridiculously high quote for a job. When you talk about money with your doctor, remind yourself that you are paying for a service and you have a right to know the cost of the service. If it sounds high, mention that fact. Ask whether the doctor has any kind of sliding fee scale. Maybe an installment payment plan can be arranged. Maybe the doctor has more discretion than you realize in what he or she charges. Most fees are not set in stone.

In our last book, we described a farmer in Indiana who fell out of his barn and suffered serious injury. He had some hefty medical bills, and his insurance didn't cover 100 percent. He could have accepted his fate as more bad luck. Instead, he took a proactive approach. He called one of the surgeons who had submitted the highest bill and explained the situation. The doctor agreed to reduce his fee to the amount the farmer's insurance would cover. That one phone call saved him several thousand dollars.

Another way to save money is to use the phone more often for garden-variety illnesses and questions. Don't assume you need an in-person visit, especially in the case of follow-up appointments and prescription refills. If you were scheduled to be seen two weeks after an illness, for example, and you're absolutely convinced you're fine, try to do a phone check-in with the doctor. Same with a visit simply to get a prescription refilled. If the medication is working well and no circumstances have changed since your last visit, most doctors will be happy to phone you in a refill.

Whenever you call, don't ask immediately for an appointment. Instead, describe your symptoms and then ask to speak to the doctor. Let the doctor decide if you need to come in or not. Don't leave it up to the receptionist, your husband, or a co-worker to decide. Obviously, you need to use good judgment yourself too. If you are running a high fever or having severe pain anywhere, don't try to save the cost of an office visit. But if you know darn well you just have a bad cold, chances are your doctor will agree all you need is the proverbial bed rest, fluid, and aspirin. By avoiding a visit, you'll get more rest and save money.

You often receive a discount for paying cash up-front for certain purchases. The same principle may apply to doctors' bills. Let's say your health insurance deductible is $500 a year. An average doctor's visit costs you $50. You're very healthy and only need to go the doctor a few times a year. Year after year, you don't meet the deductible. Yet your doctor's office has to keep billing you and filing claims. In order to reduce all that paperwork, your doctor may be so delighted to have you pay on the spot for your visit that you'll get a substantial discount as an incentive to pay cash next time too.

Low- or No-cost Care

Sometimes you can get above-average medical care by highly trained physicians for zero cost. Research studies sponsored by prestigious medical institutions and organizations often offer free care in exchange for participation. You need to qualify for an individual study, and studies don't last forever, but for the duration of the study, you can save quite a bit of money for very little time or effort. Living near a university medical center or a large urban area increases the likelihood of finding such studies. Ask your doctor for referrals or read local newspapers, especially campus publications.

State and county health services also offer free or very low-cost care. Immunizations are available for children in every state, for example. Flu shots are often provided as well. Anyone can participate in such programs, regardless of income, so there is no need not to take advantage of them to save hundreds of dollars. To find out about these programs, call your local health agency, then work your way up until you reach the right agency: town, city, county, state.

Hospitals

Avoiding hospitals is the only foolproof way to cut costs. Our first rule of thumb is to make absolutely sure you need to be in a hospital. If a doctor suggests you need to be "observed," be assertive and ask lots of questions. Unnecessary hospitalization not only costs unnecessary money, it may wind up producing a secondary problem while you are in the hospital and exposed to infection, overtired personnel, or risky anesthesia.

Even if you require surgery, you may be able to avoid a hospital stay. Ask whether or not your procedure can be done on an "outpatient" basis. More and more physicians are willing to send patients home shortly after simple operations. This single change can save you hundreds, or even thousands, of dollars. Simple surgery such as cyst removal or a breast biopsy may be done right in your doctor's office. Other operations may be better performed in facilities connected with a regular hospital.

If you must be hospitalized, and you have a choice, shop around as you would for anything else. Hospital charges vary tremendously. Only one thing is for certain: They are uniformly high. The average for one night in a hospital is almost a thousand dollars. You can very quickly wind up spending as much as you would on a house for an extended stay. The problem is that it can be difficult to compare costs. It's similar to comparing insurance policies: You have to be sure you're not comparing apples to oranges. A good idea is to visit a hospital beforehand to get a sense of its staffing and general atmosphere. Does it seem as if there are plenty of nurses? Is it clean and orderly?

Hospital Tests

Always try to check first with your own doctor before letting a hospital run tests you may not need—after all, you're the one who will pay for them! Don't take anything for granted. It's possible that one hospital doctor will order a test you just had performed. Or that an insecure medical resident will order more tests than necessary. You don't have to be rude or aggressive when questioning the necessity of tests. But you owe it to yourself to be careful in requesting information about the reason for every test.

Hospital Bills

You don't necessarily get what you pay for in a hospital. Unfortunately, time and again studies have shown that hospital bills contain errors and the errors are rarely in the patient's favor. If you accept them at face value, you could wind up paying for procedures you never received. In one case, a man got a bill with a code next to a fee for several thousand dollars. It turned out the code stood for a hysterectomy!

Hospitals don't automatically provide an itemized bill. Always ask for one. Then go over it carefully. Your bill will no doubt contain many line items that you can't possibly interpret on your own. Call the hospital's billing office with any questions regarding what abbreviations stand for or to break down any charges listed under general categories such as "miscellaneous." Keeping a notebook while in the hospital—or asking a relative to do so—will come in handy when checking your bill. You can verify dates and times of doctors' exams, tests, supplies provided, etc.

Some people don't take the time to review a hospital bill because they figure their insurance will cover everything anyway. They should think again. In the end, they are most definitely paying for extraneous charges in the form of higher insurance premiums. We all pay for waste, one way or another.

There may be ways to receive help with very large hospital bills. Start with the hospital's financial counselor or credit agent. They can help you set up manageable payment plans and even help you fill out insurance forms. Organizations such as the American Cancer Society, the Leukemia Society of America, the American Red Cross, and the U.S. Department of Veterans Affairs may offer financial aid. Again, ask for referrals at your hospital.

In the Hospital

Hospitals are notorious for outrageous charges. We wouldn't be surprised to get a bill for the air we breathed while in the hospital. To keep costs to a minimum, pay attention to these details:

- *Check-in time*. Are you being admitted over the weekend even though your tests won't be performed until Monday? That's an extra few thousand dollars right there. Make sure you don't go to the hospital any earlier than is absolutely necessary.

- *Check-out time*. Have you just had a baby? Do you feel tip-top? Why wait around with the hospital bill meter ticking when you could be enjoying your baby at home—for free? Our mothers thought it routine to spend a week in the hospital after each baby. Our daughters needn't assume that long a stay is necessary. Many healthy women go home with their healthy babies after only 12 hours.

On a less joyous note, when you have a loved one who is terminally ill, does it make sense to keep him or her in the hospital? Or would he or she prefer to be in familiar surroundings? No matter how much you spend on medical care, your loved one is going to die. Don't let your emotions get the better of your good sense. If the doctors don't object, concentrate on spending time with a dying relative at home or in a hospice rather than spending money on a hospital.

- *Beds and beyond*. You pay for a lot more than your hospital bed.

You pay for the sheets, blankets, and pillows that go on the bed. You also pay for towels, hospital gowns, toothpaste, soap, mouthwash, sanitary pads, tissues, and aspirin. Call your hospital billing office *ahead of time* to make arrangements to bring your own supplies and have some of these charges removed from your bill. They may discourage this practice, since it's how hospitals remain profitable, but if you stay firm you should be able to succeed in reducing your bill by several hundred dollars. At the very least, take everything home with you. After all, you paid for it!

- *Food.* Did you know it's possible to bring in your own meals? A young woman in Florida had just had a baby in the hospital. She was starving after hours of labor, but the last thing she felt like eating was institutional food. Her sister ran out and brought her back some Chinese food and her favorite cupcakes. All for far less than a hospital meal would cost. Unless you have special dietary needs while you're in the hospital, check to see if you can provide your own food.

- *Just say no.* Think twice before accepting that nice nurse's offer of a sleeping pill or bottled mineral water. You'll be charged for it, whether you needed it or not. If you don't need it, why pay for it?

Medication

Does it seem as if you're spending more and more on drugs your doctor prescribes? Well, you are. The cost of drugs increased three times the rate of inflation in the last decade.

Few customers even think of comparison shopping when it comes to prescriptions, but doing so can really pay off. The price of medicine can vary by as much as 75 percent depending on where you buy it. Just like consolidators who get discounts on airline seats by buying in bulk, large chain drugstores and mail-order houses pass on discounts to consumers. When we checked the price of 60 tablets of Zantac recently, for instance, it cost $96.99 at a large chain, $129.05 at a small independent pharmacy, and $92.38 through a mail-order house. The larger pharmacies don't always have the best prices, however. The point is it's worth it to call around for each prescription to find the lowest

HOW MUCH DOES COMPARISON SHOPPING FOR PRESCRIPTIONS SAVE YOU?

MEDICINE 60 TABLETS	SMALL, INDEPENDENT PHARMACY	LARGE CHAIN DRUGSTORE	MAIL ORDER
AMOXIL	18.15	19.39	13.02
DARVON	49.70	44.99	29.94
PROPOXYPHENE	24.65	15.79	7.38
PROCARDIUM	99.45	76.59	68.37
SELDANE	76.00	67.59	55.68
ZANTAC	129.05	96.99	92.38

cost. How much can you save? See the chart above for the difference in a representative sampling.

You can save by buying in bulk yourself, too. A bottle of 100 ibuprofen tablets, for example, costs $10.93 while 24 tablets cost $4.13. You save 70 percent by buying the larger quantity. Just be sure you will use that much medicine before the expiration date—otherwise you'll be wasting money instead of saving money.

Generic drugs, like generic cereal or generic toilet paper, also cost a lot less—up to half off. In the majority of cases, a generic version of a brand-name drug is equally effective. Whenever your doctor is about to write a prescription, ask if a generic is available. Then ask again when you're in the drugstore. We provide a short list of some of the more common prescription drugs and their generic equivalents on page 206.

Doctors also receive samples from pharmaceutical companies as a matter of course. Don't be embarrassed to ask your doctor to pass these free samples on to you. That's exactly what they're for!

BRAND-NAME DRUGS AND THEIR GENERIC EQUIVALENTS

Brand Name	Purpose	Generic
Amoxil	Antibiotic	Amoxycillin
Ventolin	Asthma	Albuterol
Darvon	Pain relief	Propoxyphene Hydrochloride
Tenormin	Hypertension	Atenolol
Zantac	Ulcers	Ranitidine Hydrochloride
Ritalin	Attention Deficit Disorder; Narcolepsy	Methylphenidate Hydrochloride
Esimil	Hypertension	Combined tablet: Monosulfate and Guanethidine Hydrochlorathiazide
Seldane	Allergies	Terfenadine
Percodan	Pain relief	Oxycodone
Xanax	Anti-depressant	Alprazolam
Valium	Tranquilizer	Diazepam
Lanoxin	Heart	Digoxin
Premarin	Estrogen replacement	Conjugated Estrogens

PREVENTION IS
THE BEST MEDICINE

The healthier you are, the less you need to spend on your health. It pays to do what you can to maintain your good health. You already know that. But maybe thinking of eating well and exercising as a way of *paying yourself* will help to motivate you. Every time you go for a walk or get enough rest, it's as if you're making a deposit in a "well" bank. Joining a health club or buying a bicycle is an investment. Health investments don't have to cost much either. Who says you have to join an expensive health club? Try the local YMCA for equipment that is just as good. Take up running, which is free. Keep your eyes open to low-cost alternatives. Buffy is devoted to maintaining her health. "I am a fitness fanatic," she says. "I work out four days a week on my lunch hour. I'm very faithful and alternate my workouts: running, lifting weights, aerobic dance. I'm serious about it."

THE COST OF EXERCISE

If you haven't chosen a form of exercise or want to think about switching, consider the following as a rough guide to how some alternatives stack up in terms of cost. All dollar amounts are averages for mid-range products:

WALKING — $50 shoes

RUNNING — $70 shoes

AEROBICS — $75 for a three-month class

YOGA—$85 for 10-week series

ROLLERBLADING — $100 + $75 for knee and elbow pads and helmet=$175

HEALTH CLUB — $275 for year-long membership

BIKING —$450 for bike + $100 clothes and helmet=$550

GOLF — $400 for clubs and bag + $100 for year-long membership=$500

SKIING — $900 equipment (skis, boots, snow gear) + $200 (weekend stay)=$1,100

STATIONARY BIKE — $239 and up

NORDICTRACK — $300 and up

FREE WEIGHTS (150 LBS.) — $125

We know a family who had a six-year-old with asthma. The boy needed expensive medication that had no generic equivalent. When the child's mother was waiting for the doctor, she noticed a cabinet filled with this medicine. She was hesitant, but finally forced herself to ask the doctor for some samples. The doctor was happy to give them to her and on every subsequent visit always asked whether the child needed more samples. Since the boy had to take this medicine daily, the family saved hundreds of dollars.

Here's to your healthy body and healthy bank account!

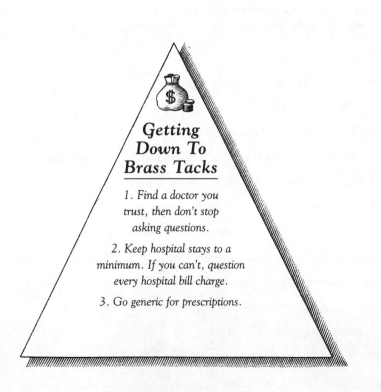

Getting Down To Brass Tacks

1. *Find a doctor you trust, then don't stop asking questions.*

2. *Keep hospital stays to a minimum. If you can't, question every hospital bill charge.*

3. *Go generic for prescriptions.*

THE TIMES OF
YOUR LIFE

*All those special occasions when we
mark important milestones don't
have to bankrupt us.*

ANYONE WHO HAS EVER PLANNED A LARGE public gathering, whether to celebrate the living or to mourn the deceased, can tell you it isn't easy. Weddings and other big parties, funerals and other rituals, are filled with so many details. Emotions run high. It can be hard to keep sight of the important elements. It's common for people to spend far more than they wanted to as they lose track of the big picture and get lost in a mountain of engraved invitations or white lace or sprays of flowers. These are occasions when people want to please each other more than usual. Some might even want to impress others.

One of us will never forget a wedding held at a Palm Springs country club. A struggling young actress was marrying a struggling young model. There were eight bridesmaids and eight ushers. The photography took more time than the ceremony itself as the wedding party posed and then posed again. There was a full, sit-down dinner, an orchestra, a river of champagne, and 300 guests. The reception lasted for hours. The bride's parents spent close to $50,000 on what turned out to be a performance more than a celebration. Sadly, the couple divorced after one year of marriage— the wedding cost more than $1,000 for each week of marriage!

The groom's sister had a very different kind of wedding. Held in an historic old church in the country, the ceremony was grace-ful and lovely. A friend took professional-quality photographs with-out interrupting the flow of events. The reception was in a com-munity hall, with the groom's band providing Dixieland jazz. A smorgasbord dinner was simple but satisfying. The bride wore a rented dress and her three attendants made their outfits. The cou-ple and their families shared the cost of this wedding, which totaled about $1,000. Sixteen years later, this couple fondly remembers their wedding—together.

STOP!

Consider that the reasons you spend money on weddings, funer-als, and other special occasions may include:

1. *Celebration.*
2. *Religious customs.*
3. *Family expectations.*
4. *Tradition.*
5. *Social obligation.*

We're not saying not to splurge occasionally on a momentous occasion. "Sometimes spending money is a wise choice where family is con-cerned," Carnell explains. "You can detract from life if you get too focused on skimping, if that becomes the only goal. We've been conser-vative, but at the same time quality of life is an investment too."

You don't have to throw caution to the wind and go overboard to have a successful event. The way not to overspend on such occasions is to *STOP, LOOK*, and *LISTEN*. You need to keep coming back to *why* you're having an event. What is its purpose? Is it a performance or a party? Is it to bring together all those you care about in cele-bration of an achievement? Is it to pay respect to someone? Do you want a dignified, elegant gathering or a festive, joyous bash? Is the goal to have fun or to make a big splash? Would you rather have a luxurious reception for a tiny group or a potluck dinner so you can invite everyone you know? Before you spend a cent, you need to stop and consider what your "dream" event would be like. Then you can begin to plan a way to get as close as possi-ble to your fantasy without spending a fortune.

If you find yourself asking, "What will so-and-so think?" you're probably not designing the event for yourself. Let so-and-so think whatever she wants—if she cares about you, she'll have a fine time at your event.

The more you *LOOK* before you leap and plan ahead, the less you have to spend on last-minute, impulse purchases and the more time you have to shop around for the best values. This is true whether you're choosing a reception hall, a caterer, or a funeral home. Doris, who plans big events frequently in her position as a school principal, sets a certain price to spend and sticks with it. "I've figured it closely so we don't overspend or have a lot of refreshments left over," she says.

Shirley describes her daughter's wedding as meeting both her daughter's expectations and serving its purpose. "My daughter had a church wedding with a reception at the church and a dinner afterwards at my home, all very reasonable. We had maybe 30 or 40 out-of-town guests and the wedding party at my home. Somebody helped cater and we had ham. The house was full; some were sitting out on the front steps or cushions on the floor. It was not very expensive, but it was a nice informal wedding. She was quite pleased with it. It was what she wanted. And we got her married."

That is the main point, isn't it?

Weddings, Christenings, Bar Mitzvahs and Other Parties

In this section, we'll focus mainly on weddings because that's where most people spend the largest amount of party dollars. Many of the concepts can be applied to any type of celebratory event. There is a lot of room for creativity and ingenuity when it comes to planning a party or reception. In fact, some of the most truly celebratory occasions we've attended weren't necessarily the most lavish affairs. Carnell's daughter had such a wedding. For guests, its charm lay in its combination of down-home earthy qualities mixed with the novelty of being on a real working farm.

"Our second daughter was married at home," recalls Carnell. "She was living in Chicago at the time, so many of her friends had never been on a farm. They wanted to do everything we do on a farm. We roasted a pig in the ground. We had a hayrack ride as part of her reception. Some of them toured the hog houses. Many of her friends stayed all night at our house with sleeping bags scattered throughout the house. It was different."

Carnell's oldest daughter had a more traditional wedding yet still managed to economize without sacrificing any of the basic ingredients. She made her own dress, because she sews well. Her sisters were the bridesmaids and made their own dresses, too. The wedding was in the local church, and the reception dinner was grilled pork chops at the Elks Club in Beardstown.

If you have unlimited funds, of course, the sky's the limit. But even if you happen to be quite well off, refer back to your Personal Priority Pyramid. Do you really want to spend 25 percent of your annual income on this one event? Will a $20,000 wedding—not unusual in this country—be that much more satisfying than a $10,000 wedding? Keep in mind the law of diminishing returns here, too. Will you enjoy a $30 champagne more than a $20 champagne? Will your wedding be that much better? Is it worth the $500 difference you'd spend on 50 bottles? What about a dress? If you spend $1,000 instead of $250 will you feel more beautiful? Will your guests care? Will they even know?

After all, a wedding is a onetime occurrence, not an investment in your future. It's not like picking a college or a house, which has long-term consequences. Your marriage won't be any better or worse depending on what kind of wedding you have. Whether you go with cheese puffs or caviar, engraved or printed invitations, roses or Peruvian lilies—none of these details will seem important to you or your guests in the big scheme of things.

Here's a suggestion. Figure out the most you can afford to spend. Then write down the least you could spend and still have a nice wedding. Agree with yourself that any money you save (the difference between the two) you'll put aside in a splurge account, to be used for a car, a down payment on a house, or your future child's college education. It's much easier to save money when you know that the money you save is going somewhere special.

The Place

Once you know the basic theme or mood for your event and how many guests you'll be inviting, you can choose a location. At one end of the spectrum is your own home, if it is suitable. The advantages are that it is free, you don't have to worry about "booking" it, and you are familiar with its good and bad points. The disadvantages are that you may have to do some major rearranging or decorating and you won't have professional help on staff. The other end of the spectrum is a fully-equipped hotel, restaurant, country club, or other reception venue. These are the most expensive locations. They usually offer a complete package deal with food, liquor, and staff included in one price. The price is calculated on a per-head, or per-guest, basis.

If your home cannot accommodate the size of your event and if you would rather not spend thousands of dollars on a hotel, restaurant, or country club, there are many alternatives. In Beardstown, for example, many of us use our church, the Elks Club or Union Hall. Some other possibilities are a community center, college, or even a public space such as a park. Maybe you live in a condominium complex with a clubhouse. Perhaps you belong to a boat club or know someone who could lend you a boat! We've heard of wedding receptions and parties held in an art gallery, a rose garden, a theater, a greenhouse, and a photography studio. By holding a large gathering in an unusual location, you often accomplish more than saving money. You can set the mood for an even more joyous occasion, as people behave differently depending on where they are. We suggest you use word of mouth as your best source of a possible inex-

BEARDSTOWN TALES

My daughter Karen wanted a champagne wedding on a beer budget. But we found a place that had complete packaged weddings. They rented everything including the wedding gown. They had all of the wedding paraphernalia. They had the men's tuxedos. She picked out a wedding gown that she loved. She picked out the tuxedos and they were up-to-date. She picked out her attendants' gowns. She had a fairly large wedding. She had a flower girl and a little ring bearer. She had four attendants. She had the cake, the punch, mints, nuts, the flowers, and the pictures, and we spent $1,000. That included all the decorations. This was several years ago, but we thought it was a bargain. I was skeptical at first, but everything was fine. Only the flowers could have been a little better. As a matter of fact, I rearranged her bouquet. She was happy with everything. It wasn't tacky. They went out of their way to make it nice. They knew I had four daughters so they wanted some repeat business.

MARGARET HOUCHINS

pensive location. Mention it to everyone you know and sooner or later you'll hear about a good spot.

If you want to go the more traditional route, try asking for times and dates that aren't the most sought after. Many places will give you a better rate on a weeknight in February than a Saturday in June. It's the law of supply and demand at work again. The same principle applies to cancellations. If you can be flexible enough to set a date for three months away instead of planning your party six months to a year in advance, you might be able to slip into a canceled slot at a big discount.

Food and Drink

What you feed your guests can seem like the crux of the party. People have such complicated relationships with food and what it means. Breaking bread together is one of life's more meaningful moments. So when you plan the refreshments, it's easy to get carried away in a wave of wanting to make the guests feel extra special—and well-fed. The key here is to keep in mind that your tastes and appetite don't change because you happen to be at a party.

Remember Carnell's advice to think in terms of buying *transportation* instead of buying a *car*, or buying *shelter* instead of buying a *house*? This thinking comes in handy when planning parties too. Try to think about providing *food* rather than finding a *caterer*. If you don't mention the word "wedding," right off the bat you'll be quoted a lower rate. Instead of looking for wedding food, search for good food. A local deli might be just the ticket if you love its homemade lasagna or six-foot heroes.

They say don't go grocery shopping when you're hungry because you'll shop with your stomach instead of your head. The same applies to planning a big party. Wait until you're sure you're thinking as clearly as possible. Set a budget for yourself. Then, and only then, figure out what will satisfy both you, your guests, and your pocketbook.

We know a young couple who were working full-time and trying to plan their own wedding. They both had large families and wanted to give the rehearsal dinner themselves. They lived in Maryland and thought serving soft-shelled crabs would be an appropriate treat. By the time they thought about the food, they were exhausted with all the details. They wound up ordering enough crabs for three times the number of people they were feeding. They also neglected to realize how many of their midwestern relatives wouldn't touch such fare. Not only did they spend unnecessary money, they had to deal with disposing of the crabs the night before their wedding, since shellfish does not keep.

Think through what to serve very carefully. If a full-course sit-down dinner means you don't get a honeymoon, is it worth the trade-off? Maybe serving good champagne and huge bowls of fresh strawberries would seem even more special—at a fraction of the cost.

We know a couple who had a potluck wedding supper. The bride's sister was enlisted to call about twenty of her closest friends. She asked each one to bring a substantial dish to the reception in lieu of a gift. Her friends were happy to contribute in such a personal way. This works especially well if the bride and groom already have plenty of material objects and don't need more silver or toasters or china.

You can also do a lot of the food yourself, if you are so inclined. Carol was spared the expense of a big wedding when her son eloped. When the spontaneous newlyweds came home, however, "We footed the bill for their reception," she says. "I'm happy with what we spent, but then, I baked the cake. We did most of it ourselves."

They also saved money by serving beer in kegs. Is there a law that says you must serve hard liquor? One of the most delightful weddings we ever attended was at a Quaker meeting house where alcohol was not permitted. The family saved money and had the kind of wedding they felt most comfortable with, too. The point is not to get locked into thinking there is only one "right" way to do things.

On the other hand, perhaps great food is one of the most important parts of your life. We know another couple who are self-proclaimed "foodies." They plan vacations around sampling various cuisines. Their idea of fun is to find the best price for sun-dried tomatoes and fresh salmon. They happen to be public defenders and don't have a lot of money. When it came time to plan their wedding, they knew they wanted to have delicious food above all. Their solution was to be married at city hall and then take only their immediate families to one of the best restaurants in New York. Everyone there agreed it was a memorable meal and a wonderful wedding. Best of all, the couple didn't have to start out their married life heavily in debt.

Flowers

Are you sure you need them? While that may sound downright un-American at first, it might make sense if your wedding is in a garden blazing with blooms or in a huge ornate church where any flowers would be lost. If you're having a winter wedding, maybe simple greens would be effective. Perhaps a bouquet of something other than flowers would work: balloons, dried herbs and leaves, or candles—you're really only limited by your imagination.

For more traditional flower arrangements, here are some tips to keep costs to a minimum:

- Tell your florist exactly how much you want to spend and listen to his or her advice on what you can expect for that amount.

- Don't say the "W" (wedding) word to your florist until after you've negotiated a price.

- Stay natural. Don't try to have hothouse roses, stiff, wired arrangements, or out-of-season flowers. You wouldn't buy raspberries for $10 a pound in the middle of the winter, right? So stick with whatever is in abundance and in season whenever possible.

- Think double-duty. Consider using bridesmaids' bouquets for your buffet table.

Margaret is a former florist. She suggests that one of the most important things a bride can do is to get written estimates from florists she is considering. "If you have a car wreck, they make you get two or three estimates. I would get at least three. I would want to have it all in writing because a lot of florists have hidden charges. I would want to know if they are going to set this up at the church and if that's an extra charge."

Another point is to check and determine the quality of flowers according to your budget. Margaret explains there might be a communication gap. You say "purple" and the florist thinks of a different purple. Or your expectations are beyond what your budget can achieve. "Maybe a girl is thinking, 'I want flowers just like at my friend's $5,000 wedding,'" Margaret says. "Well, her friend has used a $5 silk rose on a $5 stem to start. But this girl only has $1.50 to spend on a rose. I want her to come pick the flowers that we're going to use that fit within her budget. Then she won't be disappointed."

The Dress

Let's say ordinarily you spend from $50 to $150 on an outfit. Then you start shopping for a wedding gown. Why are you suddenly looking at dresses that cost thousands of dollars and that you're going to wear exactly one time? Even if you find a "bargain"—a dress that is on sale from $5,000 marked down to $1,000—do you really want to spend that much on one dress? Try not to let your mother, your friends, or all those bridal magazines inspire temporary insanity. You want to look your best, but that doesn't mean you have to spend beyond your means. Decide what a reasonable amount is as part of your wedding budget. *STOP, LOOK,* and *LISTEN.* Don't limit yourself to specialty stores or designer racks. Check regular dress shops for classically cut, flattering clothes at a fraction of the cost of gowns labeled "wedding." That one little word in front of an article of clothing immediately inflates the price.

Consider, too, having your dress made. It can be far less expensive, and you have a better chance of getting exactly what you want. A bride in California had her dress made by a good friend who was an excellent seamstress. Making the dress was her friend's wedding gift; the bride paid only for the material. Besides saving quite a bit of money, there were several other benefits. Shopping together with her friend for the pattern and fabric was far less stressful than trying on dress after dress in stores all over town. The bride wanted the material to be comfortable and carefree so she could dance to the steel-drum band at her reception without worrying about ruining her dress. She was able to find a very fine Italian cotton that looked like silk and was half the cost. Finally, since her friend did the final fitting a few days before the wedding, it wasn't a disaster that the bride had gained a couple of pounds!

A wedding dress is not an investment. It won't appreciate, and you'll never earn interest on it. So renting your wedding gown makes very good sense, especially if you want a lavish, traditional gown that you would never wear again. This is where sentimentality often clouds your ability to make a good sensible decision. You think, "Oh, but my wedding is a once-in-a-lifetime event. I will want to keep my dress as a family heirloom." Well, maybe you do. But think it through first. What is the likelihood that your daughter will want to wear this dress in thirty years? Most women want to wear the most flattering outfit more than they want the sentimental connection. A woman we know who was married in Sweden rented her dress and spent the money she saved on flying her sister to her wedding. Her sister's presence was more important to her than owning a dress she'd never wear again. (Besides, that's why there's wedding photography!)

Another way more and more modern-day women are economizing when it comes to clothes is to choose outfits they can wear more than once. If you calculate an outfit on a cost-per-wear basis, the more often you wear it, the less expensive it becomes. Maybe a beautiful suit would look elegant on your wedding day—and on many future occasions.

Funerals

Wealthy ancient Egyptians had a custom of burying their dead in elaborately decorated caskets with as many earthly possessions as possible, including gold and precious jewels. Then they topped it all off by building huge pyramids to contain their bodies and booty. Well, we'd rather build a Spending Pyramid than an Egyptian tomb. As Elsie says, echoing a thought we're sure you've heard many times, "You can't take it with you." Considering how much we spend on funerals, it seems a lot of us still believe you *can*.

Grief is a powerful emotion that can cloud the clearest minds and hearts. The time to think about funeral costs is long before a period of grief and mourning. Obviously, this is not always possible in the case of sudden or accidental death or the death of a young person.

Carol says that when her father died, the worst part was picking out the casket. "You go through 'Would you like this one? This one's $3,000, this one's $5,000. This is the public aid casket.' You're in shock because somebody's died. It's a trauma to then have to decide what you want and what you think they'd want. If you plan your own funeral, it's great for your survivors."

Shirley's brother was a funeral director, so she learned early on how helpful it is to plan ahead. You get to *STOP, LOOK,* and *LISTEN* instead of making your loved ones have to do it while they are in mourning. "I've already talked to the funeral director who bought my brother's business," says Shirley. "He knows where my cemetery lot is, where I want to be buried, what kind of a casket I want, and that I want a funeral service in my church. I wanted to make sure that he knows what I want. There will be enough money out of my insurance policy to pay for my funeral."

Elsie has a special book in which she has specified what type of arrangements she wants. "You think about that more when you get as old as I am. I don't think it's necessary to have an expensive funeral. What good does it do? You go into the ground. Why

BEARDSTOWN TALES

I very seldom send flowers to a funeral. You spend $50 to $60 for a bouquet of flowers and you look at them for one afternoon. Instead I give to a scholarship fund or church project. Then that money is used for a long time. That's what I did for Helen. Helen Kramer was one of my best friends and a Beardstown Lady. We gave programs on investing at the high schools around here. Every Thursday noon for years we went out to dinner. There was never a week that Helen didn't walk in my front door with that great, big smile. She lived to be over 80 years old. She had a very nice funeral in her church where she had been very active. Very well handled. I did not send flowers because I knew she was so well known in town that there would be flowers everyplace. If it had been a very small family, maybe I would have sent flowers. I thought, I'd rather write a check that's going to be used. Helen would approve of me giving to the scholarship fund.

SHIRLEY GROSS

put all that money into it? One casket is just as good as the other. I don't want the cheapest, but I don't want the best either."

What You Pay For

In the midst of dealing with death, it might seem odd to think of yourself as a consumer. But the average cost of a funeral is $5,000, so you certainly want to spend that money wisely. Carnell has a very firm idea of what her priorities are regarding her own funeral arrangements. She says, "I think money is for the living. We have grandchildren to educate and we have one grandchild who is handicapped, so he's not able to live independently. I think money for those things is more important than for a funeral. It's a time of trauma, so it should be done in a manner that brings comfort, but there's no need for extravagance."

You have certain rights, and the funeral industry is more carefully monitored than it used to be years ago. Federal regulations enacted in 1984 by the Federal Trade Commission are referred to as the Funeral Rule. There are plenty of resources for any consumer inquiries or complaints you may have. See page 275-276. The Funeral Rule states that when you ask about costs, the funeral provider must inform you of your rights in writing. Ask for such disclosure if you don't receive it.

Shopping for a funeral is a little like buying a car. There is the cost of the base model and then there are a myriad of options and services you can "add on." Don't assume you need the "fully loaded" funeral. When you ask for prices, be sure you understand exactly what is included in the amount so you compare accurately.

The casket is the most expensive part of any funeral, amounting to half the total cost. Caskets are made of heavy steel, oak, plastic, fiberglass, or unfinished pressboard. Cardboard or even canvas containers may be purchased for bodies which will be cremated without a viewing or other ceremony.

Shirley was recently at a funeral where they had a casket she thought was much too big and elaborate. "It could have been a nice simple little casket," Shirley says. "The funeral director no doubt sold them the most expensive casket he had. They have lost a loved one and the funeral director leads them right down the merry old path. He's going to make as much money as he can from that funeral. I do resent that. I don't believe in this wasted money."

Other funeral costs include legal documentation fees, embalming, cosmetic treatment and transportation of the body, use of the funeral home, tent and chair rentals for the graveside, limousine, and memorial booklets or programs. Flowers, obituary notices, pallbearers, and clergy honoraria may be charged to you in advance by the funeral provider. For every charge, *STOP*, *LOOK*, and *LISTEN*. Then decide what you need and what you can do without.

Ways to Save on Funerals

Here are a few cost-saving tips you may not be aware of:

- If the deceased was a member of the military, past or present, he or she may qualify for burial reimbursement. Check with the U.S. Department of Veterans Affairs.

- Other burial assistance may be available from Social Security or a fraternal organization.

- Like anything else you buy, it's a good idea to shop around for caskets. Once you find one you like, jot down the brand and model. Then shop by phone to find the lowest price. In most states, funeral homes cannot prohibit you from bringing in a casket purchased somewhere else. Check first.

BEARDSTOWN TALES

I've planned ahead for my funeral—I know where I'm going to be put to rest. Our church cemetery is just down the road from our home. We purchased six plots at a bargain price. We bought them just before they doubled the price on burial plots. We got extra plots that will be available for our children and their family if they want to use them. This just happened to occur on our 23rd anniversary so for our anniversary present my husband said "Let's go pick out our burial plot." I wanted to pick out the location. Mom and Dad's plot is up the hill and I wanted to be able to see them. We got our plot where I can see them and they can see me. For our 25th anniversary, Bill was going to get me a tombstone, but we needed an air-conditioner instead. We know a gentleman that sells tombstones and is going out of business. My husband is getting a real deal on our tombstones so we'll be all set.

Carol McCombs

- There is no law, unless it's part of your religion, that says you have to use a funeral home for everything. You can save money by having a graveside service or a memorial service at your home or church.

- Funeral homes and cemeteries often charge less for weekday services than for weekends. If you have any choice, ask whether there's a difference or not.

- Cremation is the least expensive burial option. Be aware that the container will be destroyed during the cremation process, so you especially don't want to spend a lot of money on it.

Plan, but Don't Pay, Ahead

Planning what sort of funeral arrangements you would like is always a good idea, but paying for them in advance may not be the best choice. For one thing, you're definitely not earning interest on any money you give a funeral home. Instead of paying a funeral company in advance, it's better to set aside a certain amount in an interest-bearing account or insurance policy. Then you don't have to worry about the company going out of business by the time your survivors need the services you paid for.

If you do decide to go with a prepaid funeral contract, read the fine print extra carefully. Then keep the following points in mind before you sign:

1. You might move. Does the contract "move" with you? Will it cover your funeral in a new location? Will you have to pay a fee for the transfer?

2. Avoid door-to-door funeral contract sales. Beware of being pressured into signing on the dotted line before you can do any comparison shopping.

3. Are there penalties for changing your mind? What if you want to cancel or decide on cremation?

4. The contract might have an "inflation" clause, in which case your estate will be liable for additional fees. Ask whether the price of your funeral is "guaranteed" for as long as you live.

5. Prepayment installment plans are doubly costly. You wind up paying interest to the funeral provider as well as not earning interest on that money. We would seriously question this choice.

Getting Down To Brass Tacks

1. Remember: The amount you spend on an event doesn't have to have anything to do with how important it is! It's the people that make it special, not the country club.

2. Never mention the word "wedding" or "bar mitzvah" until after you've gotten estimates for food, flowers, clothes, or locations.

3. Think like a consumer even when planning a funeral. Don't prepay your funeral costs.

CHAPTER THIRTEEN

AND WHILE WE'RE AT IT— SHOPPING FOR EVERYTHING ELSE

No matter what you're buying, STOP, LOOK, and LISTEN can become second nature if you practice.

THIS CHAPTER IS ABOUT THE KIND OF SPENDING that makes up the base of most people's pyramids: food, clothes, and furniture. It's a good place to practice smart spending because you buy groceries or underwear more often than you buy a house or a car. Again, you might have heard many of these tips before but haven't taken them to heart. By now we hope you have absorbed the lessons we've been trying to teach in this book. If you have, you will be more inspired to incorporate the following money-stretching techniques. You will have realized that every dollar you don't spend on an unnecessary purchase is a dollar you can invest and turn into many dollars. It doesn't take much extra time or effort to save money. It takes being aware that you *always have a choice* about how to spend your money.

So read on, and make a commitment to yourself to spend smart and save more. You'll feel richer than you ever dreamed possible.

General Shopping

We've said it before and it bears repeating: Do not shop if you are tired, hungry, hot, cold, unhappy, or bored.

- Take advantage of seasonal sales. Certain products go on sale at regular times of the year. If you wait until the right moment, you can save 25 to 50 percent or more. (See the chart on page 229 for a month-by-month breakdown.)

- Make lists. You probably know already that keeping a running grocery list is a big money-saver. It also works to apply the same principle to all your consumer needs. Keep a little notebook accessible. Jot down whatever you need to replace or purchase. Then, when you're at a department store sale, warehouse club, or yard sale, you can refer to your notebook and remember what it is you need to buy.

- Plan each shopping trip to focus only on what you need. Don't get sidetracked into impulse buying. Group together errands and purchases to reduce the amount of opportunities you provide yourself for "extra" spending.

- We've seen over and over how you can save money by taking advantage of middlemen who buy products in bulk, from airline tickets to hotel rooms. You can buy in bulk yourself and save. The key is to buy only those products that you can and will use before they go bad and for which you have enough storage space. Nonperishables such as toilet paper, canned food, and panty hose are good examples of bulk-buying opportunities.

- Don't be reluctant to return anything that is not satisfactory. You might as well throw your money away if you hold onto spoiled goods. As a consumer, you always have a right to return something and get a refund, credit, or exchange.

- Don't assume you can't return an item because you've already used it, either. If it fell apart after one use, return it. Just be polite and clear about why you are returning the item. We've returned everything from a down jacket with a zipper that broke to a piece of bad meat. Try not to make a special trip just for a small return, though. Hang onto your receipts and call the store to ask if you can wait until your next shopping day rather than waste time and gasoline.

- You can often get a refund or credit over the phone. Many food companies list toll-free customer service numbers on their packages. If you are unhappy with a certain product, you can call the number to complain. One woman we know called an ice cream manufacturer after discovering her container of vanilla fudge swirl had apparently melted and refrozen before she purchased it. The company sent her coupons for $20 worth of any of their products.

Food

The first step in saving on your food budget is to figure out what you spend. Start saving all receipts in an envelope. Include convenience store purchases, take-out food, vending machines, and snack bars. If you don't get a receipt, write down what you spent on the outside of the envelope. After one month, take out the receipts. If you bought nonfood items, cross them off the receipt. Now add up everything. Chances are you will be surprised by the amount you and your family spend on food. Once you know, however, it's easier to start whittling down the amount. Repeat this exercise in three or four months to see how you're doing.

Supermarkets have made a science out of getting you to spend more than you intended to when you first walked in the door. They have special consultants and newsletters devoted to studying consumer behavior and then profiting from the knowledge. By arming yourself with similar knowledge, you can defend against these gimmicks and save money. The first thing you should know is that the longer you spend in a grocery store, the more you spend. That's because you buy items that weren't on your list. These unplanned impulse purchases account for an average of $3,500 a year for a small family. No, we don't mean you should speed-shop your way into a frantic tizzy. But a little organization can go a long way in keeping your time in the store, and therefore spending, to a minimum.

- *Shop with an organized list.* Making a list and sticking to it is a great start. But grouping your grocery list according to the layout of your store will make you even more efficient. By making just one clean sweep through the store, you will eliminate backtracking and the temptation of more unplanned impulse buys. Don't believe us? Well, try the following experiment to prove it to yourself. Write your family's grocery list in any old order. Now write the same list but grouped into categories such as fresh fruit, dairy products, meat, frozen foods, canned vegetables. Go shopping with the first list. Time yourself. Keep track of anything you buy that is not on the list. Add up the amount of those unplanned purchases. Next time, time yourself again and shop with the organized list. Keep track of unplanned purchases and total your cost. Which trip was shorter? Which trip did you spend more on?

- *Buy generic.* Buying store or house brands instead of national name brands will save you 25 percent—more in many cases. But, you think, the quality is not as good so it's not a true bargain. We beg to differ. It turns out that most generic products are made by the *same manufacturers* of the name brands! In fact, they are the same exact product put into a different package with a different label—and hence, a lower price. Once again, you are paying more for a company's advertising budget, not necessarily for better quality.

- *Watch for specials.* Take advantage of store specials when you plan your family's menus. This requires checking store flyers ahead of time and then staying flexible while shopping. If you see a great deal, for instance, on ground turkey and you have ground beef on your list, consider substituting the turkey, assuming your family likes it. Then go beyond saving on that night's dinner by buying extra meat and freezing it.

  That's how Ruth shops. She says, "I buy meat seasonally and put it in the freezer. In the summertime, I always shop at the farmer's market. It's fresh and the price is better." Ruth also is on to some of the tricks supermarkets use to get us to spend more. "I watch the ad in the paper for groceries on sale. I try to make a list. But you go down the aisle, they set things out, that sometimes you don't really need. You think it's a sale, and you pick it up."

- *Warehouse Shopping.* You probably have heard of membership or warehouse clubs, those huge stores that buy everything in bulk and pass on the savings to members who pay a fee of $25 to $35 a year. You've wondered if they're worth the fee. The

BUY THE SEASON

Here is a month-by-month chart which tells you when the best bargains are available at outlet stores. In some cases, the same items are on sale in regular stores at surprisingly different times.

January
Lingerie, linens, fall and holiday women's clothes, Christmas supplies.

February
Fall and holiday women's clothes, red lingerie.

March
Wicker items, leotards and tights, silk flowers.

April
Silver, sleepwear, swimsuits, outdoor accessories.

May
Glassware, china, silver, sleepwear, swimsuits, outdoor accessories.

June
Summer and spring women's clothes, china, glassware, linens, swimsuits.

July
Women's underwear, summer and spring women's clothes, swimsuits, linens.

August
Children's clothes, women's underwear, swimsuits.

September
Children's clothes.

October
China, glassware, Christmas decorations.

November
Christmas decorations, linens china, glassware.

December
China, glassware.

answer is yes, and no. Yes, if you can use huge quantities of what you buy or split it with other families, if you prefer name brands to house or generic, if you have plenty of refrigerator, freezer, and cupboard space, if you can avoid impulse buys, and if you don't mind sore feet. You need to shop with a good knowledge of how much things cost in a regular store so you can compare. You also can't expect to do 100 percent of your grocery shopping in a warehouse store. The selection tends to be incomplete, and you'll probably have to stop by a regular store to find everything you need.

The best way to take advantage of these clubs is to buy only what you will use and not to assume the club's prices are cheaper across the board. Otherwise they are no bargain. On a recent trip to our local warehouse club, we were all set to buy a lot of seltzer for a party. Turned out the house brand at our regular supermarket was much less expensive than the name brand sold at a "bargain" at our club. Then there was the glue stick we needed. They came only in packages of 12. Well, it's going to take so long to use 12 glue sticks, we doubt that was a wise purchase. On the other hand, at least a glue stick lasts longer than 12 pounds of cheese!

- *Food storage*. Store food properly to make it last as long as it was meant to. We'd hate to think about all the infested flour and sprouted potatoes we could have avoided if we had paid more attention to where we kept them. Pay attention to freshness dates. It's no fun to open a gallon of almost-sour milk. It's worse to realize you're pouring almost three dollars down the drain!

Clothes

Many people have a closet full of clothes and nothing to wear. That's because the closet is filled with clothes that are shoddy in quality, unflattering, out-of-date, or for the wrong occasions. Do you find yourself constantly trying to buy an outfit for a certain event? Or on an endless quest to be dressed in the latest fashion? You can't win by buying this way, unless you're independently wealthy or have a personal shopper and a crystal ball. Thinking of clothes as an investment will prevent you from buying as many clothes as before.

GROCERY STORE GIMMICKS

Don't let any of the following tricks be your food budget's downfall:

- Making the price big and easy to read, while the unit price, or cost per unit of weight or volume, is hard to find.

- Putting products at the end of each aisle to make you think they are on sale when they are not.

- Placing staples such as bread or milk at the far end of the store so you have to trek through the tempting treats first.

- Limiting the quantity of a given product one customer may buy. These "limit three to a customer" signs make you think you *should* want more so you go ahead and buy the maximum even if you don't really need it.

- Using bakery aromas to entice you into buying more than you need.

- Locating big displays or frozen-food cases in awkward positions to make you slow down.

- Creating a relaxing mood with music, fresh flowers, and pleasant lighting to put you in a spending mood.

- Placing expensive convenience foods, such as puff pastry shells or bottled salad dressing, next to inexpensive seasonal items, such as fresh strawberries or lettuce.

- Last, but not least, is waiting on the check-out line, where you are tempted to throw candy, razor blades, gum, and magazines into your cart—at an average markup of a few hundred percent!

Our best tip on clothes *buying* is to stop right now. We don't mean you should run around in rags. We mean you should *invest* in your wardrobe rather than buy a dress here or a shirt there. We mean planning a wardrobe for the way you live, finding the best quality you can afford at the lowest possible price, and avoiding trendy fashion fads. Shopping for clothes with this mental approach will save you a lot of money in the long run. Follow these simple guidelines.

1. Establish a personal style that works well for you.

2. Stick with it. Refine it. Keep it simple.

3. Buy a few basic pieces of the highest quality. Make sure they fit perfectly. Then wear them over and over again. You'll always look well-dressed, your closet won't be crammed with "bargains" you never wear, and you'll spend less time shopping.

4. Buy only clothes that you can wear in more than one setting, with more than one other piece, and in more than one season. Avoid spending a lot on an outfit you will wear once a year or that doesn't match anything else you own.

5. Vary your look with lower-priced accessories.

6. Wait to replace worn parts of your wardrobe until the item goes on sale.

Doris has always applied these rules. She buys only clothes that don't seem to go out of style. "I can wear them one season to the other, one year to the next," she says. "I bought clothes on sale last spring for next fall. They had a good markdown. I plan ahead. I do a lot of mix and match."

Here are some tips to help you assemble your "investment portfolio" of clothes:

- *Buy for quality*. Quality over quantity in apparel is cheaper in the long run. Think of clothing on a cost-per-wear basis. If you buy a pair of shoes for $60 and wear them three times a week for three years, they've cost you only 12 cents each time you've worn them. If you buy a pair for $20 and they fall apart after two months, they've cost you almost a dollar for each time you've worn them. One may seem like a bargain, but the other is good value. Good value is what you want in clothes and everything you buy.

Don't be fooled into thinking that a designer label guarantees quality or that lower-priced clothes are necessarily poorly made. Many factors go into the quality and price of a given article of clothing. You always need to check a piece before you buy it. Look for small, even, straight stitches (unless it's a hand-sewn garment, which is a plus); flat seams with no puckering; roomy armholes and pockets; even dye; matching patterns at seams; and a good cut or drape.

One of our granddaughters recently bought a top-designer-label coat, thinking she'd get years of use from it to justify its cost. After wearing it through one season, the material had pilled, the lining had ripped out, and the buttons had fallen off. She would have been better off and $300 richer with a nondesigner coat.

- *Buy "on sale."* Avoid paying full price on clothes. Department stores have very high initial markups. Their "sale" prices are really like "regular" prices. We'd buy clothing from a department store only if it had been marked down. The markdown would represent the first true "sale" price. Betty says, "I don't pay full price for anything. If it isn't on sale, I don't buy it."

Take advantage of outlet stores and malls. They buy factory samples, overruns, or discontinued clothes and sell them at greatly reduced prices—20 to 70 percent off retail. The more expensive an item you are buying, the more incentive you have to shop the outlets.

- *Buy machine-washable.* Be mindful of dry-cleaning costs when you shop for clothes. If you have to wear business clothes every day and they all have to be dry-cleaned, you can easily spend more than a thousand dollars a year on this service. With more and more machine-washable linen and

BEARDSTOWN TALES

We try to find quality furniture. It's not the cheapest, but it's also not the most expensive. We want things that will last. If we could, we would spend a lot more time at auctions. I love the glasswork, I'm not opposed to something that's used, and we both love antiques. My husband refinishes furniture. Probably one of the nicest pieces we have is an antique walnut chest that we bought for $15. Bob refinished it. It has a mirror that turns around. It's beautiful. I wouldn't sell it for any amount of money.

BETTY SINNOCK

silk available, there is no reason to spend a fortune on dry cleaning.

Along the same lines, don't have clothes dry-cleaned when all they really need is to be pressed. Pressing not only costs less, your clothes will last longer with less exposure to harsh dry-cleaning chemicals.

Furniture

Buying quality furniture may or may not be important, depending on where and when you will use it. Consider whether you are buying furniture for function, furniture for aesthetic pleasure, or some combination of the two. If it's a sofa in your living room that you want to last for years, then by all means buy the best quality possible. If you have toddlers who might do permanent damage to a good piece of furniture, you might want to buy very inexpensive shelves for their rooms.

BEARDSTOWN TALES

I don't buy too much. I'm just satisfied with what I have. I do have to buy new drapes, which will be a large undertaking because the windows in my mobile home are real wide. When I buy something like that, it's a term investment. You have to look at them for a long time. I'm a very conservative shopper and I want to be satisfied. I don't want anything cheap. I've got good taste, but you don't always have the pocketbook for it. My family wants me to get new carpeting for my trailer, but the other isn't worn out. My daughter, Carol, says, "Mom, you might as well spend your money and enjoy it." I don't like to spend money on anything I don't need.

ELSIE SCHEER

Ann Corley and her husband always bought quality merchandise because it lasted longer and looked better longer. "I used to go into the furniture store and see something on the floor that I liked," Ann recalls. "The salesman would say, 'You don't want that.' It looked pretty to me, it would be bright and shiny. He'd say, 'Let me order you something.' So we would get good quality. The only thing is, you might get tired of something before it wears out."

Hazel's first furniture was a complete set of used pieces that the previous apartment dweller sold her for $40. She went on to buy other furniture, including her most memorable purchase: a rounded davenport. "My husband and I lived in a small house in Smithfield," Hazel explains. "I decided I wanted one of those, but the room was small and it was a mistake. It just didn't work out in the room like I had pictured it. But we used it. I wasn't sorry. My attitude was well, that's too bad. As my uncle used to say, 'We don't have to drink that kind of tea again.' Of course we had to sit on that davenport for a while."

When you're ready to buy your own davenport or whatever strikes your fancy, keep in mind the following:

- You can bargain with a furniture store staff member almost as much as with a car dealer. A high school history teacher we know was shopping for a dining room set. He found one on sale that he and his wife liked. But he still thought it was overpriced. He told the sales clerk it was over his budget and started walking out of the store. He hadn't gone far when the salesman tapped him on the shoulder and offered that set to him for $100 less.

- Furniture you assemble or finish yourself can be a real cost-saver. Not only that, you don't have to wait for weeks or months until it's delivered. If you enjoy that sort of project, it might be a good choice. Self-assembled furniture pieces are usually lower in quality than assembled furniture.

- Mixing very good quality pieces with flea-market finds can make the flea-market items look more like interesting antiques.

- Scotchguarding furniture is like rustproofing cars. You might not need it. Check the fabric label on the furniture to see whether it has been treated already.

- Display or floor models are sold at discounts. Stores don't usually advertise this fact, so if you see a couch you love in a display window, ask how much lower the salesperson can go on it.

- Don't assume you have to have a piece delivered. Delivery charges can add anywhere from $50 to hundreds of dollars. If you have a minivan or can borrow a pickup truck, would it be worth it to save the delivery fee?

- Always get a delivery date in writing. If that date comes and goes with no satisfactory, reasonable communication from the store or manufacturer, you have the right to ask for your money back. If you have any problem, contact your local better business bureau or consumer office.

- When a piece of furniture is delivered, check it carefully before you sign for it. If you see any scratches, missing parts, wrong upholstery, or other defects, ask the delivery person to take the item back. If the person won't do that, ask him or her to let you write "damaged goods" or "subject to inspection" on the bill and then have the person sign it as well. As soon as possible, call the store's customer service department and explain the situation.

Getting Down to Brass Tacks

1. Always make a list when you shop for more than one item.

2. Don't take for granted that brand names or designer labels guarantee quality. Consider lower-priced alternatives for good value.

3. Return anything that is not acceptable quality, whether it's food or furniture.

CHAPTER FOURTEEN

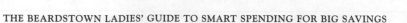

TIME WELL SPENT: THE VOLUNTEER HABIT

WE BEARDSTOWN LADIES FIRMLY BELIEVE that if life were *only* about saving and spending money, it wouldn't be worth living. We've been blessed with good health and just enough wealth to give time, money, and energy back to our community. From teaching Sunday school to teaching art, from 4-H to the three R's, among us we've been involved in every conceivable volunteer activity Beardstown needs. Varied as our activities are, we share a belief that whenever we volunteer, we get back far more than we give. In the hopes of inspiring more volunteerism among our readers, we've each picked a volunteer effort or two to describe for you.

Ann Brewer

When my children were growing up, I was involved with volunteering my services for the baseball program, Cub and Brownie groups, Boy and Girl Scouts, and school activities. I probably enjoyed helping out the organizations involving my children the most. Since they were active, it was fun.

These days, I get great enjoyment out of sharing a friendship with an older person who lives alone in the country. I try to check on her several times a week. This is a one-on-one situation and not a community project, strictly because I want to and because I care for her.

I am a deaconess in our church as well as treasurer of the Women's Fellowship. I try to help at church dinners (for fund-raising), rummage sales, etc. I try to save time for church volunteer activities. I have had to skip a few since the Beardstown Ladies have been so busy these past two years. Since my husband has retired, he is an active volunteer for both of us for Meals on Wheels.

Ann Corley

I have been secretary and treasurer of my United Methoist Church Circle. We have a regular business meeting at which we take minutes, give the treasurer's report, have a Bible lesson and refreshments. We take a collection and donate it to the United Methodist Women of which we are all members and then we decide how we want to spend the money. Helen Kramer, U.M.W. treasurer at the time, was one of our Beardstown Ladies Investment Club members. I was scholarship chairman of the hospital auxiliary for five years. The auxiliary gave scholarships to persons interested in a career in some medical field.

Doris Edwards

I'm the coordinator of religious education for the children, ages kindergarten through high school, of St. Alexius Catholic Church, of which I am a member. This involves scheduling of classes, registering students, setting up the class lists, ordering the books and supplies, and securing the teachers.

For people to know their religion, they need to study and become educated. There is much to be understood about one's religion by children and adults of all ages. I believe everyone should have a knowledge of their faith. Everyone has a conscience. Those who have had religious training seem to have a better understanding of right from wrong. They seem to make better choices in their conduct. Not only do we see it at school but in all walks of life.

In a Christian community, volunteers are always needed. For the past 25 years, I have felt comfortable volunteering for religious classes for my church, because it's an area in which I have some expertise.

Sylvia Gaushell

I was an art major in college. I've been drawing and painting ever since I was 12 years old. There are so many people who don't know anything about art. I wanted to help them. I used to have art classes in the Congregational Church basement. The first thing I would do with the little ones is say, 'How many of you have seen an elephant?' They'd all hold up their hands. And I'd say, 'Okay, draw one for me.' Well, some of them were a little nonplussed. They didn't know where to start, but it made them think. The older ones would bring their watercolor paints or chalk and I would give them lessons. They usually had an idea of what they wanted to draw or paint, so I'd try to tell them about primary colors, secondary colors, and tertiary colors. I'd try to acquaint them with all the colors. Teaching art was satisfying because I'd been doing it all my life.

Shirley Gross

I have been a Girl Scout leader and a Cub Scout den mother. I have served on the hospital board and Head Start board. At present, I am serving on the Beardstown Library board and I am a trustee of the Congregational Church, taking care of any stocks that are given to the church.

Margaret Houchins

I have been president of the Auxiliary at St. Luke's for eight years. It used to be a hospital. Now, it's a long-term care facility for developmentally disabled children and senior adults. We started quite a few programs at St. Luke's. When it was still a hospital and Cabbage Patch dolls were real popular, we did a Cabbage Patch clinic where little girls or boys brought their dolls. We had a nurse show how we would admit the doll to the hospital and what would happen. This would take the fear away from children going to the hospital. We started Adopt-a-Grandparent. We had children in the schools adopt an older patient. The grandparents who didn't have people visit them at least had little kids visit, bring them their report cards, and other things. That worked out great. We started the Carrier Watch program where we had post office carriers watch senior citizens' mailboxes. If the mail hadn't been picked up, then they were to alert the police. We've given scholarships to young people to further their education in the medical fields. We raised money to buy equipment and we remodeled all the rooms. That's been rewarding. We raised $10,000 for a special, streamlined tub. They lower patients in without having to touch them. $10,000 is a lot of money for a small community like this. I think to see everyone come together, to work hard to raise the money, to see the tub in use—it's a real sense of accomplishment.

Ruth Huston

I think that Meals on Wheels is a wonderful thing. Meals on Wheels is one of the most valuable things I do. These poor people who are shut in and can't get out, they're just happy to see a smiling face, someone to say hello. I do it through the Methodist Church and for the Business and Professional Women's Club. Helping someone always makes you feel good. I wish I could do more for people who can't do for themselves, but I have a hard time keeping up with everything. I do feel so guilty because I think maybe I've put me first, and I wish I could do more.

Carnell Korsmeyer

Rather than say there was one thing I was impassioned about, I guess my children influenced what I was doing while they were growing up. Both my husband and I taught Sunday School and were both 4-H leaders. We lived in a different era. Volunteering was more of an expected thing. It usually fell to women. Now women are so busy, it's hard for them to work that into their lives. I understand that. But we all take from society; we all have to give to society. Actually, in the big picture if you volunteer, that's a savings, too. Because if all those things are hired, that cost has to be passed on to the consumer in some way. I think anything you do, you get back. It's not all giving. You gain. You learn from others with whom you associate. And then, you're part of the bigger picture, which certainly provides satisfaction.

Hazel Lindahl

I spent a lot of time at our local Bread is Love. In different areas, it has different names. It's the noon program that the government sponsors and subsidizes. Anyone over 55 can eat with the senior citizens. The government would only hire one person, and if she didn't have volunteer help, the program would go down the drain. I helped serve and did the dishes. You felt like you were really helping somebody. I also belong to the Lutheran Women's Missionary League, a group of older women. We have a business meeting once a month and we contribute to helping a student preacher. We have a bake sale once a year. That money generally goes for some project in the church. Along with that, of course, you save your mite, it goes for missions. Since it's a national organization, they choose which churches or which missions we want to help.

Carol McCombs

I'm a huge 4-H supporter. My family has been involved in 4-H since before I was born. You could say I've been raised with 4-H. My brother and sister were in 4-H, my parents were leaders, my son was in 4-H, and my daughter is still an active member. We raise sheep for a 4-H project, then they are sold after the fair. Parents help kids with 4-H. My mother helped me. Now I'm helping my daughter. She'll probably in turn help her children someday. "Learn by doing" is the 4-H motto, and you do learn. You help them, they help you. There are all kinds of programs for youth aged 8 to 19. Dog care, cat care, computer projects. It's not strictly livestock, cooking, or sewing. It is for city kids and country kids. There are also school programs in which students become members for just a few weeks and learn to build rockets, about manners, etc. I'm active in the extension program and am a member of the county extension council. We are the administrators of the country program and the board sees that things operate in the proper manner.

My husband is president of our local Lions Club. It is an international organization which helps people with sight problems and blindness. They have programs in local communities to help people who can't afford glasses obtain them through an application program. We have a big fall festival in Beardstown in September where the Lions and a lot of other organizations have booths to raise funds for their groups. The club meets twice a month with a dinner before the meeting. This is a good way to get out, have fun, and help the community.

Elsie Scheer

I was a 4-H leader for over 30 years, teaching girls how to cook and sew and "learn by doing." The club would have as many as 15 girls or more each year. Years ago, when 4-H first started, there were mostly country boys and girls in the clubs, but now they include those living in the cities and urban areas, which has really made it grow.

4-H stands for Heart, Head, Hands, and Health, which has a lot of good training for children to learn from. Working with the girls was most satisfying, and I learned right along with them. They were required to give talks and demonstrations, and it was hard for them, but they received a lot of encouragement. I have found out just what they went through, now that I have to speak myself.

I saw three of my own children through 4-H, 10 grandchildren, and I have great-grandchildren who started this year.

I didn't spend any of my married life in the business world, except to keep the farm records. My years have been devoted to volunteering for 4-H, my church, and my community. Teaching four-year-olds in Sunday School has kept me familiar with the younger generation and helps me to stay active.

Betty Sinnock

I have taught Sunday school since I was in high school. I was a Brownie and Girl Scout leader and have volunteered for many things in our community. I have been active for 40 years in the American Heart Association. There had been a history of heart-related problems in our family so I was personally interested and found it was most gratifying. You're giving back. I probably got more than I ever gave to anybody through learning and friendships. I was treasurer in the Cass County Affiliate for over 30 years. When I moved to Mason County, I was secretary and later president of that affiliate office. As open-heart surgery and the bypasses were developed, we had doctors come from Springfield to share slides of what they were doing in surgery. The first time I saw them, I about lost my dinner, but I was glad that I knew what was going on. When my mother got a call that her brother had a 95 percent blockage and was going to have surgery, everyone was about to go to pieces. I could tell them that his problem wasn't something that couldn't be taken care of. I could even explain the surgery process. It was nice to know those things. I felt like we were making a contribution by being out there, collecting money, and being a part of the fund-raising for heart research. A heart specialist was at one of the first meetings that I attended. He told us that when he was in pre-med and they were opening up calves to operate on their hearts, he didn't realize that the money for those calves had come from the Heart Association. He was coming that night to thank us for providing those calves. The Heart Association started CPR training and provides education all over the world.

Maxine Thomas

I enjoy volunteering a great deal, after becoming a widow and then watching my youngest son fight cancer and pass away at an early age. I have been so very blessed by so many wonderful people, I know what a smile, a hug, a pat on the back, and "What can I do to help?" can mean—this is my "Thanks" and "Pass it on."

St. Luke's Health Care Center is a residential facility for disabled children and also senior adults. It is such a joy to see the children's faces when we fly kites, blow bubbles, or just wheel them outdoors to see nature. The same is true with the senior adults. I help our pastor with a church service and old familiar hymns sing-along.

For three years, I have served as a Long-Term Care Ombudsman, for a program with the Illinois Department of Aging. Ombudsman volunteer goals are to improve long-term care services, help resolve resident complaints, needs, and concerns, encourage them to speak for themselves, and help protect residents' rights.

I'm very active in the First Lutheran Church, having served two three-year terms on our church council. Our church volunteers make tapes and videos of our church services which we deliver to "shut-ins" and all of Beardstown's nursing homes.

I was a class leader for eight years with Explorers Bible Study until my eyesight began to fail. I still volunteer to help if I'm able. This is a great educational study of the Bible. Beardstown has a community choir of which I am a member, and I also sing in my church choir. Community choir performs several times a year including a Christmas Canata. All of this is so rewarding.

Buffy Tillitt-Pratt

I am on the Board of the Beardstown United Way and am active with my husband in volunteer work for Ducks Unlimited. I guess the most important volunteer work I do is that for the past 15 years I have played the organ at church. The church has to pay an organist for the other mass, so I like the idea that I am saving them money. Sometimes I wish I had accepted a check for playing the organ, then invested that money to be able to return the nest egg to the church when they had a major expense. It would have been fun to have seen if I could have helped more in that manner than in just playing the few chords.

Although it may not be considered strictly volunteer work, it has been rewarding doing the presentations for The Beardstown Ladies around the country. Almost every time someone (usually female) comes up to us afterwards and remarks, "I was afraid to invest, but now that I've seen you Ladies, I think I can do it." Whenever someone says something like that, I feel so thankful that we wrote the books.

YOUR LETTERS

DOING THESE BOOKS HAS BECOME VERY PERSONAL for all of us. We feel very proud each time a book is published and we hear from many of you. We get letters saying "You've really touched me. I'm going to start saving just a little bit." Thank you for taking the time to tell us. Writing these books has been an inspiration for us as well. In letters, phone calls, and in person, readers let us know what they think and what they want to know.

We have enjoyed reading our mail, and thought that others might like to see a sampling of the letters we receive. Here are some of our favorites.

Dear Doris:

I hope this letter finds you well. I read all you gals' book *The Beardstown Ladies' Stitch-in-Time Guide* and it is full of wonderful information. I am 38, married with two children. I have always been a saver of some sort. I would really like to invest in stocks or mutual funds, but when I call or write companies most of them want to start with $3,000, which I don't have. Do you know of any place I could get started at say, $250 minimum and $25 a month? Someone told me you could but I can't find the company that offers that. I wrote to you because you like to write letters. Could you ask your buddies? Maybe they can give me some names of companies. I really want to save for me and my family.

Good luck and much more success and happiness!!!! Can't wait to read the next book.

Sincerely,
Terri G. Spring
Salem, Virginia

Dear Elsie and Carol:

The only good reason for the long delay in writing to you, is my 80th birthday. I have been "celebrating" nonstop since I saw you and to tell you the truth, I am tuckered out. But I could not let another minute go by without writing to tell you what a treat you gave Rochester this past week. My phone was ringing when I got home, and I have had notes and calls all week telling me how much they enjoyed you!

And as for me, I never met two people I liked more on sight! You are just the most comfortable celebrities I have ever met. And I want to tell you right off that my CORN HUSK DOLL is my favorite gift! I wrapped her in tissue and put her in a little plastic bag, and I have taken her every place I have gone this week. I JUST LOVE HER. I call her Elsie, and she stands on my table, propped up against my little daily devotional book, and I see her first thing each day and last thing at night. She is my good luck charm. And when I tell people one of the Beardstown Ladies made her...well, they have more respect for me! She's just WONDERFUL! Thank you! I never had a corn husk doll before and I purposely didn't put her on my refrig because I wanted her closer to me when I sit down to eat. That was such a nice thing for you to do. I will always remember you.

We were so fortunate to have the only Mother-and-Daughter team as our guests. That made it super-special. You two work off each other so well as you give your presentation. You kind of toss the ball back and forth, in a completely relaxed, easy way. You are both such nice people to be with.

So thank you for the great send-off for my big week, and for being a completely charming, wonderful couple. I wish we could bring you back again...maybe after the next book, and we could have a cooking demonstration. That would be different, wouldn't it?

I am enclosing a copy of my introduction, in case you keep a file. I know Debbie plans to send you some things, too. Meanwhile, bless you and I hope you both have a happy year of storming the country for the Beardstown Ladies.

Happy Springtime,
Margaret Thirtle
Scottsville, New York

Dear Margaret:

Thank you so much for your delightful letter—little wonder you are so successful—your creative venture is most unique! I see a group of enterprising women surpassing the expectations of the world—my applause!!

Since you mentioned your Joliet visit March 15th to a Women's Expo, I've called the Chamber of Commerce, *Herald News*, both hospitals—these *have not* been informed of your coming to "Expo." Please do tell me where and when we might find you. Your books have a waiting list in our three libraries so you can be sure many will want to mark their calendars for your coming—you all have stirred up a terrific interest by your expertise.

WGN-TV morning news and News Time showed Ann and Carnell in their business-interest time. Who in the world would expect Carnell to know anything about hogs—she reminds me of someone I'd met at a P.E.O. gathering.

About to conclude when I got a call from Joliet Junior College—I mentioned this Expo—"Oh yes" was the reply—I nearly dropped. I shall spread the word—no need to reply but let me assure you this will be a spectacular event from what I'm told. I can hardly wait to meet you. Since I'm a member of the Alumni Board the activities hold a special interest for me. Thank you again for your thoughtful letter—the ides of March have just lost their meaning.

Sincere best wishes,
Clarice Engelman
Joliet, Illinois

Dear Ms. Edwards:

At 2:00 A.M. I finished your club's latest book. It's written—as was your first book—in such a down-to-earth manner. The fact that none of you put on airs makes your books so readable. Parlin Library in Canton has your videotape which we've watched several times. For two years (since we've retired) we've wanted to start an investment club, but have decided against it until we're settled in Indiana. That way we wouldn't have the problem of pulling out our shares.

I'm writing you for several reasons. First, we are retired teachers, and when I read that you have been teaching since 1942, I though, "Zowie." We went out with the 5/5 Plan and we love retirement! Second, I too, am a letter writer, and I agree with you: It does appear to be a lost art. For my last several years of teaching I had my students read the paper to find anniversaries, weddings, births, awards, etc. Then they wrote to that person and included the article along with a short report on a book they had read. You can't imagine the response we received! People sent letters, pencils, pens, candy, and pictures. The students could hardly wait for the mail! You know, I agree with Margaret Houchins that the years DO fly by, but hopefully, the students will remember how important it is to write letters.

I chuckled when I read about Ann Corley's $1 yard sale find of the dolphin-stemmed dish. For years I've bought clothes, furniture, greeting cards, etc., at a tremendous savings. In fact, both my children now practice the "art of yard sales" to buy for their homes and their growing children. Ruth Huston could probably find some pink items (her favorite color, and mine, too!), and Carnell Korsmeyer has received some pigs for her collection from some yard sales, I'd bet! I have a neighbor who has hundreds of elephants. Yet each summer I seem to find about 10 that she doesn't have (at yard sales, of course)!

I feel that I have something in common with each of you. Like Helen Kramer, I bake bread, and like Sylvia Gaushell, I quilt. I didn't learn to quilt until I retired, but it does get under your skin.

Shirley Gross paints to relax and to tune out her bad days while Carol McCombs dresses her lawn goose. Isn't it wonderful that we all have such unique interests?

Ron, my husband, watches me as I read and watch TV because, like Betty Sinnock's husband, he sees me cry and hears me laugh. People ask me all the time, "Aren't you bored with retirement?" My reply, "Who could ever be bored if one can read?"

My heart went out to Maxine Thomas when she was faced with blindness—only to know the joy of sight after surgery. Her thankfulness in giving back by volunteering was inspiring! I have a degree from ISNU (in '62 the word "Normal" was still included in Illinois State University!) in Special Ed—Blind. I'm enclosing a braille note I received from a former student.

Buffy Tillitt-Pratt is enjoying her son to the fullest. We, too, enjoyed our children, Tim age 29, head tennis coach at Purdue, and Anne Marie, 28, a stay-at-home mom of two little girls. Both of our children graduated from University of Wisconsin (of Madison). We traveled to Colorado several times each year, and like Elsie Scheer, we were thrilled to be going and never worried about a crash because when your time is up your time is up. Hazel Lindahl would be pleased to know that we both love airplane food because we don't have to cook it!

Ann Brewer said she would have killed her kids if they had married at age 18; at age 28 my son and his wife heard the story of my engagement after only two weeks of courtship. (We didn't get married for a year, though, and we've been married for 33 years) Tim said, "Why didn't I ever hear this before?" I replied that, although I was 21, I didn't want him to follow that lead.

I've enjoyed your tape, your books, and your down-home educational methods. Thank you for sharing your knowledge with us! I taped *20/20* and shared it with others!

In 1967 a man tried to sell us mutual funds. Unfortunately, we didn't buy. But within the last several years, we have tried to educate ourselves, and we now have stocks (after doing our homework!) and mutual funds. What an eye-opener it is to read about the business world.

Thanks again, Ms. Edwards, for helping ALL of us!

Kathy Madden
Lewiston, Illinois

Dear Shirley:

Having just read the story in *People* magazine about the Beardstown Ladies' Investment Club, I would like to congratulate you and your fellow members on the publication of your book. As an NAIC member, I am familiar with the great success that your club has enjoyed and was glad to see the recognition you have received.

Since 1990 I have been teaching Investing 101 to my junior high students, working in conjunction with Peter Lynch. During the past five years the Wall Street Wiz Kids have had many accomplishments. In January of this year we beat Peter in a year-long stock-picking contest sponsored by *USA Today*, and just recently we came in second in the "Dateline NBC" Challenge, beating NY stockbroker Frank Curzio.

With the investment background my students have received, I have high hopes that they are well on their way to planning for their financial future. And your club has shown them that investing is a lifelong pursuit that can, with hard work, reap big benefits.

Once again, the Wall Street Wiz Kids congratulate the Beardstown Ladies' Investment Club and hope that they will do as well when "real money" is involved.

Sincerely,
Joan K. Morrissey
Watertown, Massachusetts

Dear Ladies:

I would like to offer you my warmest congratulations both on your book, *The Beardstown Ladies' Common-Sense Investment Guide*, and on your success in investing.

I read about your club in the *Cleveland Plain Dealer* and saw you on television and I am frankly impressed by your enthusiasm and acumen. While I was treasurer of Ohio, for 12 years, and before that treasurer of Marion County, Ohio, I too enjoyed investing money. Now as treasurer of the United States, I also manufacture the money we all invest!

If any of you, either individually, or as a club, visits Washington, D.C., I would enjoy meeting with you. I find your success inspiring.

> Sincerely,
> Mary Ellen Withrow
> Treasurer of the United States

Well, there you have it. We surely do look forward to hearing from you, too!

> The Beardstown Ladies

WORKSHEETS

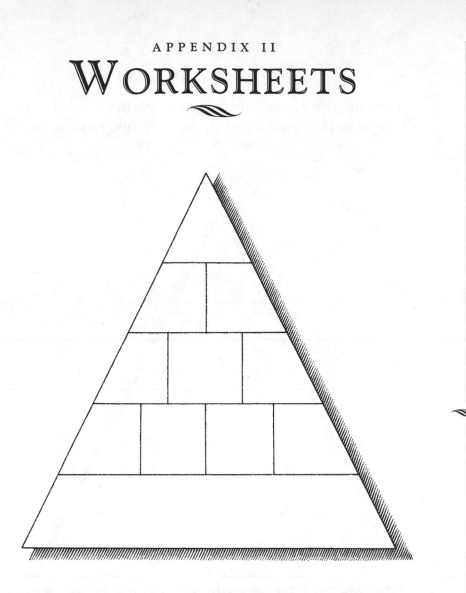

Your Spending Pyramid

Where do you spend most of your money? Fill in this pyramid with your largest actual expenses at the top.

Your Spending Pyramid

Where do you spend most of your money? Fill in this pyramid with your largest actual expenses at the top.

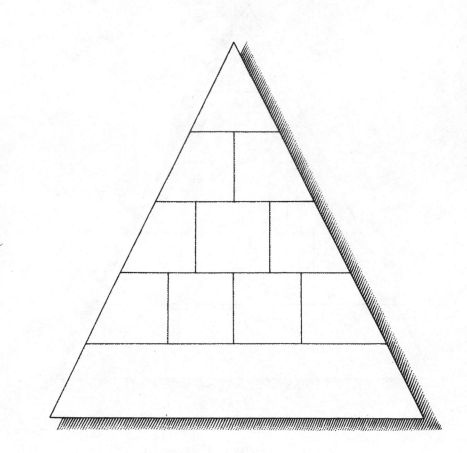

Your Priority Pyramid

Where would you like to be spending your money? Fill in this pyramid with your most important categories at the top.

Your Priority Pyramid

Where would you like to be spending your money? Fill in this pyramid with your most important categories at the top.

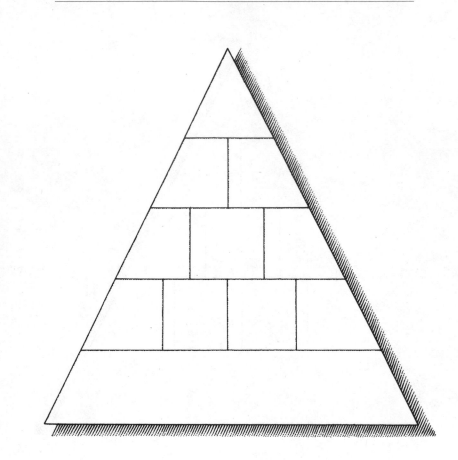

WORKSHEET

MORTGAGE REFINANCING

Here is a sample worksheet to help you calculate how long before you realize savings from refinancing.

1. Present principal and interest payments on $ _____
at _____ % interest: _____

2. Proposed principal and interest payments on
$ _____ at _____ % interest: _____

3. Subtract Line 2 from Line 1 for your monthly savings: _____

4. Total closing costs from Bank Disclosure Statement: _____

5. Amount of interest included in Bank Disclosure Statement: _____

6. Subtract Line 5 from Line 4 for actual closing cost: _____

Actual closing cost (Line 6): _____
Divided by monthly savings (Line 3): _____

Equals number of months before you start
saving after refinancing: _____

WORSHEET

PROPERTY TAX ASSESSMENT REDUCTION REQUEST

Assessment Subject _____

Address _____

Assessment # of Subject _____

Name of Owner _____

	ASSESSMENT	÷	SQUARE FEET IN HOUSE	=	ASSESSED VALUE
Subject	$_____	÷	_____	=	$_____
COMPARABLE ASSESSMENTS					
Comp #1	$_____		_____		$_____
Comp #2	$_____		_____		$_____
Comp #3	$_____		_____		$_____

Average of three assessments = $_____ per square foot

Request assessment for _____ at ____ assessed valuation based on square feet in subject and average assessment per square foot.

RESOURCES WE RECOMMEND

CHAPTER TWO: HOUSE-PROUD AND HOME FREE

ORGANIZATIONS

AMERICAN HOMEOWNERS
ASSOCIATION
1801 Westport Road
Kansas City, MO 64111
800-822-3215
A fee entitles members to: early mortgage payoff analysis; free CAP advice; materials on topics from roofing to remodeling; newsletter; environmental testing kit at cost.

CONSUMER FEDERATION OF AMERICA
1424 16th Street, NW
Suite 604
Washington, DC 20036
202-387-6121
A nonprofit public interest group which represents and lobbies for legislation on behalf of consumers.

COUNSELORS OF REAL ESTATE
430 N. Michigan Avenue
Chicago, IL 60611
312-329-8427
For names of real estate counselors, who for a fee, will provide expert, experienced advisory services, such as litigation support, asset management, valuation, feasibility studies, and general analysis.

FANNIE MAE (FEDERAL NATIONAL
MORTGAGE ASSOCIATION)
3900 Wisconsin Avenue, NW
Washington, DC 20016
800-7-FANNIE
For mortgage investing information.

NATIONAL ASSOCIATION OF EXCLUSIVE
BUYER AGENTS
7652 Gartner Road
Suite 500
Evergreen, CO 80439
800-986-2322
An independent alliance of real estate professionals. Will provide names, addresses, and phone numbers of exclusive real estate brokers (agents whose companies do not accept seller-property listings).

NATIONAL ASSOCIATION OF HOME
BUILDERS
1201 15th Street, NW
Washington, DC 20005
202-822-0200
For home-building information and educational materials.

NATIONAL COUNCIL FOR STATE
HOUSING AGENCIES
444 North Capital Street, NW
Suite 438
Washington, DC 20001
202-624-7710
Lobbies for affordable housing for first-time home buyers.

U. S. DEPARTMENT OF HOUSING AND
URBAN DEVELOPMENT
Program Information Center
451 7th Street, SW
Room 1104
Washington, DC 20410
202-708-0700
For HUD publications and information; also provides Notifications of Funding Availability for HUD programs.

PUBLICATIONS

A Good Place to Live; A Guide to Settlement Costs; A Home of Your Own: The HUD Homebuying Guide; Finance Manufactured Homes; Home Buyer's Vocabulary; Should You Rent or Buy a Home
U.S. DEPARTMENT OF HOUSING AND URBAN DEVELOPMENT
451 7th Street, SW
Washington, DC 20410
800-767-7468

The Banker's Secret by Marc Eisenson.
New York: Good Advice Press, 1989.

Buying a Home: What Buyers and Sellers Need to Know About Real Estate Agents
Published jointly by the American Association of Retired Persons and the Consumer Federation of America.

AMERICAN ASSOCIATION OF RETIRED PERSONS
601 E Street, NW
Washington, DC 20049
202-434-2277

CONSUMER FEDERATION OF AMERICA
1424 16th Street, NW
Suite 604
Washington, DC 20036
202-387-6121

Consumers Guide to Mortgage Settlement Costs
FEDERAL RESERVE SYSTEM
Publications Services
Mail Stop-127
Washington, DC 20551
202-452-3244

Land Buying Checklist; Production Checklist
NATIONAL ASSOCIATION OF HOME BUILDERS
1201 15th Street, NW
Washington, DC 20005
202-822-0200

What Should I Know Before I Buy a House?
CALIFORNIA BAR ASSOCIATION
555 Franklin Street
San Francisco, CA 94102
415-561-8200

SERVICES AND HOTLINES

APPRAISAL INSTITUTE
875 N. Michigan Avenue
Suite 2400
Chicago, IL 60611
312-335-4458
For free information about appraisals.

BUYER'S AGENT, INC.
1255 Lynnfield Street
Suite 273
Memphis, TN 38119
800-766-8728
This office represents buyers on a fee or commission basis; there are over 50 locations in 26 states.

BUYER'S RESOURCE REAL ESTATE
6099 S. Quebec Street
Suite 200
Englewood, CO 80111
800-359-4092
Will provide listings of exclusive brokers free of charge.

COMPUTER LOAN NETWORK
2944 Hunter Mill Road
Suite 203
Oakton, VA 22124
800-816-2870
Provides a free service which allows home owners and realtors to post loan requests on the Internet for access by local, regional, and national lenders. Computer Loan Network receives a fee from the lender if the loan is successful.

HSH Associates
1200 Route 23
Butler, NJ 07405
800-873-2837
For a fee, this office will send a list of rates, terms, and fees of 25 to 50 lenders in your area.

Chapter Three:
Saving on Auto
Spending

ORGANIZATIONS

The Center for Auto Safety
2001 Street, NW
Suite 410
Washington, DC 20009
202-328-7700
Consumer advocate group that monitors the automobile industry and automobile safety in an effort to heighten government and consumer awareness.

Consumer Information Center
PO Box 100
Pueblo, CO 81009
719-948-3334
Provides information and materials relating to the automobile industry.

Greater NY Automobile Dealers
Association
18-10 Whitestone Expressway
Whitestone, NY 11357
718-746-5900
Trade association representing new car dealers.

Office of the Comptroller of
Currency
250 E Street, SW
Washington, DC 20219
202-622-2000
For complaints if you lease from a financial institution.

PUBLICATIONS

Automotive News
Crain Communications, Inc.
800-678-9595
A weekly trade journal available at newsstands, bookstores, and most libraries.

The Car Book: The Definitive Buyer's Guide to Car Safety, Fuel Economy, Maintenance and More by Jack Gillis. New York, Harper, 1993.
Available in bookstores or from the Center for Auto Safety.

Consumer Reports Annual Auto Issue
Consumers Union
914-378-2000
Published each April; available at libraries, newsstands, or from Consumers Union.

How to Buy a Car; a Former Car Salesman Tells All by James R. Ross. New York: St. Martin's Press, 1992.

The Kelley Blue Book Used Car Guide. California: Publishers Group West, 1996.

The Lemon Book: Auto Rights for New and Used Cars by Ralph Nader and Clarence Ditlow. Mount Kisco, NY: Moyer Bell Limited, 1990.

National Automobile Dealers Association (NADA) Official Used Car Guide
National Automobile Dealers
Association
800-544-3123
Published monthly; available at libraries, newsstands, or directly from National Automobile Dealers Association.

New Car Buying Guide; Buying a Used Car
Consumer Information Center
PO Box 100
Pueblo, CO 81009
719-948-3334

Shopping for a Safer Car
INSURANCE INSTITUTE FOR HIGHWAY
SAFETY
PO Box 1420
Arlington, VA 22210
703-247-1500

Used Car Book: The Definitive Guide to
Buying a Safe, Reliable, and Economical
Used Car by Jack Gillis. New York:
Harper Perennial, 1993.

SERVICES AND HOTLINES

AMERICA ONLINE
keyword: CHECKBOOK
Computerized auto buying service.

AUTO INSIDER
800-446-7433
Auto buying service.

CARBARGAINS
800-475-7283
Auto buying service.

CONSUMER REPORTS NEW CAR PRICE
SERVICE
800-933-7700
Will print out a list of retail and wholesale prices of a car, its various options,
and current offers.

CONSUMER REPORTS USED CAR PRICE
SERVICE
900-446-0500
Touch-tone phone is required. Price
information on 1987-1995 used vehicles
only.

CREDIT UNION NATIONAL
ASSOCIATION
800-358-5710
For referrals to credit unions in your
area.

THE KIDNEY CARS PROGRAM
800-488-CARS
800-488-2277
Through this program you can donate
your old car to help raise money for
organ transplant patients.

LEMON LAW HOTLINE
800-771-7755
Connects you with the local Attorney
General's Office.

THE U.S. DEPARTMENT OF
TRANSPORTATION AUTO SAFETY
HOTLINE
800-424-9393
The National Highway Traffic Safety
Administration.

CHAPTER FOUR:
HOW TO MAKE
APPLIANCES
WORK FOR YOU

ORGANIZATIONS

BETTER BUSINESS BUREAU
800-877-3152
The regional offices take consumer complaints.

THE ELECTRONICS INDUSTRIES
ASSOCIATION CONSUMER ELECTRONICS
GROUP
2500 Wilson Boulevard
Arlington, VA 22201
703-907-7500
Trade association representing different
electrical product manufacturers. A division of EIA available for consumer questions and complaints.

PUBLICATIONS

Consumer Guide to Finding Reputable
Service Companies
THE PROFESSIONAL SERVICE
ASSOCIATION
71 Columbia Street
Cohoes, NY 12047
518-237-7777

Extended Warranty Service Contracts:
Good or Bad?; Getting Good Service for
Electronic Equipment; Consumer
Complaint Checklist for Electronic
Equipment Repair
THE NATIONAL ELECTRONICS SERVICE
ASSOCIATION
2708 West Berry Street
Fort Worth, TX 76109
817-921-9061

Service Contracts; Warranties
FEDERAL TRADE COMMISSION
Public Reference Branch
6th and Pennsylvania Avenues
Suite 130
Washington, DC 20580
202-326-2222

The Wholesale-by-Mail Catalog
HarperCollins
PO Box 588
Dunmore, PA 18512
800-331-3761

SERVICES AND HOTLINES

APPLIANCE CLINIC
http://www.phoenix.net/~drapline/

APPLIANCE CONSUMER CONNECTION
http://www.appliance.com/app/con-
sumer.htm

THE CONSUMER ELECTRONICS
CYBERSPACE COMPANION
http://w3.the group.net/~cema/

CONSUMERS UNION
Dept. DY
101 Truman Avenue
Yonkers, NY 10703
914-378-2000
Provides you with a free worksheet for
cooling-capacity estimates.

FRIGIDAIRE CUSTOMER SERVICE
800-451-7007

GENERAL ELECTRIC CUSTOMER
SERVICE
800-626-2000

KENMORE CUSTOMER SERVICE
Contact a local Sears store.

MAYTAG CUSTOMER SERVICE
800-688-9900

PHILIPS CUSTOMER SERVICE
800-531-0039

SEARS CUSTOMER SERVICE
847-286-5188

WHIRLPOOL CUSTOMER SERVICE
800-253-1301

CHAPTER FIVE:
THE INSURED LIFE

ORGANIZATIONS

FEDERAL DEPOSIT INSURANCE
CORPORATION
Office of Consumer Programs
550 17th Street, NW
Washington, DC 20552
202-393-8400
Provides insurance information.

NATIONAL ASSOCIATION OF
INSURANCE COMMISSIONERS
444 North Capitol Street, NW
Suite 701
Washington, DC 20001
202-624-7790
Oversees and gives support to state insur-
ance regulators. Can direct consumers if
they need help in that area.

PUBLICATIONS

Guide to Health Insurance for People
with Medicare; Nine Ways to Lower
Your Auto Insurance Costs; Twelve
Ways to Lower Your Home Insurance
Costs; What You Should Know About
Buying Life Insurance
CONSUMER INFORMATION CENTER
PO Box 100
Pueblo, CO 81002
719-948-3334

Product Report: Life Insurance for
Older Adults
AMERICAN ASSOCIATION OF
RETIRED PERSONS
601 E Street, NW
Washington, DC 20049
202-434-2277

SERVICES AND HOTLINES

EQUIFAX
800-456-6004
Will provide you with a copy of your
C.L.U.E. (Comprehensive Loss
Underwriting Exchange) Report. This
contains your claim history and information about any claims placed against your
policy over the last five years.

INSURANCE INFORMATION, INC.
23 Route 134
South Dennis, MA 02660
800-472-5800
For a fee, will provide quotes on five low-
est-price term life policies suited to your
needs.

INSURANCE INFORMATION INSTITUTE
110 William Street
New York, NY 10038
800-331-9146
For general insurance questions.

INSURANCEQUOTE SERVICES, INC.
3200 North Dobson Road
Building C
Chandler, AZ 85224
800-972-1104
Free service that provides five of the low-
est-cost term life insurance plans in the
U.S.

JACK WHITE & CO. INSURANCE DEPT.
9191 Towne Centre Drive
Suite 220
San Diego, CA 92122
800-622-3699
Provides quotes on life insurance companies best suited to your needs.

NATIONAL INSURANCE CONSUMER
HELPLINE
800-942-4242
For general insurance questions.

QUOTESMITH CORPORATION
8205 South Coff Avenue
Suite 102
Darien, IL 60561
800-556-9393
Offers a free insurance price comparison
service.

SELECTQUOTE INSURANCE SERVICES
800-343-1985
Term life insurance broker that provides
lowest cost comparison best suited to a
customer's insurance needs.

TERMQUOTE
800-444-TERM (8376)
Offers quotes for lowest term life
insurance.

THE WHOLESALE INSURANCE
NETWORK
800-808-5810
Offers quotes for low-load policies.

INSURANCE COMPANY RATING FIRMS

A.M. BEST COMPANY
Ambest Road
Oldwick, NJ 08858
908-439-2200

DUFF & PHELPS CREDIT RATING
COMPANY
55 East Monroe Street
Chicago, IL 60603
312-368 3157

MOODY'S INVESTORS SERVICE
99 Church Street
New York, NY 10007
212-553 0300

STANDARD & POOR'S CORPORATION
25 Broadway
New York, NY 10007
212-425-2606

WEISS RESEARCH, INC.
PO Box 2923
West Palm Beach, FL 33402
561-627-3300

CHAPTER SIX:
UTILIZE YOUR UTILITIES

ORGANIZATIONS

AMERICAN SOLAR ENERGY SOCIETY
2400 Central Avenue
Unit G-1
Boulder, CO 80301
303-443-3130
Nonprofit membership group representing companies that deal with and individuals who are interested in solar and renewable energy.

THE ENERGY EFFICIENCY AND
RENEWABLE ENERGY CLEARINGHOUSE
PO Box 3048
Merrifield, VA 22116
800-363-3732
Provides literature on energy efficiency and renewable energy technology.

NEW YORK PUBLIC INTEREST
RESEARCH GROUP
9 Murray Street
New York, NY 10007
212-349-6460
Watchdog organization that represents a variety of consumer groups.

PUBLICATIONS

The Consumer Guide to Home Energy Savings by Alex Wilson and John Morrill (also available at bookstores); *The Most Energy-Efficient Appliances; Saving Energy and Money with Home Appliances; Publications Catalog*
THE AMERICAN COUNCIL FOR AN
ENERGY-EFFICIENT ECONOMY
2140 Shattuck Avenue
Suite 202
Berkeley, CA 94704
510-549-9914

Cooling Your Home Naturally; Energy-Efficient Windows
CONSUMER INFORMATION CENTER
PO Box 100
Pueblo, CO 81002
719-948-3334

Energy-Efficient and Environmental Landscaping
APPROPRIATE SOLUTION PRESS
Dover Road, Box 39
South Newfane, VT 05351
802-348-7441

Mother Earth News
Sussex Publishers
PO Box 56302
Boulder, CO 80322
800-234-3368
Also available at libraries, bookstores, and newsstands.

SERVICES AND HOTLINES

CONSUMER HOME ENERGY EFFICIENCY
RATING SYSTEM
800-4-CHEERS (800 -424-3377)
A nonprofit corporation that will determine the energy-efficiency of your home and advise you about how to save on your utility bills.

DEPARTMENT OF ENERGY'S
CONSERVATION AND RENEWABLE
ENERGY INQUIRY AND REFERRAL
SERVICE (CAREIRS)
800-523-2929

CHAPTER SEVEN:
BANK ON THIS

ORGANIZATIONS

BOARD OF GOVERNORS OF THE
FEDERAL RESERVE SYSTEM CONSUMER
AND COMMUNITY AFFAIRS
20th and C Streets, NW
Washington, DC 20551
202-452-3000
Writes and amends consumer laws and examines state member banks for violations of and compliance with these laws. Also administers a community outreach program through a Community Affairs Officer at each Federal Reserve Bank nationwide.

COMPTROLLER OF THE CURRENCY
Compliance Management
U.S. Department of the Treasury
250 E Street, SW
Washington, DC 20219
202-622-2000

CREDIT UNION NATIONAL
ASSOCIATION
PO Box 431
Madison, WI 53701
800-358-5710

FEDERAL DEPOSIT INSURANCE
CORPORATION
Division of Consumer Compliance
and Consumer Affairs
550 17th Street, NW
Washington, DC 20552
202-942-3100
800-934-3342
For information on deposit insurance, how to obtain financial reports on FDIC institutions, and foreclosure.

HOUSE COMMITTEE ON BANKING,
FINANCE, AND URBAN AFFAIRS
2129 Rayburn Office Building
Washington, DC 20515
202-224-3121

THE NATIONAL FOUNDATION FOR
CONSUMER CREDIT
800-388-2227
Has regional offices that offer credit counseling.

OFFICE OF THRIFT SUPERVISION
CONSUMER AFFAIRS
1700 G Street, NW
Washington, DC 20552
800-842-6929
Will take banking complaints when you can't get results dealing with a bank's branch manager.

STATE BANKING AUTHORITIES
National Center for Financial
Education
PO Box 34070
San Diego, CA 92163
619-232-8811

PUBLICATIONS

The Banker's Secret Quarterly
800-255-0899.
Newsletter explaining benefits of early payment on consumer loans.

Making Sense of Savings; Choosing and Using Credit Cards; Consumer Handbook to Credit Protection Laws; How to Dispute Credit Report Errors; Shop...The Card You Pick Can Save You Money; 66 Ways to Save Money
CONSUMER INFORMATION CENTER
PO Box 100
Pueblo, CO 81009
719-948-3334

Questions and Answers About Your Insured Deposits
FEDERAL DEPOSIT INSURANCE CORPORATION
Office of Consumer Programs
550 17th Street, NW, Room F-130
Washington, DC 20429
202-393-8400
800-934-3342
Also available at most banks.

SERVICES AND HOTLINES

BANK RATE MONITOR
407-627-7330
Low-interest-rate credit cards.

BANXQUOTE ONLINE
100 Passaic Avenue
1st Floor South
Fairfield, NJ 07004
800-765-3000
Will provide CD rates.

CARDTRAK
RAM Research
Box 1700
Frederick, MD 21702
301-695-4660
Will provide complete information on low-interest, no-fee, and gold credit cards currently available.

CHECKFREE
PO Box 2168
Columbus, OH 43216
800-882-5280
Complete information on a plan to pay bills electronically.

CHECKS IN THE MAIL
800-733-4443
For low-cost checks.

CURRENT, INC.
800-533-3973
For low-cost checks.

EQUIFAX CREDIT INFO SERVICE
PO Box 105873
Atlanta, GA 30348
800-685-1111
Will provide you with a free credit report.

FDIC PUBLIC INFORMATION CENTER
801 17th Street, NW
202-416-7358
Washington, DC 20434
Provides reports on financial institutions, including press releases and customer testimonials.

TRW
PO Box 8030
Layton, UT 84041
800-392-1122
Will provide you with a free credit report.

VERIBANC
PO Box 461
Wakefield, MA 01880
800-442-2657
Rates banks on financial soundness.

CHAPTER EIGHT:
TAX BREAKS FOR ORDINARY PEOPLE

ORGANIZATIONS

AMERICAN INSTITUTE OF CERTIFIED PUBLIC ACCOUNTANTS
1211 Avenue of the Americas
New York, NY 10036
212-596-6200
For a free list of CPAs in your area, ask for product G00616.

NATIONAL ASSOCIATION OF
ENROLLED AGENTS
200 Orchard Ridge Drive
Suite 302
Gaithersberg, MD 20878
800-424-4339
301-212-9608
*Professional membership organization
that represents and promotes enrolled
agents. Enrolled agents are tax practition-
ers who are required to maintain their
credentials through continuing education
reported to the IRS.*

PUBLICATIONS

Ernst & Young Tax Guide
John Wiley & Sons
1 Wiley Drive
Somerset, NJ 08875
800-225-5945
Also available at bookstores and libraries.

*Guide to Free Tax Service; Your Federal
Income Tax; Your Rights as a Taxpayer*
INTERNAL REVENUE SERVICE
4300 Carolina Avenue
Richmond, VA 23222
800-829-3676

J. K. Lasser's Income Tax Guide
201 West 103 Street
Indianapolis, IN 46290
800-858-7674
Also available at bookstores and libraries.

SERVICES

VITA (VOLUNTEER INCOME TAX
ASSISTANCE)
Internal Revenue Service
1111 Constitution Avenue, NW
Washington, DC 20224
202-283-0195
*Free volunteer tax assistance. Call for the
phone number of the center in your area.*

CHAPTER NINE:
FIRST-CLASS TRAVEL
AT HALF THE PRICE

ORGANIZATIONS

AMERICAN AUTOMOBILE ASSOCIATION
(AAA)
1415 Kellum Place
Garden City, NY 11530
800-222-4357
*Offers benefits to members including
emergency road service, personal trip
planners, travel discounts, and loan/leas-
ing options.*

AMERICAN HOTEL & MOTEL
ASSOCIATION
1201 New York Avenue NW
Suite 600
Washington, DC 20005
202-289-3100
*Trade association that represents and lob-
bies for the lodging industry. Information,
research, and magazine available for
members.*

AMERICAN SOCIETY OF TRAVEL
AGENTS (ASTA)
1101 King Street
Alexandria, VA 22314
703-739-2782
*Trade association that represents travel
agents and those who service the travel
industry.*

COUNCIL ON INTERNATIONAL
EDUCATIONAL EXCHANGE
205 E. 42nd Street
New York, NY 10017
212-822-2600
*Offers three International Identity cards
for young travelers (especially those
working or studying abroad), that provide
eligibility for discounts on transportation,
accommodations, attractions, and sick-
ness, accident, life, and emergency medical insurance.*

HOSTELING INTERNATIONAL-
AMERICAN YOUTH HOSTELS
733 15th Street, NW
Suite 840
Washington, DC 20005
202-783-6161
*International nonprofit organization that
provides lists of 5,000 hostels in over 70
countries. Services available to both
members and nonmembers, although discount hostel rates are available to members, as well as publications, brochures,
and maps.*

NATIONAL TOUR ASSOCIATION
Consumer Protection
546 E. Main Street
Lexington, KY 40508
800-682-8886
*To register complaints about tour
providers who are members of the NTA.*

OFFICE OF CONSUMER AFFAIRS
U.S. Department of Transportation
Aviation Consumer Division
C75
Washington, DC 20590
202-366-2220
To register recorded complaints by phone.

U.S. TOUR OPERATORS ASSOCIATION
211 E. 51st Street
Suite 12B
New York, NY 10022
212-750-7371
*To register complaints about tour
providers who are members of the
USTOA.*

PUBLICATIONS

Best Fares
1301 South Bowen Road
Suite 490
Arlington, TX 76013
800-635-3033

Budget Lodging Guide
CAMPUS TRAVEL SERVICE
Box 5486
Fullerton, CA 92635
714-525-6683

A Consumer's Guide to Renting a Car
McCool Communications
PO Box 13005
Atlanta, GA 30324
404-814-1936

*Consumer's Guide to Resort and
Urban Timesharing*
AMERICAN RESORT DEVELOPMENT
ASSOCIATION
1220 L Street, NW
Suite 500
Washington, DC 20005
202-371-6700

*Consumer Reports Travel Buying Guide;
Consumer Reports Travel Letter*
CONSUMER REPORTS BOOKS
SUBSCRIPTION DEPT.
PO Box 53629
Boulder, CO 80322
800-234-1970
Also available at bookstores.

Facts and Advice for Airline Passengers
AVIATION CONSUMER ACTION PROJECT
PO Box 19029
Washington, DC 20036
202-638-4000

Frequent Flyer
2000 Clearwater Drive
Oak Brook, IL 60521
800-323-3537

Guide to Vacation Rentals in Europe,
By Michael and Laura Murphy
Old Saybrook, CT: Globe Pequot
Press, 1994.

InsideFlyer
4715 Town Center Drive
Suite C
Colorado Springs, CO 80916
800-333-5937

The Insider's Guide to Air Courier Bargains by Kelly Monaghan
New York: Intrepid Traveler, 1996.

Small Hotel Directory
TRAVEL SMART
40 Beechdale Rd.
Dobbs Ferry, NY 10522
800-327-3633

Travel Discounts Newsletters
PO Box 3396
Carmel-by-the-Sea, CA 93921
408-626-1212

World-Wide Home Rental Guide
3501 Indian School Road, NE
Suite 303
Albuquerque, NM 87106
505-255-4271

SERVICES AND HOTLINES

ACCOMMODATIONS EXPRESS
801 Asbury Avenue
Ocean City, NJ 68226
800-444-7666
Discount hotel reservation service.

AMERICAN AIRLINES
http://www.americanair.com/

AMTRAK
60 Massachusetts Avenue, NE
Washington, DC 20002
800-USA-RAIL

COURIER TRAVEL
516-763-6898
For low airfares.

ENCORE
4501 Forbes Boulevard
Lanham, MD 20706
800-638-8976
Comprehensive travel savings club which, for an annual fee, offers discounts at 4,000 hotels, motels, and resorts, and 300 restaurants around the world. Also available are discounts on car rentals, airfares, tours, cruises, and theme parks.

ENTERTAINMENT PUBLICATIONS
300 West Schrock Road
Westerville, OH 43081
800-477-3234
For discount hotel and resort services.

FREEFLIER
Bowling Green Station
PO Box 844
New York, NY 10274
212-727-9675
For a small fee, Freeflier will enroll you in over 20 frequent-travel programs, including auto rental upgrades and complimentary lodging.

GREAT AMERICAN TRAVELER
PO Box 26573
Salt Lake City, UT 84127
800-548-2812
Offers 50% discounts at moderately priced hotels for an annual fee.

HOME LINK & VACATION EXCHANGE CLUB
PO Box 650
Key West, FL 33041
800-638-3841
International home-exchange service which, for a fee, will help you arrange a vacation.

HOTEL RESERVATIONS NETWORK
800-634-6835
http://www.hoteldiscount.com
Discount hotel reservation service.

INTERVAC U.S. INTERNATIONAL AND
U.S. HOME EXCHANGE
30 Corte San Fernando
Tiburon, CA 94920
415-435-3497
email: IntervacUS@aol.com
*International home-exchange service
which, for a fee, will help you arrange a
vacation.*

INVENTED CITY HOME EXCHANGE
41 Sutter Street
Suite 1090
San Francisco, CA 94104
800-788-2489
415-252-1141
Fax: 415-252-1171
E-mail: invented@aol.com
*A domestic and international home-
exchange service.*

LOAN-A-HOME
7 McGregor Road
Woods Hole, MA 02543
508-548-4032
*International home-exchange service
which, for a fee, will help you arrange a
vacation. Specializes in long-term
exchanges.*

NOW VOYAGER
74 Varick Street
New York, NY 10003
212-431-1616
*Offers very low airfares for couriers will-
ing to make do with just one carry-on
bag, measuring no more than 9"x 14" x
22". Although the luggage compartments
on these flights are generally used to carry
freight, occasionally you will be permitted
to check a bag through.*

QUEST INTERNATIONAL CORPORATION
402 East Yakima Avenue
Suite 1200
Yakima, Washington 98901
800-560-4100
800-638-9819
*Offers discounts for members of up to
50% at over 2,000 hotels; 25% discounts at restaurants nationwide; and
airline and cruise discounts. A relatively
high membership fee makes this a better
bet for the frequent traveler.*

QUIKBOOK
381 Park Avenue South
New York, NY 10016
800-789-9887
*Discount hotel reservation service for
hotels in Atlanta, Boston, Chicago, Los
Angeles, New York, San Francisco, and
Washington, DC.*

RENT-A-WRECK
800-535-1391
For low-cost rental cars.

SOUTHWEST
http://www.iflyswa.com/

TWA
http://www.twa.com/

UGLY DUCKLING
800-843-3825
For low-cost rental cars.

UNITED AIRLINES
http://www.ual.com/

U SAVE
800-272-8728
For low-cost rental cars.

USAIR
http://www.usair.com/

CHAPTER TEN:
How to Love Your Children for Less

ORGANIZATIONS

CHILD CARE ACTION CAMPAIGN
330 Seventh Avenue
New York, NY 10001
212-239-0138
A nonprofit advocacy group that promotes quality child care. Publishes a newsletter and other reports.

NATIONAL ASSOCIATION FOR FAMILY CHILD CARE
206 Sixth Avenue
Suite 900
Des Moines, IA 50309
515-282-8192
A national membership organization working with the more than 400 state and local family child care provider associations in the United States to promote quality family child care through accreditation and to promote training and leadership development through specialized technical assistance.

NATIONAL CHILD CARE ASSOCIATION
1029 Railroad Street
Conyers, GA 30207
800-543-7161
A professional trade association representing the private, licensed early childhood care and education community. NCCA has a dual advocacy for quality, affordable child care as well as the child care business.

NATIONAL CHILD CARE
INFORMATION CENTER
301 Maple Avenue West
Suite 602
Vienna, VA 22180
800-616-2242
Fax: 800-716-2242
http://ericps.ed/uiuc.edu/nccic/
nccichcme.html
Promotes child care linkages and supports quality, comprehensive services for children and families through dissemination of information, publication of the Child Care Bulletin, *collection of data, and online Internet access.*

NATIONAL HEAD START ASSOCIATION
1651 Prince Street
Alexandria, VA 22314
703-739-0875
Fax: 703-739-0878
Helps to meet the needs of all people involved in the Head Start community, including directors, parents, staff members, and agencies.

PUBLICATIONS

Bunting and Lyon Blue Book
BUNTING AND LYON
238 N. Main Street
Wallingford, CT 06492
203-269-3333
Annual directory of private schools in the U.S. and abroad.

Employer Tax Credit: Assets or Liability; Child Care Primer; Liability Insurance and Child Care
CHILD CARE ACTION CAMPAIGN
330 Seventh Avenue
New York, NY 10001
212-239-0138

Free Money For College by Laurie Blum. New York: Facts on File, 1994.

Fund Your Way Through College by Debra Kirby. Detroit, Michigan: Visible Ink, 1994.

Guide to the College Admission Process
NATIONAL ASSOCIATION OF COLLEGE
ADMISSION OFFICES
1631 Prince Street
Alexandria, VA 22314
703-836-2222

Peterson's Guide to Four-Year Colleges; Peterson's Guides to Graduate Programs (six volumes arranged by area of specialty); *Peterson's Guide to Two-Year Colleges*
PETERSON'S
PO Box 2123
Princeton, NJ 08543
609-243-9111

A Practical Guide for Parents: Advertising, Nutrition, and Kids; Self Regulatory Guidelines for Children's Advertising
THE CHILDREN'S ADVERTISING REVIEW
UNIT OF THE BETTER BUSINESS
BUREAU
845 Third Avenue
New York, NY 10022
212-705-0114

The Scholarship Book by Daniel Cassidy. Canada: Prentice Hall, 1996.

You Can Afford College, Kaplan Books. New York: Simon & Schuster, 1997.

Zillions
101 Truman Avenue
Yonkers, NY 10703
914-378-2000
The Consumer Reports *magazine for kids and their families.*

SERVICES AND HOTLINES

AMERICAN COUNCIL OF NANNY
SCHOOLS
c/o Joy Shelton
A-74
Delta College
University Center, MI 48710
517-686-9417
Nonprofit coalition of accredited nanny schools. Will provide listings of nanny agencies and training programs nationwide.

CHILD CARE AWARE
2116 Campus Drive NE
Rochester, MN 55904
800-424-2246
Will provide information on family day care anywhere in the country, including tips on choosing child care, referral agencies, and classes available for child care providers.

EDUCATION RESOURCES INSTITUTE
(TERI)
800-245-8374

KNIGHT TUITION PAYMENT
PLAN (ABLE)
800-225-6783

NATIONAL ASSOCIATION FOR
CHILDCARE RESOURCE AND REFERRAL
AGENCIES
1319 F Street, NW
Suite 810
Washington, DC 20004
800-570-4543
A membership association that promotes the growth and development of quality child care resources and referral services.

NELLIE MAE (EXCEL)
800-634-9308

CHAPTER ELEVEN:
YOUR HEALTH:
PHYSICAL AND FISCAL

ORGANIZATIONS

AMERICAN ASSOCIATION OF
RETIRED PERSONS
601 E Street, NW
Washington, DC 20049
202-434-2277
*A small fee entitles members to Modern
Maturity, a bimonthly magazine, and
discounts on many products and services,
including a group hospitalization plan,
Medicare supplement, and benefits of leg-
islative and consumer advocacy.*

JOINT COMMISSION ON THE
ACCREDITATION OF HEALTHCARE
ORGANIZATIONS
One Renaissance Boulevard
Oakbrook Terrace, IL 60181
708-916-5600
*Evaluates and accredits more than
14,000 health care organizations in the
U.S. The Joint Commission has developed state-of-the-art standards and evaluates the compliance of the health care
organizations against them. Current
accreditation status of an organization is
available to the public on request.*

PUBLICATIONS

Better Health Care for Less
by Neil Schulman. New York, NY:
Hippocrene Books, 1993.

Consumer Reports on Health
PO Box 52148
Boulder, CO 80322
800-234-1645

Directory of Medical Specialists. New
Providence, NJ: Marquis, 1991
*Check here to see if your doctor is board
certified; available in most libraries.*

*Directory of Physicians in the U.S., 35th
edition (4 volume set).*
Chicago, IL: American Medical
Association, 1996.
*Lists over 700,000 doctors across the
country; available in libraries and book-
stores and can be ordered from the
American Medical Association.*

The Health Robbers by Stephen Barrett
and William Jarvis. Amherst, NY:
Prometheus Books, 1993.

Long-Term Care Insurance Buyers Guide
NATIONAL ASSOCIATION OF
INSURANCE COMMISSIONERS
120 West 12th Street
Suite 1100
Kansas City, MO 64105
816-842-3600

Medical Records: Getting Yours by The
Public Citizen's Health Research
Group Staff. Washington, DC: Public
Citizen Health Research Group, 1992.

*150 Ways to Be a Savvy Medical
Consumer* by Charles B. Inlander, and
the staff of People's Medical Society.
Allentown, PA: People's Medical
Society, 1992.

Physician's Desk Reference, (PDR)
Montvale, NJ: Medical Economics
Data Production Company, 1995
Available at most libraries.

The Rights of Patients
AMERICAN CIVIL LIBERTIES UNION
PO 186
Wye Mills, MD 21679
800-775-ACLU

*Take This Book to the Hospital With
You: A Consumer Guide to Surviving
Your Hospital Stay* by Charles B.
Inlander. Allentown, PA: People's
Medical Society, 1993.

SERVICES AND HOTLINES

AARP PHARMACY
800-456-2277
An affordable mail-order service that offers nonprescription and prescription drugs. Available to members and non-members of American Association of Retired Persons. Call for the location nearest you.

ACTION PHARMACY
PO Box 787
Waterville, ME 04903
800-452-1976
Sells low-priced prescription and nonprescription drugs through the mail; will send catalogs and quote prices through the mail.

AMERICAN BOARD OF MEDICAL SPECIALTIES
47 Perimeter Center East
Altanta, GA 30346
800-776-CERT (2378)
Will tell you if your doctor is board-certified, the year of certification, and the specialty.

AMERICAN MEDICAL ASSOCIATION'S PHYSICIAN DATA SERVICES
515 North State Street
Chicago, IL 60610
312-464-5000
Will confirm your physician's education, specialty, and location of practice.

CHILDREN OF AGING PARENTS
1609 Woodbourne Roard
Suite 302A
Levittown, PA 19057
215-345-5104
National resource and referral organization for caregivers of the elderly. Offers supports groups to adult children of aging parents.

MEDI-MAIL
PO Box 98520
Las Vegas, NV 89193
800-922-3444
Sells low-priced prescription and nonprescription drugs through the mail; will send catalogs and quote prices through the mail.

NATIONAL ASSOCIATION OF AREA AGENCIES ON AGING
1112 16th Street, NW
Washington, DC 20036
800-677-1116
A nationwide organization dedicated to helping family and friends find information and services for older people. The "Eldercare Locator" will point you towards government agencies and service providers in your area.

CHAPTER TWELVE:
THE TIMES OF YOUR LIFE

ORGANIZATIONS

FUNERAL AND MEMORIAL SOCIETIES OF AMERICA
PO Box 10
Hinesburg, VT 05461
800-765-0107
Monitors funeral industry for consumers. Will provide information about local memorial societies in your area.

FUNERAL SERVICE CONSUMER ASSISTANCE
2250 East Devon Avenue
Suite 250
Des Plaines, IL 60018
800-662-7666
Offers general consumer assistance with funeral planning problems.

NATIONAL FUNERAL DIRECTORS
ASSOCIATION
PO Box 27641
Milwaukee, WI 53227
414-541-2500
*The world's largest organization repre-
senting funeral professionals.*

PUBLICATIONS

The Bridal Registry Book by Leah
Ingram. Chicago, IL: Contemporary
Books, 1995.

Caskets and Burial Vaults
FEDERAL TRADE COMMISSION
6th and Pennsylvania
Avenue, NW
Washington, DC 20580
Attn: Public Reference Room 130
202-326-2222

*Dealing Creatively with Death: A
Manual of Death Education and Simple
Burial* by Ernest Morgan. Bayside, NY:
Excelsior Music Publishing Co., 1994.
*Final Celebrations: A Personal and
Family Funeral Planning Guide* by
Kathleen Sublett and Marty Flagg. San
Bernardino, CA: Borgo Press, 1992.

Final Details
AMERICAN ASSOCIATION OF
RETIRED PERSONS
601 E Street, NW
Washington, DC 20049
202-434-2277

SERVICES AND HOTLINES

DISCOUNT BRIDAL SERVICE
800-874-8794
*Personal buying service for brides; offers
discounts on invitations and nationally
advertised bridal gowns.*

CHAPTER THIRTEEN
SHOPPING FOR
EVERYTHING ELSE

ORGANIZATIONS

CONSUMER FEDERATION OF AMERICA
1424 16th Street, NW
Suite 604
Washington, DC
202-397-6121

CONSUMERS UNION
101 Truman Avenue
Yonkers, NY 10703
914-378-2000

FEDERAL TRADE COMMISSION
HEADQUARTERS
6th Street and Pennsylvania
Avenue, NW
Washington, DC 20580
202-326-2222

BRANCH LOCATIONS:
1718 Peachtree Street, NW
Suite 1000
Atlanta, GA 30367
404-347-4836

101 Merrimack Street
Suite 810
Boston, MA 02114
617-424-5960

55 East Monroe Street
Chicago, IL 60603
312-353-4423

668 Euclid Avenue
Cleveland, OH 44114
216-522-4207

100 N. Central Expressway
Suite 500
Dallas, TX 75201
214-767-5501

1405 Curtis Street
Denver, CO 80294
303-844-2271

11000 Wilshire Boulevard
Los Angeles, CA 90024
310-235-7575

150 William Street
New York, NY 10038
212-264-1207

901 Market Street
San Francisco, CA 94103
415-356-5270

2806 Federal Building
915 Second Avenue
Seattle, WA 98174
206-220-6350

DEPT. OF HOUSING AND URBAN
DEVELOPMENT
451 7th Street, SW
Room 9266
Washington, DC 20410
202-4708-1422

PUBLICATIONS

The Book of Inside Information by the editors and experts of *The Bottom Line*. Greenwich, CT: Boardroom Books, revised annually.

Consumers Digest; Guide to Federal Government Sales; How You Can Buy Used Federal Personal Property; U.S. Real Property Sales List
CONSUMER INFORMATION CENTER
PO Box 100
Pueblo, CO 81002
719-948-3334

Consumer Reports Magazine; The Bottom Line/Personal
SUBSCRIPTION SERVICE CENTER
PO Box 50379
Boulder, CO 80323

Consumers Research Magazine
CONSUMERS RESEARCH INC.
800 Maryland Avenue NE
Washington, DC 20022
202-546-1713

Cut Your Spending in Half Without Settling For Less, by the Editors of Rodale Press. Emmaus, PA: Rodale Press, Inc. 1994.

Joy of Outlet Shopping
VALUE RETAIL NEWS
PO Box 17129
Clearwater, FL 34624
800-344-6397
For information on outlet stores.

Kiplinger's Personal Finance
1729 H Street, NW
Washington, DC 20006
202-887-6400
Fax: 202-331-1206

Money
Time Inc.
1271 Avenue of the Americas
Rockefeller Center
New York, NY 10020
212-522-1212
Fax: 212-522-0189

SmartMoney
1790 Broadway
New York, NY 10019
212-649-3766

INDEX

Accountants, 30, 40, 134, 139-142
CPAs, 141, 267; enrolled agents,
268; fees, 141; how to get the
most from, 141
Advertising, 1
Air conditioners, 78, 80, 107, 114
Air travel, 151, 270
consolidators, 152; couriers, 155,
270, 271; discounts, 152, 156;
"fare wars", 152; frequent-flier
programs, 129, 153, 154, 158,
164, 270; low-fare search programs, 151, 152; no-frills airlines, 152; refunds, 152; travel
agents, 151; travel savings clubs,
270, 271
Allstate, 90
A.M. Best 97
American Association of Retired
Persons (AARP), 51
AARP Pharmacy, 275; advocacy,
274; discount hotel rates, 163;
funeral information, 276; life
insurance, 264; medical insurance, 274

American Automobile Association
(AAA), 130
discount hotel rates, 163, 165;
diagnostic test center, 59; emergency road service, 268; hotel
ratings, 161
American Cancer Society, 203
American Heart Association, 242
American Red Cross, 203
American Society of Heating,
Refrigeration, and Air-
Conditioning Engineers, 109
Annuities, 137
Appliances, 4
air conditioners, 78, 80, 107,
114; brand names, 67; compari-
son shopping, 70; consumer
complaints, 262; *Consumer
Reports*, 67, 75; discounts, 70;
dishwashers, 77, 82, 107, 114;
dryers, 69, 78, 74, 82, 115; ener-
gy efficiency, 71, 82, 105, 265;
EnergyGuide label, 71, 73;
Estate, 68; floor models, 70;
Frigidaire, 68, 263; General
Electric, 68, 263; Gibson, 68;
Hotpoint, 68; Jenn-Air, 68;

Kelvinator, 68; KitchenAid, 68; lawn mowers, 69; life-cycle costs, 79; Magic Chef, 68; Magnavox, 68; markups, 69; Matsushita, 68; Maytag, 68, 263; microwave ovens, 114; Montgomery Ward, 68; Norge, 68; online information, 67, 263; owner's manual, 82; Panasonic, 68; 263; Prism, 68; Quasar, 68; RCA, 68; refrigerators, 69, 71, 75, 114, 115; repairs, 74, 80, 82; Roper, 68; Sears, 68, 263; service, 263; service contracts, 72, 263; shopping tips, 75-78, 80; stoves, 70, 76; Tappan, 68; toaster ovens, 114; VCRs, 70; warranties, 19, 72, 74, 75, 82, 84, 263; washing machines, 20, 68, 76; Whirlpool, 68, 263; White-Westinghouse, 68

Appraisers, 37, 260

Attic fans, 113

Auctions, 233

Automated Teller Machines (ATMs), 119, 120, 131

Automobiles, 3, 5
American Automobile Association (AAA), 59, 268; base price of, 53; Buick, 48, 51; Buyer's Guide sticker, 58; buying new, 46, 47, 49-53, 262; buying services, 262; buying used, 2, 17, 46, 49, 56-59, 262; Cadillac, 48, 49; Chevrolet, 57; *Consumer Reports*, 51, 52; dealers, 261; dealer sticker price, 53; demonstrators, 57; donating used, 262; Edmunds' New Car Prices, 52; *Edmunds' Used Car Guide*, 52; expenses, 10; financing, 54, 59, 262; Ford, 56; insurance, 62, 85, 87, 88, 97-101, 130; invoice price, 53; leasing, 61-64, 261; Taurus, 56; Lincoln, 49, 50, 56; Mercury, 49; Monroney sticker, 53; National Automobile Dealer's Association, 100; Oldsmobile, 52; options, 54;

owner's manual, 58; Pontiac, 49, 51; pre-owned, 56, 63; rental, 269-271; Rolls-Royce, 16; safety, 261; selling your car, 52, 54; service records, 58; test driving, 58; Toyota, 49; warranties, 56, 58, 60, 63

Baby equipment, 177

Banks
401(k) plans, 136; ATMs, 119-122, 124; average daily balance, 123; certificates of deposit, 121, 123, 267; checking accounts, 119, 120, 122-124, 131, 132, 267; choosing, 118; club accounts, 120; complaints about, 266; debit cards, 131; direct deposit, 124; electronic banking, 267; insured deposits, 266, 267; interest rates, 118, 119, 123; IRAs, 132, 135-138; Keoghs, 135, 138; loans, 123, 266; minimum balances, 119, 123; money market deposits, 121; mortgage, 30; night deposits, 125; NSF, 122, 124; overdrafts, 122-124; safe deposit boxes, 128, 144; savings accounts, 119, 121, 123, 267; service charges, 118, 119, 124; statements, 9, 118

Bar mitzvahs, 211
choosing a place, 214, 224; clothing, 217, 224; food and drink, 214, 224; flowers, 216, 224

Beardstown Ladies' Common-Sense Investment Guide, 184

Beardstown Ladies' Investment Club, 251

Beardstown Ladies' Stitch-in-Time Guide to Growing Your Nest Egg, 2

Bed-and-breakfasts, 168

Best Western, 161

Bonds, 19

Brewer, Ann, 46, 50, 59, 67, 86, 98, 124, 125, 143, 237, 249

Brokerage firms
    IRAs, 132, 135, 136; no-bank
    banking, 131
Buick, 48, 51

Cadillac, 48, 49
Central Illinois Public Service
Company, 106
Certificates of deposit, 121, 123,
138, 267
Checking accounts, 119, 120, 122-
124, 131, 132
Child care, 174, 194, 272
    classes for providers, 273; types
    of, 175; nannies, 273; referral
    agencies, 273; ways to reduce
    cost of, 175
Christenings, 211
    choosing a place, 212; clothing,
    217; food and drink, 214, flow-
    ers, 216
Classes and lessons for children,
179, 180
Cleveland Plain Dealer, 251
Clothes, 10, 230
    designer labels, 232, 236; factory
    samples, 233; markups, 233; out-
    lets, 233; overruns, 233; plan-
    ning a wardrobe, 231
Colleges, 19, 43, 272
    accelerated degrees, 192; admis-
    sion process, 273; choosing, 180;
    cost of, 181-184; Federal
    Methodology Analysis, 188;
    grants, 9, 189, 190; investing for,
    184-187, 194; junior or commu-
    nity, 192, 273; loans, 184, 189-
    191; pre-paid tuition plans, 186;
    saving for, 180, 184; scholar-
    ships, 184, 191, 192, 273; work-
    study, 188
Comfort Inn, 162
Consumer complaints, 269
    appliances, 82; sample letter to a
    manufacturer, 81

Consumer Reports, 277
    appliances, 67, 75; automobiles,
    51, 52; health care, 274; travel,

269; *Zillions*, 273
Corley, Ann, 4, 10-12, 35, 55, 59, 70,
74, 90, 101, 110, 157, 234, 238, 248
Costs
    calculating, 19
Courtyard by Mariott, 162
Credit, 16
    counseling, 266; protection laws,
    267; rating, 31; reports, 267
Credit cards 9, 13, 132, 267
    annual fees, 126, 127; annual
    percentage rate (APR), 125-127,
    131; credit limits, 127; emer-
    gency roadside help, 130; fre-
    quent flier miles, 129, 153, 154,
    158; gold cards, 267; insurance,
    130; loss of, 130, 131; lost lug-
    gage assistance, 130; low-interest
    rate, 267; MasterCard, 126; no-
    fee, 267; price protection, 129;
    purchase protection, 129;
    rebates, 130; rental car collision
    damage waivers,129; travel acci-
    dent insurance, 129; Visa, 128
Credit unions, 118, 266

Debt, 2, 13, 17
Diapers, 176
Dishwashers, 77, 82, 107, 114
Disney resorts, 164
Doctors, 197, 208
    certification of, 274, 275; fees, 199;
    directory of, 274; government ser-
    vices, 201; medical records, 274;
    medical research, 201; office visits,
    198; patients' rights, 274; phone
    consultations, 200; second opin-
    ions, 199; surgery, 199; tests, 198,
    202
Dry-cleaning, 233, 234
Dryers, 68, 78, 82, 115

Edmunds' New Car Prices, 52
Edmunds' Used Car Guide, 52

Education, 9
    college, 19, 43, 180-194
Edwards, Doris, 15, 23, 46, 51, 55,
57, 59, 125, 126, 135, 150, 166,

211, 232, 238, 245, 248, 249
Elder care, 275
Elderhostel, 168
Emergency road service, 268
Emergency rooms, 197
Energy efficiency, 71, 82, 105, 265, 266
  energy audits, 107, 116; Energy
  Guide label, 71, 73;
Estate, 68
Exercise, 207
Expenses
  monthly, 10

Farm Business Farm Management
Association, 140
Farmers Home Administration, 38
Federal Housing Administration, 38
Federal Trade Commission, 58
  appliance service contracts and
  warranties, 263; branches, 276;
  Funeral Rule, 220
Fireplaces, 115
Food, 227
  brand names, 236; cost per unit,
  231; generic brands, 228; grocery
  store gimmicks, 231; impulse
  purchases, 227, 230; shopping
  lists, 227; storage, 230; store specials, 228; warehouse clubs, 228,
  230
Frequent-flier programs, 129, 153,
154, 158, 164
Frigidaire, 68
Funerals, 218
  burial plots, 221; burial vaults,
  276; caskets, 218-221, 276;
  cemeteries, 221; clergy, 221;
  consumer assistance, 275; cost-
  saving tips, 221; cremation, 222;
  embalming, 221; federal regulations, 220; flowers, 219, 221;
  graveside ceremonies, 221, 222;
  legal documentation fees, 221;
  limousines, 221; memorial booklets and programs, 221; memorial services, 222; obituary notices,
  221; pre-payment of, 222; Social
  Security, 221; pallbearers, 221;
  tombstones, 221; transportation

of the body, 221; U.S.
  Department of Veterans Affairs,
  221; weekday services, 222
Furnaces, 110
Furniture, 10, 233, 234
  bargaining, 235; defects, 236;
  deliveries, 235, 236; floor models, 235; unassembled, 235;
  unfinished, 235

Gaushell, Sylvia, 11, 12, 48, 49,
106, 125, 181, 239, 248
General Electric, 68
Gibson, 68
Gross, Shirley, 10, 15, 26, 57, 59,
88, 91, 134, 139, 144, 180, 190,
211, 219, 220, 239, 248, 251

H&R Block, 139
Health care, 274
Heat pumps, 110
Holiday Inn, 161
Home building and construction, 259
Home equity loans, 126, 186
Home exchanges, 168
Hospices, 203
Hospitals, 201
  bills, 202, 203, 208; check-in,
  check-out, 203; emergency
  rooms, 197; food, 204; insur-
  ance, 203; outpatient surgery,
  199, 201; patients' rights, 274;
  terminal illness, 203; tests, 198,
  202; bringing your own supplies,
  204
Hostels, 168, 269
Hotels
  advance reservations, 162; Best
  Western, 161; Comfort Inn, 162;
  consolidators, 165; Courtyard by
  Marriott, 162, 164; discount
  reservation services, 270, 271;
  Disney resorts, 164; Holiday
  Inn, 161; La Quinta, 162; rates,
  163-165; ratings, 161; *Official
  Hotel Guide*, 161; Motel 6, 162;
  small, 270; toll-free numbers,
  163; travel savings clubs, 270
Hotpoint, 68

Hot water heater, 111
Houchins, Margaret, 12, 27, 43, 50, 57, 66, 68, 120, 125, 128, 213, 216, 217, 239, 247, 248
Huston, Ruth, 11, 27, 46, 57, 95, 108, 125, 150, 158, 228, 240, 248

Income, 10
    tax, 25
IRAs, 132, 135, 136, 142, 186
Insulation, 108
    R-value, 108, 109
Insurance, 4, 7, 9, 10, 17, 31, 264, 265
    Allstate, 90; A.M. Best, 97, 265; annuities, 137, 138, 186; auto-mobile, 62, 87, 85, 88, 97-101, 130, 264; claim adjusters, 103; claims, 264; credit, 61; credit card, 130; deductibles, 87, 98, 100, 103, 104; direct-response companies, 89; disability, 61; discounts, 90, 97, 103; earth-quake, 101; home owner's 85, 86, 131; Farmers Home Administration, 38; Federal Housing Admin-istration, 38; fire, 92; flood, 101; group policies, 89, 96; health, 100, 200, 264; home owner's, 37, 39, 86, 87, 101-103, 264; how to buy policies, 88; independent agents, 88-90; individual plans, 89; interest-adjusted net cost index, 95; life, 19, 61, 86, 91-97, 120, 185, 264; low-load policies, 265; medical, 203, 274; Moody's Investors Services, 97, 265; mortgage, 30, 38; National Insurance Consumer Organization, 96; no-fault, 98; no-load policies, 96; premiums, 89, 92-94, 96, 99, 100, 103, 203; ratings, 96, 97, 265; rental cars, 159; riders, 96; shopping for, 86, 89; Standard & Poor's, 97; travel accident, 129; U.S. Department of Veterans Affairs, 38

Interest rates, 25
    mortgage, 19, 30, 31
Internal Revenue Service, 138, 139, 144, 145, 268
Investing
    mortgage, 259; municipal bonds, 18; mutual funds, 18; stocks, 18

Jenn-Air, 68

Keoghs, 135, 138
Kelvinator, 68
KitchenAid, 68
Korsmeyer, Carnell, 6, 9, 48, 49, 54, 69, 89, 92, 107, 109, 110, 118, 119, 125, 126, 132, 133, 140, 144, 182, 210-212, 214, 215, 219, 220, 240, 248
Kramer, Helen, 219, 238, 248

La Quinta, 162
Lawn mowers, 69
Lawyers, 30, 144
    appraising your property, 37; real estate closing, 39; tax, 141
Leukemia Society of America, 203
Lightbulbs, 106, 115
Lincoln, 49, 50
Lindahl, Hazel, 11, 13, 57, 59, 86, 125, 126, 191, 234, 235, 240, 249
Lynch, Peter, 250

Magic Chef, 68
Marriott, 162, 164
MasterCard, 125
Matsushita, 68
Maytag, 68
McCombs, Carol, 28, 46, 74, 80, 87, 88, 91, 92, 101-103, 125, 140, 143, 192, 221, 241, 246, 248
Medication, 198, 204
    brand-name, 205, 206; buying in bulk, 205; chain drugstores, 204; free samples, 205; generic, 205, 206, 208; mail-order, 204, 275; *Physician's Desk Reference*, 274
Mercury, 49
Merrill Lynch, 131
Michelin Guide hotel ratings, 161

Microsoft, 181
Microwave ovens, 114
Money market acounts, 121, 131
Montgomery Ward, 68
Moody's Investors Services, 97
Mortgages, 11, 23, 24, 86, 260, 261
    banker, 30; biweekly, 35; closing
    costs, 39, 260; Fannie Mae, 259;
    interest rates, 19, 24, 31, 33, 40,
    43, 44; term, 31, 33; payments,
    30, 32; points, 31, 34, 39; pre-
    approved, 28, 30; pre-payments,
    31, 144, 259; refinancing, 40, 41,
    43, 44, 257
Motel 6, 162
Municipal bonds, 18
Mutual funds, 4, 18
    college funds, 184; IRAs, 132,
    135, 136; Keoghs, 138; tax-sav-
    ing strategy, 135

National Automobile Dealer's
Association, 100
National Insurance Consumer
Organization, 96
Norge, 68

Oldsmobile, 52
Owner's manuals
    appliances, 82; automobile, 58

Panasonic, 68
Paychecks
    automatic deductions from, 4
Pell grants, 189, 190
Pension plans, 137, 186
People Magazine, 250
Perkins student loans, 190
Pontiac, 49, 51
Preventive medicine, 207
Prism, 68
Property tax, 21, 22, 35-38
Pyramids
    Personal Priority, 15, 18-20, 255,
    256; Spending, 8, 15, 20, 253,
    254

Quasar, 68
RCA, 68

Real estate, 4, 9
    agents, 37, 44, 260; appraisals,
    260; buyer's brokers, 29, 44, 259,
    260; buying and selling without
    real estate agents, 28, 43, 44; clos-
    ing costs, 39, 260; down pay-
    ments, 25, 26, 38; estate sales, 27;
    Federal Housing Administration,
    38; foreclosures, 27; insurance,
    37, 39; mortgages, 11, 30, 40, 41,
    43, 44, 259-261; motivated sell-
    ers, 27, 28; negotiating, 7; owning
    your home, 21; selling checklist,
    42; taxes, 35-38
Refrigerators, 69, 71, 75, 105, 114, 115
Renewable energy, 265, 266
Rental cars, 157
    additional drivers, 159; cancella-
    tion fees, 160; discounts, 158; drop-
    off charges, 160; free upgrades, 157;
    insurance, 159, 169; unlimited free
    mileage, 159
Renting your home, 25
Retirement
    plans, 132, 135-138, 142, 186;
    Retirement Plans for the Self-
    Employed, 138; savings, 2, 9, 46
Retreats, 169
Rolls-Royce, 16
Roper, 68

Savings accounts, 119, 121, 123
Scheer, Elsie, 51, 59, 80, 130, 140,
218, 219, 234, 242, 246, 249
Schools, 21
    college, 19, 43, 180-194, 272;
    private, 22, 272
Schwab, 131
Sears, 17, 68
Shopping, 2, 226
    bargain-hunting, 12; buying in
    bulk, 226; comparison, 5, 13;
    impulse, 12, 24, 226; lists, 226,
    236; outlets, 233, 277; profile, 12,
    14; returning merchandise, 226,
    236; seasonal sales, 226; toll-free
    customer service numbers, 227
Simplified Employee Pension Plans
(SEPs), 138

Sinnock, Betty, 11, 12, 49, 52, 74, 86, 88, 105, 112, 122, 126, 130, 136, 150, 151, 162, 163, 185, 233, 242, 249
Social Security, 91, 142
Solar energy, 265
Spending, 1
  emotion-based, 5, 24; paying cash up-front, 16; Pyramid, 8, 15, 20, 253-256; rules, 16
Stafford student loans, 190
Standard & Poor's, 97
Stocks, 19
  college funds, 184; funds, 9; common, 18
Stoves, 70, 76
Supplemental Educational Opportunity Grant (SEOG), 189
Supply and demand, 16
Surgery, 199
  emergency, 199; getting a second opinion, 199; outpatient, 199, 201

Tappan, 68
Taurus, 56
Taxes, 10
  401(k) plans, 136, 186; accountants, 139-142; annuities, 137; assistance with, 268; audits, 134, 143-145; deductions, 61, 133, 134, 142-144, 145, 146; estate, 91; estimated, 135, 140,142; federal, 135; forms, 139, 142; guides, 268; income, 25, 133, 185, 268; Internal Revenue Service, 138, 139, 144, 145, 268; IRAs, 133, 135, 136, 142; Keoghs, 135, 138; laws, 141; lawyers, 141; loopholes, 141; penalties, 135; preparers, 139-142, 144; property 21, 22; real estate, 31, 35; records, 141, 144; refunds, 133, 134, 140, 144; returns, 142, 145; SEPs, 138; state, 135; tax-deferred retirement savings plans, 135, 146; taxpayer rights, 268; tax-shelters 134, 142; withholding, 134, 146
Thermostats, 111

Thomas, Maxine, 11, 15, 30, 46, 49, 57, 69, 89, 101, 107, 139, 142, 166-168, 174, 243, 249
Tiffany & Co., 13
Tillitt-Pratt, Buffy, 10, 31, 43, 48, 49, 56, 59, 89, 100, 133, 135, 173, 175, 178, 207, 244, 249
Timesharing, 269
Toaster ovens, 114
Toyota, 49
Toys, 178
Travel agents, 151
  low-fare search programs, 151, 152
Travel savings clubs, 270, 271

USA Today, 251
U.S. Department of Energy, 105
U.S. Department of Veterans Affairs, 38, 203, 221
U.S. Savings Bonds, 185
Utilities, 10, 105
  billing options, 107; cost-reduction programs, 116; energy audits, 107; energy-saving programs, 106, 266; rebates and subsidies, 106

Vacations
  car rentals, 269-271; couriers, 155, 270, 271; home-exchanges, 168, 271; home rentals, 270; hostels, 168, 269; hotels, 161-165, 270, 271; tours, 166, 167, 269, 270; travel agents, 151, 152; travel savings clubs, 270, 271
VCRs, 70
Visa, 128
Volunteering, 237-244

Wall Street Journal, 149
Warranties
  appliance, 19, 72, 74, 75, 82, 84; automobile, 56, 60, 63
Washing machines, 68, 74
Water restrictors, 114
Weddings, 211
  bridal registry, 276; choosing a place, 212, 214, 224; discount

bridal service, 276; dress, 212, 217, 276; food and drink, 214, 224; flowers, 216, 224; invitations, 276
Whirlpool, 68
White-Westinghouse, 68
Withrow, Mary Ellen, 252

YMCA, 207

Zero coupon bonds, 185

The Beardstown Ladies are 14 women who are members of an investment club that was established more than 13 years ago. They all live in or near Beardstown, Illinois, and still meet on the first Thursday of every month.

Robin Dellabough is associate publisher at Seth Godin Productions. A former freelance writer, she has worked on more than a dozen books and is the co-author of *The Beardstown Ladies' Stitch-in-Time Guide to Growing Your Nest Egg*.

Seth Godin Productions creates books in Irvington-on-Hudson, New York. To date, they have more than 75 titles in print, including works on business, celebrities, computers, and more.

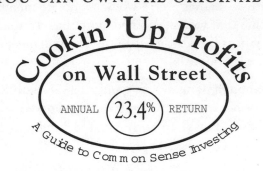